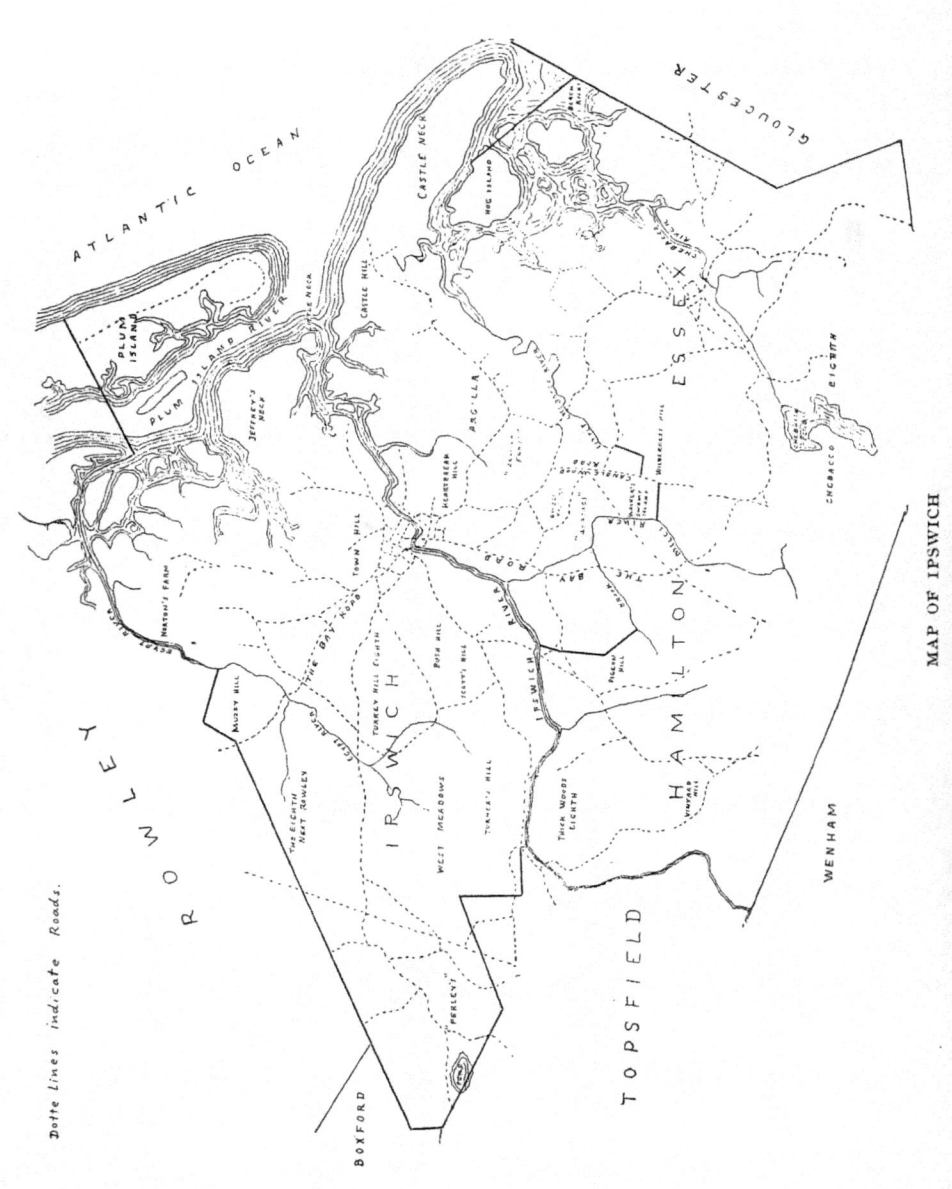

CANDLEWOOD

An Ancient Neighborhood in Ipswich

WITH
GENEALOGIES OF
JOHN BROWN, WILLIAM FELLOWS
AND ROBERT KINSMAN

T. Frank Waters

HERITAGE BOOKS
2012

HERITAGE BOOKS
AN IMPRINT OF HERITAGE BOOKS, INC.

Books, CDs, and more—Worldwide

For our listing of thousands of titles see our website
at
www.HeritageBooks.com

A Facsimile Reprint
Published 2012 by
HERITAGE BOOKS, INC.
Publishing Division
100 Railroad Ave. #104
Westminster, Maryland 21157

Originally published in Salem, Massachusetts, in 1909
as Parts XVI and XVII of the Proceedings
of the Ipswich Historical Society.

— Publisher's Notice —
In reprints such as this, it is often not possible to remove blemishes from the original. We feel the contents of this book warrant its reissue despite these blemishes and hope you will agree and read it with pleasure.

International Standard Book Numbers
Paperbound: 978-0-7884-3065-7
Clothbound: 978-0-7884-9276-1

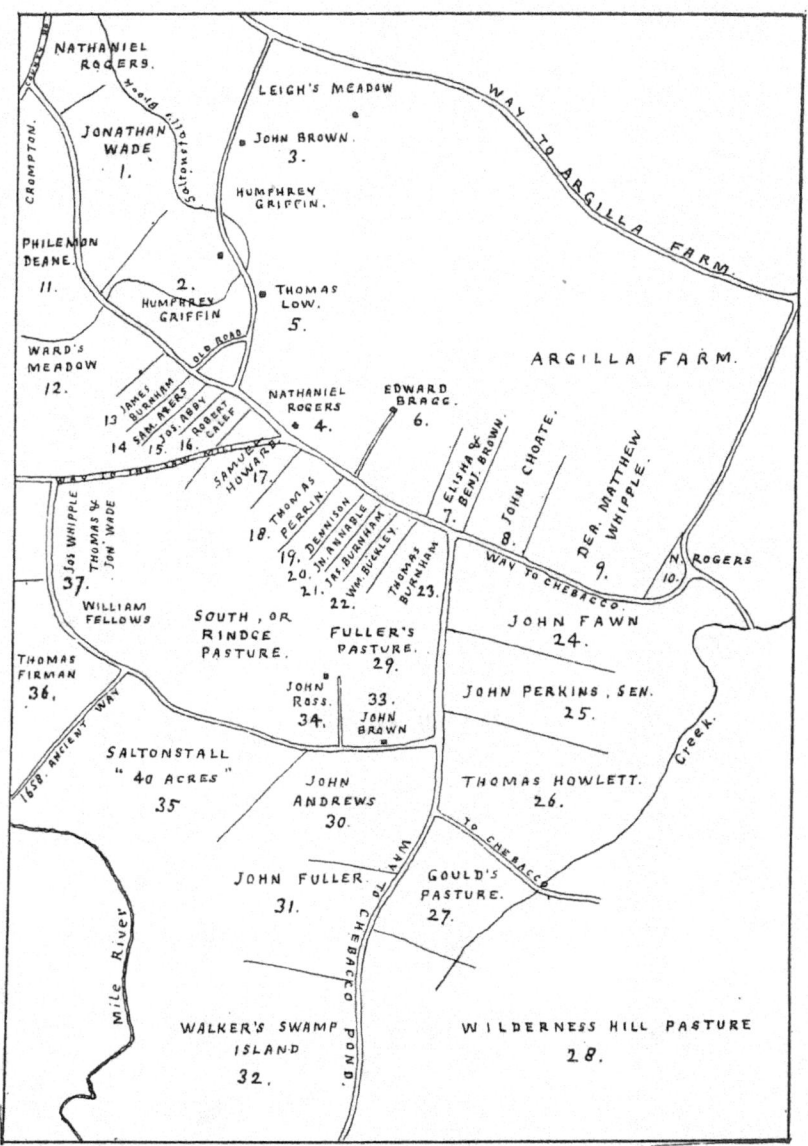

CANDLEWOOD.
Known also as "The South Eighth."

CANDLEWOOD

THE STORY OF AN ANCIENT NEIGHBORHOOD.

Why and when the name was given is largely a matter of conjecture. Pastor Higginson of Salem wrote to friends in England of the primitive way in which the earliest settlers often lighted their houses, by burning thin strips of the pitch pine trees. The suggestion is natural that this fine farming country was originally covered with a pine forest, and that it was of so clear grain and so rich in pitch, that it furnished the light for many homes. The name, Candlewood Island, was very early given to a spot in the upper river, in the present limit of Topsfield, but except a single allusion to Candlewood Street in a deed of 1812, no reference to the name occurs in any early documents. An ancient deed, drawn in 1652, speaks of a portion of this neighborhood, at least, at Mr. Joseph Marshall's, as "a place called Chebacco." The more prosaic name, The South Eighth, prevailed seventy-five years ago, but the more significant and picturesque name, Candlewood, has been common for two generations and may well be perpetuated.

Strictly speaking, the ancient neighborhood to which the name was originally applied, centered about the corner, where the Essex road and the Candlewood road divide, but for convenience sake, its bounds will be stretched and it will be taken as including the whole region east of the Old Bay road and south of the road to Argilla.

Jonathan Wade's Lot.
No. 1 on Diagram.

Beginning with the north side of the road, now called Essex Road, the whole tract from the line of division between Mr. Maynard Whittier and Mr. Samuel Gordon, to the orchard lot now owned by Mr. Wallace P. Willett seems to have belonged originally to Mr. Jonathan Wade, a substantial citizen, who owned the mills at the lower falls, and the homestead which had belonged to the eminent Rev. Nathaniel Ward. His will (proved 1669. Pro. Rec. 304: 125-6), bequeathed his land and housing and the mills to his son, Thomas. Thomas bequeathed all his landed estate to his sons, Jonathan and Thomas in equal portions (proved Oct. 3, 1696. Pro. Rec. 305: 216-7.)

Jonathan, by division with his brother, or by purchase, became the owner of this whole tract and enlarged it by the purchase of the Gravel Pit Pasture, now included in the house lots of Mr. Albert S. Brown and Mr.

(1)

Maynard Whittier, from Mr. Daniel Rogers, Dec. 20, 1727 (66: 2). He bequeathed to his wife, Jane, the use and improvement of one half of his real estate, and the use of his negro man, Dick; to his grandson, William Cogswell, "the pasture I purchased of Mr. Daniel Rogers with the common land laid out and adjoining thereto, commonly called Gravel Pit Pasture." If he should die, the will provided that it should be given to his granddaughters. The residue was bestowed upon his grandson, Dr. Nathaniel Cogswell of Rowley. The division of the ancient pasture and the eventual sale to Mr. Brown and Mr. Whittier, have been fully considered in the history of "The Old Bay Road and Samuel Appleton's Farm." [1]

In 1716, March 10, Jonathan Wade sold his brother, Thomas, 14 or 15 acres at the Windmill Hill lot (28: 265). Captain Thomas built the mansion, still known as the Col. Wade house, for his dwelling in 1727, as the family tradition has always maintained. He bequeathed to his wife, Elizabeth, one half the dwelling, his negro woman, and his silver tankard; to his daughter, Elizabeth Cogswell, "my negro girl, I account at £40," and to his son, Timothy, all his real estate. His son Thomas received £500 and his daughter Mary Wise was well remembered (proved Jan. 2, 1737. Pro. Rec. 322: 97–100). Timothy Wade left a numerous family, the widow Ruth, sons, William, John, Nathaniel and Samuel and daughters, Elizabeth Heard and Mary. The widow had the use of a third of the real estate "and my negro man, Pomp, except she finds best to sell him" (proved April 9, 1763 Pro. Rec. 340: 326). The widow, as executrix, sold 15 acres to William, Feb. 24, 1769 (131; 150) and William conveyed 11 acres 82 rods, as the deed states, though there may be an error in the figures, to Ruth, on the next day, Feb. 25, 1769 (134: 52). Thomas Wade, the son of William sold a part of the estate of his father to Nathaniel, Jan. 5, 1803 (171: 158) which he reconveyed to Thomas, Jan. 6, 1803, 3¾ acres, bounded on the east by the land of Eunice, widow of William, set off as part of her thirds in her late husband's estate (171: 158). The heirs of Thomas quitclaimed to Isaac Wade, Feb. 8, 1831 (261: 217). Isaac sold to George Haskell, Oct. 26, 1831 (261: 216) and Haskell to Charles Giddings, Jan. 9, 1835 (279: 194). Their interest in the lot set off to the widow was sold by William Wade and David and Elizabeth Choate, of Essex, to Samuel Wade, April 28, 1829 (253; 49) who sold the lot, 4½ acres, to Charles Giddings, Jan. 26, 1835 (279: 194). Giddings sold the whole lot, estimated as 8 acres, to Samuel Gordon, March 8, 1859 (583: 250). Mr. Gordon built the dwelling which he still occupies. He conveyed a small lot on the eastern side of the homestead to his son, Samuel C. Gordon, upon which he built his attractive dwelling, Aug. 6, 1903 (1715: 485).

Ruth Wade, the widow of Timothy, conveyed 6 acres to Col. Nathaniel, Dec. 10, 1772 (134: 52). In the division of Col. Wade's estate, the west half of this lot was assigned to his son, William Foster Wade, the east, to his son Nathaniel, May 17, 1827 (244: 244). The heirs of Nathaniel sold to William F. Wade Jr., March 4, 1844 (344: 129). The heirs of William

---

[1] Publications of the Ipswich Historical Society. No. xv.

F. sold to their brother, Asa, six eighths of the lot, June 13, 1853 (492: 80), the heirs of Daniel Weed sold him one eighth, April 8, 1854 (499: 295) and he inherited an eighth. William F. Wade sold the other half of the original lot to Asa, March 6, 1854 (502: 104). He conveyed to Wallace P. Willett, Nov. 9, 1880 (1051: 214). Sarah E. Willett, wife of Wallace P., sold to Enoch Bailey, Sept. 12, 1892 (1355: 88). Mr. Bailey built the house and made his home here until his death. His widow, Mary M. Bailey, sold the house and the 6 acres to Albin M. Spuyt, March 30, 1903 (1702: 222).

The widow, Ruth Wade, sold another 6 acre lot to Abraham Choate, May 4, 1764 (120: 83) which was conveyed by Samuel and John Choate to Samuel Kinsman, Jan. 2, 1775 (134: 166) who then owned the farm now owned and occupied by Mr. Carl Caverly. He sold the whole farm to Asa Andrews, April 7, 1809 (186: 48). Theodore Andrews, son of Asa, sold to Increase H. Brown of Marblehead and his brother, Asa of Ipswich, Oct. 24, 1835 (286: 196). In the division of the various pieces of real estate which they owned jointly, the "Choate lot" was assigned to Asa Brown, May 2, 1840 (318: 193). He mortgaged and eventually gave title to Benjamin Hawkes (643: 19) who conveyed to Increase H. Brown, Oct. 12, 1863 (657: 181), Brown to Theodore F. Cogswell on the same date and he, to Josiah Stackpole, June 23, 1882 (1075: 77) whose heirs still own.

The Humphrey Griffin Lot.
No. 2 on Diagram.

Humphrey Griffin was the original owner apparently of a large tract owned later by Samuel Podd, then by Thomas and James Burnham. It seems to have joined the Jonathan Wade land. The lot adjoining the Choate lot on the east was included in the estate of Dr. Nathaniel Cogswell, which he had inherited, for the most part, as has been said, from his grandfather, Jonathan Wade, in 1749. Dr. Cogswell seems to have acquired this lot, not by inheritance, but by purchase from the Burnhams, who were large land owners in this vicinity, prior to the year 1769. In the deed of conveyance from the Cogswell heirs to Theodore Andrews, the lot is called "the Burnham pasture," 18 acres, Nov. 15, 1825 (243: 18). Andrews sold to Asa and Nathan Brown, April 1, 1833 (269: 89). They divided the lot, the west half falling to Nathan. He conveyed to Perley Haskell the same described in the quitclaim deed of Asa, Dec. 2, 1837, on May 1, 1838 (312: 215). It passed successively to Epes Sargent, March 30, 1839 (312: 216), Alfred Kimball, Sept. 9, 1859 (593: 214) and Wallace P. Willett, the present owner, April 11, 1860 (603: 260).

Nathan Brown quitclaimed the eastern half to Asa Brown, Dec. 2, 1837 (304: 51), Asa sold to his brother, Increase H., Oct. 28, 1862 (643: 243). He sold to their sister, Mrs. Rhoda B. Potter, April 28, 1866 (701: 230), who conveyed to Ira B. Carlisle, April 26, 1869 (770:107). John W. Carlisle, brother of Ira, gained possession and his heirs conveyed to his widow, Nancy B., Nov. 6, 1897 (1530: 378). She included this 9 acre pasture in the sale of the farm to Lester E. Libby, Sept. 19, 1899 (1587: 137).

Alonzo B. Fellows purchased it of Libby, Jan. 29, 1900 (1601: 496) and still owns.

The Hobson lot, so called, on which the old cellar and the lilac bushes, which bloomed in the door-yard, are still seen, was undoubtedly a part of the Thomas Burnham estate. Moses Potter sold to Samuel Kinsman, 3¼ acres of upland and meadow, with a dwelling, barn and well, "reserving a way through the premises where the way formerly went for Thomas Burnham and Capt John Kinsman," April 8, 1778 (138: 167). It was owned and occupied before 1790, by Alexander Troop, who left a widow, Lucy, and son, Alexander, and minor children, Lucy, Jane, Peggy, Christian, Hannah and William (175: 117). Alexander Troop, laborer, conveyed the homestead to Daniel C. Hobson, brick maker, Sept. 7, 1801 (194: 15). The heirs of Hobson, whoever they may be, are the legal owners of the small estate to-day, but the taxes have been paid and the lot has been used as a pasture, by the owners of the adjoining lot, Thomas Low and his successors, for many years.

Old Road.
On Diagram.

A little to the east of the Hobson cellar, an old road, grass-grown and long disused, but plainly visible, leads down the slope and turns to the right toward the present Heart Break Road. This is the way reserved in Moses Potter's deed to Samuel Kinsman, "where the way formerly went to Thomas Burnham and Capt. John Kinsman," April 8, 1778. This ancient road is of especial interest, as it opened the way to a group of houses and tillage and pasture lots in the earliest times.

The first of these old settlers is Samuel Podd, to whom Humphrey Griffin, late of Ipswich, sold two parcels, a 6 acre lot "which is & hath been in the possession of sayd Samuel Pod diverse years bounded by John Brown northeast and the common west and a 10 acre lot with a piece of swamp which I the said Humphrey bought of Joseph Metcalfe" with John Lee, north, other land of Samuel Pod, west, Feb. 20, 1660. (Ips. Deeds 4: 396). On March 6, 1677, Samuel Podd conveyed to James Burnham, "a small parcel of my land about 5 rod broad between 27 & 28 rods in length," having Mr. Wade's land southwest, Mr. Nathaniel Rogers's northwest, Podd's other land northeast and southeast on the highway leading to John Brown's to the brook, and also a free passage to the common, allowing a passage 1½ rods wide from sd Burnam's land to his house, etc. (Ips. Deeds 4: 280). In the December following, articles of agreement between Samuel and Grace Podd and James Burnham were drawn, which specified:

1. A lease to James Burnham, of the house and land, and 20 acres adjoining and all the marsh and upland in the island formerly Edward Chapman's during the life of Podd and his wife.
2. Podd is to have the use of half the barn, etc., during his life.
3. At the death of the Podds, the title to rest with Burnham. (Ips. Deeds 4: 281).

James Burnham was the younger son of Thomas, who bought the house and 12 acres of George Giddings, on the Argilla road, June 3, 1667 (1:217) and his purchase from Podd was the first of a long series of conveyances, of which only the most prominent can be considered. The Podd land seems to be identical, in part, with the land now owned by Mr. Carl Caverly. It extended to the Gloucester road apparently and was bounded on one side by the Jonathan Wade land, we have already considered. It also included part of the land on the east side of Heart-break road.

John Brown's Lot.
No. 3 on Diagram.

On January 9, 1684, James Burnham bought of John Brown, his land and dwelling, some 16 acres in all. A ten acre field was bounded by Podd's land south and southwest, land of Lieut. Thomas Burnham, brother of James, and other land of James north and northwest, Joseph Lee's and Samuel Podd's land east. A six acre lot was near by. (Ips. Deeds 2: 77.)

In various later conveyances allusion is often made to the great rock in the field that was Brown's. A large granite boulder has been gradually blasted away for building stone, in a field owned by the heirs of Joseph Kinsman, on the east side of the lane. As this is the only rock that can be found in the vicinity, it may safely be identified with the rock mentioned in the deeds, and locates in a general way the house and land of John Brown.

In the division of the estate of Thomas Burnham, father of James and Thomas, the homestead and adjoining lands were apportioned to Thomas, Nov. 14, 1691 (9: 161). To James, conveyance was made of "the interest he hath in his now dwelling house, which said James liveth in, with ¾ acre about it and 14 acres upland and meadow near the homestead" 1687 (9: 168). James Burnham apparently had built a new house before this date.

Mr. Burnham added other fields to his domain from year to year; a half acre of meadow from Daniel Rogers in April 10, 1691; (Ips. Deeds 5:397) an acre "partly common" south of Podd's home lot, August 1, 1690 (Ips. Deeds 5: 329), and a two acre lot having Podd's land northwest, May 14, 1691 (Ips. Deeds 5: 380) both purchased of Samuel Rogers; 4 acres of pasture from Daniel Rogers having Captain Wade's land on the south, Feb. 13, 1693 (10: 98); a 6½ acre pasture from Rev. John Rogers, which Thomas Burnham Jr., carpenter, had sold him, on the south of his homestead, April 10, 1693 (10:97), and a 7 acre field from Joseph Lee, Aug. 9, 1695 (11: 39).

On Sept. 2, 1703, he conveyed to his son, Thomas, "a certain parcel of meadow upland and marsh with ye buildings, with my old house, barn and shop, with half an acre they stand on, joining to them as it is bounded by ye Common southwest, and by Mr. Wade's land westerly," his orchard bounded by Mr. Wade's land west, and a 6 acre pasture adjoining etc (24: 18). A few rods from the road, in the orchard now owned by Mr. Willett, a level spot amid the rolling hillocks, would have afforded ample room for an ancient dwelling, and I have often thought, that the old house alluded to in this deed, may have stood there.

James Burnham made a later conveyance to his son Thomas of about 40 acres and housing on Jan. 25, 1719 (37: 161). Thomas sold the same, enlarged to 61 acres to Samuel Bragg, Dec. 18, 1773 (135: 53). Bragg sold the house and 26 acres to Samuel Kinsman, May 7, 1784 (186: 47). Kinsman sold the house and 18 acres to Asa Andrews, "with the road running through the same," "also the right to pass and repass on that piece between the bridge and Josiah Burnham's barn, now fenced out as a way, also a piece of land adjoining the above, $1\frac{1}{2}$ rods wide 28 rods long, bounded on land we sold Asa about a year since, ... reserving a way one rod wide subject to gates and bars for those who have heretofore been accustomed to pass," April 7, 1809 (186: 48). This deed has great interest from its inclusion of the small parcel which Samuel Podd conveyed to James Burnham in 1677, and the allusion to the fact that the present Heart-break road had "been fenced out as a way."

Mr. Andrews enlarged the farm by later purchases so that it contained 47 acres when his son and heir, Theodore Andrews, conveyed it to Increase and Asa Brown, Oct. 24, 1835 (286: 196). By the deed of division the farm with the exception of the Choate lot, as was mentioned, fell to Increase H. Brown. His executor sold to J. Farley Kinsman, June 2, 1873 (882:22), who conveyed it to Dr. Sidney A. Lord, measuring 41 acres, Oct. 25, 1904 (1760: 1). He sold to Mr. Carl Caverly, the present owner.

The exact age of the house is uncertain. Its sharp roof and general architecture point to the seventeenth century. It was built probably by James Burnham, and may be the dwelling which he occupied in 1687, or the later house in which he dwelt in 1703.

On the same day that he conveyed the 40 acres and dwelling to his son, Thomas, James Burnham made similar conveyance of "the house I now live in," barn etc., the malt house and about 40 acres to his son James (37:178). His will was presented for probate, June 27, 1729 (Pro. Rec. 319: 223). It recites that his real estate had been given to his sons already. His wife, Mary, received a privilege in the west end of the house with all personal effects, servants, money, etc. The inventory includes two negro servants, valued at £100 and a calash, £7-10.

Rev. Nathaniel Rogers's Lot.
No. 4 on Diagram.

James Burnham Jr., son of James, by purchase acquired the Rogers estate. In the indenture between John Rogers, the President of Harvard College, and his brother Samuel, by which the estate of their father, Rev. Nathaniel Rogers was divided between them, Samuel received a house and 8 acres, bounded one side by Goodman Loe and by Edward Bragg at one end, March 4, 1684 (Ips. Deeds 5: 146). This included the Willard B. Kinsman property now occupied by Miss Patch and part of the Wallace farm.

Samuel Rogers also received from his father's estate, 6 acres of upland adjoining Thomas Loe and Samuel Pod, 40 acres adjoining Mr. Wade, Mr. Saltonstall and Joseph Lee (now owned by Mr. John Galbraith) and the 40 acre Ox Pasture, near the Haffield Bridge.

The inventory of Mr. John Rogers, son of Samuel, taken Nov 21, 1694 (Pro. Rec. 303: 260) included:

"ye mansion house and common right, barne and other outhouses, orchard and homestead about 6 acres and 5 acres of upland near Podds," etc. and one negro servant, valued at £30.

Martha Rogers, widow of John, married Jacob Boarman. Her account of the estate included an allowance for bringing up the three children from their father's death to the time of her marriage, about six years, "besides ye income of ye sd estate £50-0-0" (Pro. Rec. 309: 266). A double share was given to John, the oldest child, and shares to Sarah and Martha. The widow also received a part of the estate (311: 204). Jacob Boarman and Martha, in consideration of a deed of quitclaim by James Burnham Jr. and wife, Sarah, and Matthew Perkins Jr. and wife Martha, conveyed to James and Sarah Burnham and Matthew and Martha Perkins, their interest in the house and land of "our father, Mr. Samuel Rogers," "the west end of the dwelling they now dwell in," Dec. 21, 1714 (29: 192). Jacob Boarman made a later conveyance to James Burnham Jr. of five sixths of the dwelling he then occupied, March 4, 1719 (38: 110).

James Burnham, the son of James, survived his father but a few years. The inventory of his estate was filed, May 5, 1737 (Pro. Rec. 322: 379). It revealed a goodly degree of prosperity and even luxury. His apparel was valued at £60-8-0.

2 gold rings 50/	
silver buckles 25/	
silver tankard £26-4/	
gold and silver lace 25/	
things in ye garret, negroes beds, bedding, baggs etc.	9-12-0
a negro man £100	
an old negro woman £5	
8 cows and seven calves at £8 per cow and calf	£63- 0-0
2 pr oxen £42	
1 pr oxen £17	
10 2 yr old cattle at £3-15/	122-10 0
a bull £4-0-0	
a horse £22	
10 yearling cattle at 55/	
a mare and colt £8	35-10-0
66 sheep and 27 lambs £66	
3 swine, 5 piggs £9	75- 0-0

"The dwelling house, orchard, barn, mault house and other buildings where his father dwelt, ye homestead, about 40 acres with about 4 acres of land in ye mault house pasture adjoining to sd homestead   £1200-0-0 the dwelling house, orchard, etc. where he dwelt, with ¾ acre of land,

about 8 acres on y⁰ back side and about 11 acres on y⁰ front that was common £700–0–0
about 26 acres on y⁰ westerly side of y⁰ road leading to Chebacco £282–0–0"
(now owned by Geo A. Whipple)
    Real and personal estate   £5083–18–0

The estate was divided:

To the widow Hannah, was assigned one third of the real estate,
"five sixths of the house of sd deceased, that did once belong to Mr. John Rogers and about ¾ acre about it, and the 26 acres on Chebacco road."

To his daughter, Abigail, the 1st division,
part of the house that was formerly Mr. James Burnham's, "over ye stone kitchen" and various fields.

To his eldest daughter, Sarah, the 2nd division,
rooms in the house of deceased "and y⁰ part of y⁰ old house that was Pods, and y⁰ old house where y⁰ widow Comer dwelt" with various lots.

To his daughter, Mary, m. Staniford, the 3d division,
half the malt kiln and part of the homestead.

To his daughter Hannah, m. Kinsman, the 4th division,
rooms in the dwelling of James, and about 1¾ acres on the southerly side of road to Chebacco (now included in the lot occupied by T. M. Norman, owned by William J. Cameron).

It appears from this, that Mr. Burnham occupied the Rogers house and that his father's house (about where the Wallace dwelling stands, I incline to believe), the ancient Podd dwelling and another old house, perhaps the John Brown house occupied by the widow Comer, were still standing on the farm.

The legatees conveyed their interest to Capt. John Kinsman; Thos. Staniford and his wife, Mary, daughter of Mr. Burnham on Jan. 3, 1740 (81: 197) and Mar. 16, 1758 (112: 263); Martha Dodge, widow of Barnabas, Aug. 16, 1740 (80: 120); Abigail, another daughter, on April 30, 1755 (112: 264) and March 25, 1758 (115: 159); and Rev. Nathaniel Rogers[1] on May 24, 1760 (115: 160) and March 16, 1761 (115: 158).

Thomas Low's Lot.

No. 5 on Diagram.

Mention has been made of Thomas Loe or Low as abutting on the Rogers homestead on the south and facing the ancient Lane on the west. John Low, son of Thomas, was in possession in 1690 and he conveyed the homestead and 8 acres to his brother, Thorndike, May 5, 1708 (36: 218). John was then a resident of Portsmouth, N. H. Under the will of Thorndike (proved Oct. 17, 1750. Pro. Rec. 336: 425) the real estate passed to his son, Nathaniel, and his daughter, Elizabeth, who had married her next neighbor's son, Timothy Bragg Jr., received £25. The other children were Joseph, Sarah, the widow of Abraham Martin, Debo-

---

[1] He married the widow, Mary Staniford, May 4, 1758.

rah, the widow of Isaac Randall, Mary deceased, the wife of Nathaniel Foster Jr., Martha, unmarried, Dorothy, wife of Thos. Yorke and . . . wife of Jacob Carter. The inventory gives a house, barn and 6 acres (Pro. Rec. 338: 496).

Daniel Low, joyner, sold to Capt. John Kinsman, two-thirds of the Nathaniel Low homestead and 10 acres, April 22, 1761 (131: 75) and Sarah Foster, widow, Dr. Nathaniel Low and others, conveyed to him half a dwelling and 6 acres, March 25, 1779 (138: 166). By this purchase Captain John Kinsman came to own the original James Burnham farm, the ancient Thomas Low estate and the Samuel Rogers estate. He conveyed to his son, James, three fourths of a dwelling and land, evidently the Rogers dwelling, Oct. 18, 1760 (110: 133) and two parcels of upland, March 21, 1761 (110: 263).

After the death of James Kinsman, his widow, Mary, sold 18½ acres with part of a barn to Captain John, Feb. 21, 1764 (113: 182). The Captain died in 1785. His will (proved March 7, 1785. Pro. Rec. 351: 356) devised to his wife Elizabeth, the improvement of a third of a dwelling and garden and to his son, Samuel, "the house I now live in" with barn and outbuildings . . . with a portion to his grand-daughter, Mary Remick. It is more than probable that his dwelling was the spacious mansion which still stands, lately owned by Mr. Aretas D. Wallace.

Samuel Kinsman sold 79 acres and buildings to Isaac Burnham, "reserving liberty to the heirs of Dr. Joshua Burnham to pass and repass as usual, likewise a way for myself from Mr. Bragg's farm with my cattle and team to the country road which leads to Chebacco," Feb. 15, 1790 (152: 96) Isaac Burnham conveyed to Josiah, March, 18 1795 (158: 290), Josiah to his brother, Aaron, 88 acres, Jan. 9, 1812 (196: 109), Aaron Burnham to John Heard, with cider mill, press, etc., Feb. 2, 1814 (201: 282). Mr. Heard also bought 6 acres of Asa Andrews, July 7, 1819 (221: 213) which Mary Remick and James of Barrington, N. H., had sold to Andrews, "being part of the estate of James Kinsman," July 9, 1819 (221: 212). Mr. Heard sold half an acre out of this 6 acre lot to Levi Brown, Sept. 4, 1826 (244: 38) and the 88 acre farm to his son, George W. Heard, April 2, 1830 (282: 162). He conveyed to Thomas Low, 83 acres, April 1, 1835 (315: 270) and his daughter, Abby S. Stone, widow of Augustine, to Aretas D. Wallace, March 27, 1901 (1636: 517). Augustine and Abby Stone had sold a two acre lot to Robert W. Bolles, Feb. 11, 1888 (1223: 462) on which he built, at once, his dwelling and other buildings.

Mr. George W. Heard sold an acre and a half to Levi Brown, who had bought a half acre from his father, March 21, 1832. He built a dwelling and other buildings. He quitclaimed to his brother, Francis, who sold to Henry S. Holmes, 2 acres and buildings, March 9, 1842 (330: 18), Holmes to Willard B. Kinsman, April 1, 1851 (456: 112), who enlarged the house, to its present form.

The ancient dwelling, now occupied by Mr. Caverly, is the one surviving link that binds this compact group of eighteenth and seventeenth century dwellings with the present. The old brick yard on the Wallace estate has been so long disused that its existence is only indicated by the levelling of the clay field. Mr. Daniel C. Hobson, the brick-maker, who bought the Troop estate in 1801, probably worked at his trade on this spot.

Edward Bragg's Farm.
No. 6 on Diagram.

The next farm, now owned by Alonzo B. Fellows, was originally part of the great farm which was granted to John Winthrop Jr, leader of the little company which settled here in March, 1633. Dep.-Gov. Samuel Symonds bought it in 1637-8 (Ips. Deeds, 1: 45) and probably gave it the name, Argilla farm, which still holds. Mr. Symonds sold to his former servant Edward Bragg, "9 acres, as it is now fenced in with a yard where there is a barn and other buildings," 28-11-1658 (Ips. Deeds 4: 39) and another 9 acre lot and 4½ acres, April 21, 1676 (Ips. Deeds 4: 40). The administrators of the Dep.-Governor's estate sold to Bragg, 35 acres adjoining Bragg's house and barn, near the northwest corner, Feb. 8, 1679 (Ips. Deeds 4: 306). John Rogers sold to Edward Bragg and Timothy, his son, 2 acres of upland and a half acre pasture, Feb. 26, 1693 (43: 97). In his old age, Mr. Bragg conveyed to his son, Timothy, in a carefully drawn instrument, his houses and lands, 112 acres in all, the dwelling of Edward and the house Timothy had built for himself, the land he had bought of Mr. Symonds and the 40 acres of marsh and upland he had purchased from Mr. Rogers, "with all that, being about 20 acres, which Edward was possest of before he purchased the above mentioned." He bound Timothy to keep his house in repair during his own and his wife's life, care for a garden spot fenced before the door and plough an acre for his use, where he chose. Timothy was bound to provide firewood at the door, also a horse, 30 sheep, 60 bushels Indian corn, 20 bushels malt, 15 bushels rye and wheat called Messling, 4 bushels wheat, 6 barrels good cider, 10 bushels winter apples and summer apples as needful.

"He shall improve fifty rods of land yearly for flax which Timothy is to plough yearly, also if s^d Edward's now wife see good to live half a year at sd. now dwelling house after ye decease of sd Edward sd Timothy shall carry her to meeting on Sabath and Lecture days if she desire it," June 26, 1699 (14: 12).

His will was proved Aug. 23, 1708 (Pro. Rec. 310: 78-80). It devised "to the church of Christ in Ipswich of which I am a member £3 in money to be layd out by my overseers in a piece of silver plate for ye use of said church forever."

A codicil states that Timothy, the son, to whom he had given his whole estate, had died, and it was then given to the sons of Timothy, John, Timothy and Abiell. Division was made, to John, the east third to Timothy, the middle including the lower house, (the house of Edward his grandfather), to Abiel, the west third, including the house his father lived in, July 22, 1709 (Pro. Rec. 310: 162). John Bragg sold to James and Thomas Burnham, the sons of James, "my share of land given unto me by my grandfather, Edward Bragg, tillage and pasturing land with part of an orchard," Dec. 16, 1709 (22: 140).

John Bragg, of Scarboro, made conveyance to his brother, Timothy, of his interest in his father's and grandfather's estate, May 2, 1724 (50: 24). Ebenezer Bragg of Marlboro, and Nathaniel Bragg of Wenham quitclaimed to Timothy, Jan. 8, 1723–4 (50: 26) and Edward Bragg of Andover, May 22 1724 (50: 27). There is also record of a conveyance by Samuel Baker Jr. to Timothy Bragg Jr. of a house and 33 acres, Nov. 30, 1752 (108: 30), but it is likely that this was Timothy Bragg's dwelling which may have been mortgaged to Baker. This also came into the possession of Thomas Burnham Jr. who thus owned the whole Bragg farm. He sold 79¼ acres with dwelling to Francis Brown, Feb. 16, 1781 (138: 170). It was inherited by John Burnham Brown, son of Francis, who built the present dwelling, near the highway. The cellar of the ancient house, built by Bragg, is by the side of a lane, some 800 feet north of the present location.

Thomas Burnham sold to his son, James, a cooper by trade, about 30 acres and a house, the Timothy Bragg Jr. dwelling undoubtedly, and 26 acres on the other side of the road, with 11 acres of salt marsh called Saltonstall's, Nov. 10, 1783 (142: 19).[1] James Burnham conveyed this to John Willet, his father-in-law, Jan. 19, 1793 (155: 167). John Willet's will (proved Feb. 7, 1804. Pro. Rec. 371: 325) gave to his daughter, Betsey Burnham, the improvement of the property of her late husband, James Burnham; to Betsey and Joshua Burnham, children of said Betsey, all lands conveyed to him by James Burnham; to his son, Moses, his homestead, land and buildings, about 15 acres. Betsey Burnham married Jabez Richards and conveyed to him the title in the house and 1¼ acres and 3½ acres on the other side of the road, Oct. 17, 1809 (189: 14). Richards mortgaged to Moses Willett in 1817 (213: 129). David Dodge, administrator or Moses Willett, quitclaimed to Oliver Appleton Jr., Dec. 24, 1823 (234: 130). Appleton sold to Nathan Brown, Jan. 6, 1824 (234: 130). He moved the house to the lot he owned on County Road, near the Common, where it still stands (the dwelling of Mr. Everett K. Brown). Mr. Brown sold the lot formerly occupied by the house to Nehemiah Brown, Jan. 13, 1826 (272: 111), and he to John B. Brown, Aug. 23, 1833 (609: 236).

Joshua Burnham sold his half interest in 28½ acres to John Burnham Brown and his sister Mary, Dec. 6, 1823 (251: 127). Mr. Brown, now the owner of the whole Bragg farm, gave or sold 15 acres to his son, John A. Brown and sold the remaining 100 acres and buildings to Ira B. Carlisle and Joseph Huckins, Aug. 2, 1860 (610: 234). John A. Brown sold 15 acres to the same on the same date (610: 233). By mutual quitclaim, they divided the farm, Mr. Huckins taking the eastern, Mr. Carlisle, the western half, Oct. 16, 1861 (634: 51). Ira B. Carlisle conveyed his title to his brother, John C. Carlisle, May 9, 1870 (798: 136), the heirs of John to the widow, Nancy B., Nov. 6, 1897 (1530: 378), she to Lester E. Libby, Sept. 19, 1899 (1587: 137) who sold to Alonzo B. Fellows, Jan. 29, 1900 (1601: 496). Mr. Huckins bought 2 acres adjoining of Mrs. Rhoda B. Pot-

[1] Page 12.

ter, April 28, 1869 (770: 106). His heirs sold to William G. Horton 53 acres with the house, barn etc., which Mr. Huckins built when he purchased the farm, Feb. 26, 1889 (1243: 408).

Elisha and Benjamin Brown.

No. 7 on Diagram.

A second section of the Argilla farm included a dwelling remembered by the older folk, between Mr. Horton's and Mr. Marshall's, near the bars. Rev. Samuel Philips, John Philips of Boston and others sold to Elisha Brown, weaver, and Benjamin Brown, blacksmith, in equal halves, $\frac{1}{4}$ of the Argilla farm, 120 acres, "formerly set off to Mrs. Dorothy Emerson (since called Henchman) as her part of the Argilla farm," June 13, 1743 (84: 203). They built a dwelling, Elisha owning the west half, Benjamin the east. John Choate sold them 6$\frac{1}{4}$ acres, reserving a drift way, Dec. 21, 1752 (102: 140). Elisha Brown and Lydia sold the half house in which they lived and about 14 acres to Francis Brown, March 16, 1789 (228: 128) who had bought the Thomas Burnham farm, as has been said, in 1781. This half house with a small lot of land was set off to the widow, Judith. John Burnham Brown owned $\frac{18}{28}$, Mary Brown and Charles Brown owned $\frac{12}{28}$ (185: 248). After the death of their mother, John B. Brown, Mary Brown and widow Judith Manning sold the half house to John Sweet, April 18, 1836 (291: 139), he to Asa Brown, Feb. 13, 1840 (317: 184). By various conveyances Charles and Mary quitclaimed their interest in the land to John B. Brown (540: 198, 199, 200).

Benjamin Brown, the blacksmith, owner of the east side of the dwelling, had sons, Nathaniel and Benjamin, Abner and David. In his will, he gave the front chamber, part of the orchard, etc. to his son David, and to Abner, rooms in the house and 13 acres of land (proved June 13, 1809. Pro. Rec. 378:128). Nathaniel and Benjamin had lands elsewhere as will be noted. Charles Kimball, the administrator of David, sold his interest to John A. Brown, Jan. 27, 1847 (610: 96), who sold the same to Ira B. Carlisle and Joseph Huckins, July 21, 1860 (610: 234). Abner Brown conveyed 14 acres to Ammi and William Brown, April 20, 1818 (216: 116). Hannah, the widow of Ammi, and others sold to Nathaniel Kinsman, owner of the adjoining property, Nov. 26, 1835 (287: 51). Abner bequeathed his interest in the house and land about it to his grandson, William Cook, son of John M. Cook of Salem and his daughter, Sarah, (proved Feb. 2, 1819. Pro. Rec. 394: 242). Elisha Brown sold an acre of tillage and orchard ground, half a barn, quarter of a dwelling and undivided quarter of the yard in front, "conveyed to me by deed June 16, 1828, signed by Geo. Smith, guardian of William Cook, a minor," to Asa Brown, April 2, 1835 (282: 89). His purchase of the other half the house in 1840 has been noted. The house, untenanted and falling into decay, was burned, by the touch of an incendiary it was thought. The 2 acre lot was sold to Mrs. Rhoda B. Potter, Feb. 11, 1867 (743: 198) and by her to Joseph Huckins, April 28, 1869 (770: 106). Joseph Marshall relin-

THE RESIDENCE OF MR. JOSEPH MARSHALL.

See Pages 13 and 66.

quished the ancient drift-way to Huckins, April 26, 1869 (770: 106). The lot was included in the sale by the Huckins heirs to William G. Horton.

John Choate Farm.
No. 8 on Diagram.

The Joseph Marshall farm was also a part of the Argilla farm. Matthew Whipple conveyed to John Philips of Boston, John Choate Esq, and Samuel Baker "my title to one half of the westerly half of Argilla Farm, about 130 acres, salt marsh and upland, being the two quarters of sd farm which the sd John Philips and others in the right of their mother, Mrs. Mary Philips and Mr. John Emerson in his own right, recovered in law some years past as it descended to them in right of Mrs. Dorothy Henchman late of Boston," Dec. 8, 1749 (95: 50).

John Choate was the sole owner in 1752 when he sold 6¼ acres to Elisha and Benjamin Brown. William and John Choate sold the lot, measuring 28 acres, to Abraham Choate, Feb. 4, 1772 (130: 44) and he, to Elisha Brown, Feb. 6, 1772 (130: 44). Elisha built a house, and on March 16, 1789, the same day on which he sold his half-dwelling in which he lived, to Francis Brown, as we have noted, he sold the newer house, the east half, and 28 acres to Nehemiah Brown (161: 13) the west half and half an acre to Joseph Brown (157: 140). Joseph lived in the house at the time, perhaps, as he mentions his residence in his deed of sale to Nehemiah, March 29, 1798 (193: 266).

Ammi Brown of Salem sold his interest to his brother, Nehemiah, "⅔ of all the real estate of our honored father, Nehemiah, the homestead and other lots, ⅝ conveyed to me by Michael Brown, Nov. 28, 1820, (226: 249) ⅛ by my sister, Elizabeth Brown (203: 139), ⅛ I hold as heir of my father subject to the dower of our mother, Mary Brown," July 17, 1821 (248: 157).

William Brown Jr. of Salem conveyed his ninth interest to Nehemiah, Sept. 7, 1826 (248: 157). Nehemiah Brown sold the house and 29 acres to Nathaniel Kinsman, April 10, 1828 (248: 175) and Hannah, the widow of Ammi Brown and other heirs sold him the 14 acre lot adjoining, already described, Nov. 26, 1835 (287: 51). Joanna Kinsman, daughter of Nathaniel, sold her half interest to Joseph Marshall and Abby, sister of Joanna, April 5, 1866 (874: 184). Mr. Marshall bought a half acre piece of Joseph Huckins, April 6, 1869 (874: 185). The old house, which had weathered a century, was removed by Mr. Marshall to a new site, east of its original location, and the large new buildings were erected on the old spot.

Dea. Matthew Whipple Lot.
No. 9 on Diagram.

Elisha and Benjamin Brown, we have noted, bought a lot in 1743 from the Henchman heirs on which they built their house. On March 4, 1763, they bought of Matthew Whipple, 30 acres of upland, in equal shares,

adjoining the lot we have just traced (112: 121). Benjamin had the west half and he gave this to his son, David (June 13, 1809. Pro. Rec. 378 128). David Brown utilized his small property by a public bequest. After bestowing the rooms in the dwelling which were bequeathed him by his father, he proceeds,
"The rest and residue of all my estate . . . I give, devise and bequeath for the purpose of supporting a school for the small children in the school district, where I now live, in the summer season and I do order and direct that the improvement of the aforesaid property be expended for the above purpose, and that the property aforesaid be under the sole care and direction of my executor, hereafter named and the two oldest selectmen of the town of Ipswich... and if the improvement of the above interest shall be more than sufficient for a common school, what remains to go toward supporting a school in the winter season and so to continue as above, annually and forever (proved June 4, 1822. Pro. Rec. 399: 502).

A small lot, opposite the Geo. A. Whipple house, on the Candlewood road, and this 15 acre lot were included in the bequest. At a Probate Court, April 5, 1870, the trustees were authorized to sell the real estate (Pro. Rec. 426: 447). Mr. Joseph Marshall bought the larger lot, adjoining his own land, measuring 16 acres 24 rods, May 25, 1870 (874: 185) and removed the old house to a place on this lot. The interest from the fund thus provided is now used in providing transportation for the children of the neighborhood to the schools in the center of the Town.

The other half of the Deacon's Pasture as it is still called, as Matthew Whipple was a Deacon in the Hamilton church, was assigned to Elisha Brown. He sold this lot to his sons, on the same March 16, 1789, when he divided all his belongings, a half to Joseph (157: 140), a quarter to Nehemiah (161: 13), and a quarter to Francis (228: 128). Joseph sold to his son, Joseph Jr. the 8 acres he had bought of his father and about 3 acres, he had bought of the heirs of his brother Francis, Aug. 1, 1806 (191: 259). He bought the interest of Nehemiah, April 9, 1828 (249: 211). His sons, Gardiner A. and Joseph P. inherited and the heirs of Joseph P. quitclaimed to Gardiner, Oct. 12, 1858 (578: 99), whose heirs still own.

Rev. Nathaniel Rogers's Lot.

No. 10 on Diagram.

The small tract, on which the house of Mr. Charles G. Brown stands, was originally owned by Rev. Nathaniel Rogers, then by his son Samuel, apparently, by James Burnham, and by Capt. John Kinsman. He sold a 3½ acre pasture lot to his son, John Jr., July 24, 1759 (109: 56). John Jr. built a house and sold or mortgaged house and lot to his brother, Samuel, March 1, 1783 (140: 129). Samuel reconveyed to John Jr. in 1784 (142: 172) and John Jr. then sold to Moses Kinsman, May 7, 1784 (142: 173). Moses Kinsman was succeeded by his son Moses, who built the present dwelling. His widow, Jane Kinsman, sold to Alfred Smith, April 27,

1865 (683: 194), he to William S. Todd of Gloucester, Nov. 10, 1868 (759: 259), who conveyed to Gardiner A. Brown, April 5, 1877 (974: 173). The farm included beside the house lot, land on the east side of the North Gate Road, 6½ acres at Peto Point, the Woodbury marsh, 12 acres, etc.

Philemon Dane's Lot.
No. 11 on Diagram.

Returning now to Parting Paths and the Inner Common of the South Eighth[1], the Crumpton lot on the corner has been traced already.[2] Philemon Dane by virtue of one old right, owned the lot adjoining Crumpton's in 1733, which he sold to Joseph Appleton, May 1, 1742 (104: 77) who owned the lot adjoining, fronting on the Bay Road. Joseph Appleton, son of the above, sold his holdings to Alexander Troop, trader, whose dwelling was on the opposite side of the road, as has been already observed,[3] Sept. 27, 1787 (148: 114). Troop sold to the Farley brothers, John and Thomas, the tanners, Sept. 7, 1801 (175: 117) and the Farleys to Amos Jones, Feb. 17, 1820 (223: 160) Daniel Ross, the Revolutionary soldier, succeeded and conveyed to Thomas Wade, May 22, 1824. The executor of Mr. Wade sold to Symmes and Richard Potter, Sept. 18, 1838 (308: 91).

Richard Potter sold his interest in the 8 acre lot, to Ebenezer Fall, April 20, 1844 (344: 130) and Fall conveyed to Capt. Symmes Potter, Sept. 10, 1845 (358: 266). He bequeathed to his sister, Mrs. Julia P. Willett, 1859 (Pro. Rec. 420: 46) and her son, Wallace P. Willett, inherited and still owns.

Ward's Meadow.
No. 12 on Diagram.

The next lot in the ancient Inner Common of the South Eighth was the largest of all, containing about 50 acres. It was known as Ward's meadow, and is so called in the inventory of Jonathan Wade in 1749 (Pro. Rec. 330; 435). Jonathan Wade, the first of the name, bought the houselot of Rev. Nathaniel Ward and the commonage went with the homestead. It may have been granted to Mr. Ward though no record remains and continued in the Wade family to the date mentioned above. The question of these early grants in the Inner Common will be considered a little later in connection with John Tuttle's grant.

Jonathan Wade bequeathed the residue of his estate, which included this spacious meadow, to his grandson, Dr. Nathaniel Cogswell (proved Jan. 17, 1749. Pro. Rec. 329: 133). Northend Cogswell and other heirs sold it to James Brown "commonly called Ward's Meadow Pasture," Nov. 15, 1825 (240: 167). His heirs sold to George W. Brown, May 1, 1852

The Inner Common of the South Eighth has been fully described in The History of the Old Bay Road, No. XV of the Publications. It was a great pasture, held in common until about 1726, when it was divided, usually into small lots of about 8 acres.
Publications of Ipswich Historical Society. No. XV.
[3] Page 4.

(463: 118). He conveyed to Asa Wade, 38½ acres and a barn, April 21, 1862 (637: 1), and he sold in turn to Mary Quincy Kinsman, wife of Willard F. Kinsman, who still owns, March 30, 1881 (1055: 292).

James Burnham's Lot.
No. 13 on Diagram.

The lot on the east side of Ward's meadow seems to be the one described in the deed of James Burnham to Jonathan Wade, 6¾ acres, Feb. 23, 1728-9 (77: 172) Jonathan Wade sold to Joseph Manning, 5 acres, 124 poles, part of the land I purchased of Mr. James Burnham and Mr. Timothy Wade in the South eighth, July 2, 1741 (88: 131). It was bounded south by the Hamlet road, so called *i. e.*, Lakeman's Lane, and west "by the land of Jonathan Wade, to ye ditch in Ward's meadow so called and by the south side of the ditch down to Chebacco road." Its later history is given in connection with Joseph Abbe's lot.

Samuel Ayers's Lot.
No. 14 on Diagram.

The next lot was sold by Samuel Aiers and others to Joseph Fellows, about 9 acres "laid out to me in part with the heirs of Nathaniel Fuller," March 8, 1738 (88: 142). Nathaniel Fuller sold Joseph Manning ⅔ of an old right descending to Nathaniel, from his father, Nathaniel, being originally Haskell's right, lying in common with an old right, laid out to Samuel Ayers, Jan. 15, 1739 (80: 82). Dr. Manning conveyed to Joseph Fellows, whose land abutted on the south, in consideration of 1 acre 34 rods and £5, 1 acre 94 rods of upland I bought of Nathaniel Fuller, joining near to Proctor's brook, so called, June 27, 1740 (88: 142). Joseph Fellows conveyed to Joseph Manning his interest in the north end of the Ayers lot, June 27, 1740 (88: 132), and it was merged in Dr. Manning's large tract.

Joseph Abbe's Lot.
No. 15 on Diagram.

Dr. Joseph Manning purchased a third lot, one of the old lots, of Joseph Abbe, 10 acres which was bounded south west "by the way laid out from the saw mill to Brag's hill, through said Inner Common," March 26, 1743 (87: 254).

Lakeman's Lane is the way referred to, which extended originally to the saw mill.[1] The Bragg house cellar is still visible in the rear of Alonzo B. Fellow's residence. The old road may have traversed the low hill on which the old house stood to avoid the swamp, over which a causeway may have been built later.

Dr. John Manning inherited these three lots from his father, Dr. Joseph, and sold the 24 acres, comprised in them to Abraham Brown, May

---

[1] See The History of the Old Bay Road.

12, 1806(179: 50), who conveyed to Asa and John Dudley Andrews, March 31, 1815(208: 16), and they to Col. Nathaniel Wade, April 17, 1817 (215: 10). His heirs divided the estate, May 17, 1827 (Pro. Rec. 244: 243). William Foster Wade received the west half of this spacious pasture and Nathaniel Wade, the east. Joseph H. Wade and other heirs of William F. sold to Ira Worcester, March 13, 1844 (377: 256). His widow, Ruth G. sold to Willard B. Kinsman, the same which her husband had bought except a small corner of meadow sold to Asa Wade, July 12, 1876 (960: 110). Willard B. sold this to Mary Q. Kinsman, his daughter-in-law, May 10, 1883(1055: 83), Willard F. and Mary Q. conveying to Willard B. the Birch pasture on Lakeman's lane. Nathaniel Wade's portion was sold by his executor, his son Francis H. Wade, to Willard B. Kinsman, April 17, 1845 (357: 68). He sold to Mary A. Quincy, who became the wife of Willard B. Kinsman Jr., 24 acres, March 29, 1876 (951: 72). This included the 12 acre lot, bought of the executor of Nathaniel Wade in 1845, an 8 acre lot, purchased of Elisha Brown in 1848 and 3½ acres bought of Jacob B. Tenney Jr. in 1869.[1] On the eastern side of this lot the attractive farm buildings were built. Mention has already been made of the purchase by Mrs. Kinsman of the 12 acre lot, originally owned by Col. Nathaniel Wade in 1883 and the Ward's meadow pasture in 1881. These lots compose the present spacious farm.

Robert Calef's Lot.
No. 16 on Diagram.

Robert Calef owned an 8 acre lot, which was sold by his son, John, to John Kinsman, May 26, 1748 (93: 147) and by Kinsman to Benjamin Brown 3d and Nathaniel Brown, March 31, 1773 (132 : 152). Benjamin Brown, Parker Brown and other heirs sold their interest to Sarah, their sister, July 16, 1817 (281: 235), Sarah to Elisha Brown, July 7, 1835 (281: 236) and Elisha to Willard B. Kinsman, July 3, 1848 (411: 66).

Beyond this point the original ownerships and earlier transfers are very difficult to determine and the titles to some are very complicated. An attempt will be made, however, to trace the pedigrees.

Samuel Howard's Lot.
No. 17 on Diagram.

John Brown 3d was the owner of the next lot. Samuel Howard sold to John Brown 3d, carpenter, and Joseph Brown Jr., cordwainer, his right in a ten acre lot, set out to Capt. Ringe, Lt. Simon Wood and others, 9 acres on the south side of the Hamlet road and 1 acre on the north side, Nov. 21, 1737 (86: 314).

Philemon Dane and Simon Wood sold to John Brown 3d their proportionable part of two old rights in the South Pasture, 18 acres, May 26, 1742 (88: 59). John Brown Jr. sold a small lot, an acre and a half or two

---

[1] These belonged to the adjoining original lots and will be considered under that head.

acres, which he had bought of Benjamin Fellows, Oct. 12, 1742 (87: 211) to his son, John Brown 3d, with a house, Jan. 20, 1745 (89: 2). The will and inventory of John Brown 3d were filed June 9, 1746 (Pro. Rec. 327: 59). Two acres and all the buildings thereon and the remainder of the homestead on both sides of the road were devised; to the widow ⅛ the house and 3¾ acres with 7 acres of pasture on the south side of the road; to Samuel, the son, ⅔ of the house and 4 acres about it and 14 acres of pasture. Thomas Boardman sold to Benjamin Brown, his interest in the house and 14 acres, April 6, 1761 (109: 257) and he made a further conveyance of the interest which Samuel Brown conveyed to him on Dec. 19, 1758, to Benjamin, May 23, 1762 (113: 132). Benjamin Brown, it will be remembered, owned and occupied the east half of the house of which his brother, Elisha was joint owner,[1] and this house and land was left to his sons, Benjamin and Nathaniel. They bought the 8 acre lot on the west, we have noticed, March 31, 1773, and on the same date, they bought of John Kinsman the triangular lot, at the junction of the road to Essex and Lakeman's Lane (132: 152). This was owned by James Burnham and was acquired by Captain Kinsman, in his purchase from the heirs. They bought another 8 acre lot of Samuel Kinsman, east of their father's, March 20, 1783 (215: 188). On the death of their father, they became owners as well of the house where they dwelt and land about it and 14 acres of land on the south side of the lane (will proved April 3, 1797. Pro. Rec. 365: 97; land set off June 13, 1809. Pro. Rec. 378: 128). A large clump of lilacs near the line of Lakeman's Lane marks the location of the dwelling. The inventory of Benjamin (filed June 8, 1816. Pro. Rec. 389: 540) records about 20 acres, held in common with Nathaniel and the half dwelling. The heirs, Benjamin, Parker and others quitclaimed to Sarah Brown, their sister, the east end of the dwelling and 1¾ acres of land about it and land on the south side of the lane opposite the house, held in common with Nathaniel, etc., as well as the 8 acres, which was mentioned in connection with the lot just described, July 16, 1817 (281: 235). All the heirs, Benjamin, Parker, Sarah and Martha, widow of Elisha Brown, had quitclaimed to Nathaniel, their interest in 7 acres 30 poles with half the dwelling, 12 poles with part of the barn, an 18 pole lot and the 15½ acres pasture, July 10, 1817 (262: 134). Nathaniel Brown bequeathed a third of all his estate to his son, David, a third to Lucy, daughter of his deceased son, Nathaniel, and the remainder to the four children of his deceased daughter, Susanna Lakeman, William, Abigail, Susanna and Laura Ann (will proved June 1: 1830. Pro. Rec. 407: 415.) This 8 acre lot with half a dwelling was sold by George Haskell to Increase H. and Asa Brown, "the homestead of Nathaniel Brown," Nov. 6, 1835 (285: 242). The "Nat lot" 8 acres was included in the conveyance by Asa Brown to Mrs. Rhoda B. Potter, Feb. 11, 1867 (743: 198). Three acres were sold to Francis Brown and the remainder, 5½ acres, were sold by Mrs. Potter to Jacob B. Tenney, April 29, 1869 (771: 222). Mr. Tenney sold 3½ acres to Willard B. Kinsman,

---

[1] Page 12.

owner of the adjoining lot, reserving the remainder, April 29, 1869 (771: 270). The east end of the dwelling with 1¾ acres was conveyed by Sarah to Elisha Brown, July 7, 1835 (281: 236). Elisha sold to Francis Brown, 1¾ acre "beginning at the southwest corner by the road, straight through the land where a house stood," May 1, 1849 (435: 279). The house had disappeared and it was evidently torn down by Elisha and the new house built on the knoll near by.

The 18 rod lot which was quitclaimed to Nathaniel, in the apex of the triangle, was also acquired by Francis. Lucia P. Brown and others sold $\frac{9}{15}$ June 15, 1831 (261: 21), and Charles Kimball for Caroline Brown and others sold $\frac{6}{15}$ June 23, 1831 (261: 21), and on the same date, the same parties sold the 15 acres to Levi and Francis Brown (261: 21).[1]

Francis Brown sold the house and 3 acres of land and the 14 acre pasture to John Marshall, Feb. 21, 1863(651: 81), Marshall to Jacob B. Tenney April 7, 1869 (771: 221). Tenney bought the adjoining lot, as was mentioned. He sold 3½ acres to Willard B. Kinsman, April 29, 1869 (771: 270) and the house with 5 acres and the pasture to Albert Sturtevant, April 30, 1878 (998: 1). Ada L. Sturtevant, administratrix of Albert, sold to Albert S. Garland, April 27, 1881 (1057: 38), who sold to T. M. Norman, July 30, 1894 (1419:469) and he to W. J. Cameron, April 5, 1901 (1637:396).

Thomas Perrin's Lot.
No. 18 on Diagram.

Thomas Perrin owned a lot in the South Eighth, which he sold to John Brown Jr. and James Burnham, 15 acres, Nov. 26, 1729 (53: 217). Captain John Kinsman, as the heir or purchaser of the James Burnham land, came into possession. His heir, Samuel, sold 3 acres to Benjamin Brown Jr., tailor, Oct. 9, 1797 (168: 33). On this low and unfit spot near the Goose Pond, Mr. Brown built a home and reared a large family. His widow, Hannah, and the children, Edmund Brown of Lynn, blacksmith, Levi of Ipswich, cordwainer, Perley of Manchester, cabinet maker, John Brown Jr. of Ipswich, cordwainer, conveyed to Francis, another son, their interest in 17 acres, exclusive of about an acre and dwelling, barn etc., which were by deed of gift in the life time of Benjamin, conveyed to Hannah and Francis, in two equal moieties, April, 1838 (329: 295) John P. Lakeman, guardian of his children, conveyed ⅛ interest in 17 acres to Francis Brown, the estate of their grandfather, Benjamin Brown, Sept. 18, 1838 (329: 295). He conveyed to Francis their interest in the estate of their grandmother, Feb. 20, 1840 (329: 296).

Samuel Kinsman sold 15 acres, bounding the 3 acres sold to Benjamin Brown Jr., on the east and south to Josiah Burnham, Sept. 5, 1803 (191: 278). This was sold successively to John How Boardman, March 13, 1811 (191: 280); John Heard, Feb. 2, 1814 (201: 284); Geo. W. Heard, April 2, 1830 (282: 162); Thomas Low, April 1, 1835 (315: 270); John C.

---

[1]Francis Brown sold an 8 acre pasture on Lakeman's Lane to Henry S. Holmes, Mar. 9, 1842 (330: 18)

Carlisle, March 5, 1880 (1056: 260); Gustavus Kinsman, June 28, 1900 (1613:127).

Notice should be taken of a grant to Mr. John Tuttle, at the very beginning of the settlement of the Town of

"one hundred and fiftie acres about sixteene whereof are meadow having Mr. Winthrop East the Mile River West Mr. Faune John Perkins and Sergeant Howlett South and from the South part of Sergt. Howletts upland by a line to the East part of a great swamp to the River bounded on the North by great oaks marked neere the River and so to a marked tree neere to Mr Winthrop's farm."

"Memorandum, there is reserved an highway of foure rodd broad throu this farm to the Common to be layd out where the Towne shall appoint." (Town Record).

This great tract bounded by a line from the farm of Mr. Alonzo B. Fellows to Mile River, and extending to the farm of the late Gardiner A. Brown and others, much more than the 116 acres granted, was never occupied by Mr. Tuttle. It is interesting to note, however, that some large grants were made to individuals in this section of the common lands, which came to be known as the Inner Common of the South Eighth. The fifty acre Ward's meadow may have been granted to Rev. Nathaniel Ward. Mr. Saltonstall had a forty acre grant on Mile River and Thomas Firman a similar one. The highway was laid out and reserved for public use, but frequently there were no walls or fences and boundaries were dimly defined.

Denison Lot.
No. 19 on Diagram.

In this tract, originally assigned to John Tuttle, by request of Rev. Nathaniel Rogers, guardian to the heirs of Col. John Denison, a 10 acre lot was laid out to them, which he sold to James Burnham, Feb. 16, 1730–1 (137: 50).

John Annable's Lot.
No. 20 on Diagram.

Another lot was laid out to John Annable, which Robert Annable sold to Jonathan Wade, Jan. 10, 1728 (66: 20).

James Burnham's Lot.
No. 21 on Diagram.

Thomas Choate and Jonathan Wade, "specially appointed by the Commoners and Proprietors of ye common lands of Ipswich at their meeting, July 9, 1730," set off the full half part of an old supernumerary right to James Burnham, about 10 acres, having land in the possession of Thomas Burnham Jr. and the widow of Thomas Burnham deceased, son of Lieut. Thomas Burnham deceased, on the east side and John Annable's land west, equal to the other half of the right belonging to Wm. Buckley deceased, Sept. 28, 1730 (55: 250).

William Buckley Lot.
No. 22 on Diagram.

The other half of this Buckley right is undoubtedly identical with the lot which John Higginson of Salem sold to William Brown, "one half an old right about 9 acres in Brown's Pasture, otherwise Browns, Kinsmans and Choates, which was this day by Commoners laid out in part satisfaction of a common right belonging to the heirs of William Buckley dec'd by virtue of his draught the fourteenth of February, 1664," March 4, 1729 (55: 76).

Part of the land included in these grants, is contained in the meadow or pasture land, which Thomas Burnham sold to Francis Brown. Thomas Meady had his dwelling on a small lot opposite the gravel pit where some fruit trees still grow. His homestead is alluded to as early as 1808, but no trace of his title can be found. The 6 acre lot was inherited by John B. Brown and acquired in part by purchase and was included in the sale of the farm to Carlisle and Huckins, Aug. 2, 1860 (610: 233) and in the sale by Huckins's heirs to William G. Horton, a half interest in 8 acres, Feb. 26, 1889 (1243: 408).

The estate of James Burnham included 26 acres on the south side of the road, which came eventually, I presume, to Capt. John Kinsman and was sold by himself and his son Samuel as has been stated.

Thomas Burnham's Lot. [1]
No. 23 on Diagram.

Thomas Burnham 4th owned at his death 12 acres, tillage and pasture, called Brown's lot, which may be identified with the half right sold to William Brown in 1729. His estate included as well 17 acres and the buildings and 17 acres pasture land by Bragg's hill, so called (will proved May 8, 1730. Pro. Rec. 319: 149–51). It would seem that he was living then upon part of the Bragg farm, which fell to his son, Thomas, and was sold by Thomas to his son James Burnham, a cooper, Nov. 10, 1783 (142: 19). This deed conveyed 26 acres on the south side of the road. James Burnham conveyed this to John Willet, Jan. 19, 1793 (155: 167) having previously conveyed 4 acres of fresh meadow bounded on the west by a row of willow trees, July 28, 1787 (155: 200).

This row of trees or the later offshoots from the ancient stock still remains. John Willet directed in his will that his daughter, Betsey Burnham, should have the improvement of her late husband's property and that his grandchildren, Betsey and Joshua Burnham, children of Betsey, should have all the lands conveyed by their father (proved Feb. 7: 1804. Pro. Rec. 371: 325).

Betsey Burnham became the wife of Jabez Richards and the portion assigned was set off to her, Oct. 7, 1806 (Pro. Rec. 374: 285). She conveyed this fresh meadow to Richards, Oct. 17, 1809 (189: 14). Executions

[1] Page 11.

were granted against Richards and the 4 acre meadow was apportioned to Daniel Cogswell, July 23, 1819 (Exec. No. 3: 156) and to Langley Brown March 2, 1821 (Exec. No. 3: 289). William Cogswell and others, heirs of Daniel, sold to Hervey Whipple, March 24, 1866 (923: 46).

During his ownership of the 26 acre lot, James Burnham had sold a half acre to Elisha Brown, which he used as a brickyard, and 2 acres to Nehemiah Brown, Sept. 17, 1792 (155: 166). After John Willet's death his heirs sold to Joseph Brown. Moses, son of John Willet, sold him 10 acres, abutting on Daniel Brown's brickyard and Joshua Burnham sold him the remainder, 14 acres, bounded south by "Candlewood St. so called," reserving the land on which the district school now stands.[1] Both deeds were drawn on April 1, 1812 (198: 264). Mr. Brown built the house, as a dwelling for his son, James, probably that same year, and sold him the house and 3 acres, Dec. 23, 1817. The whole property eventually came to him. D. F. Brown and the other heirs sold their interest to Hervey Whipple, who had married Martha P., daughter of James Brown, July 3, 1852 (463: 116). His son, George Albert, inherited and still occupies. He bought the old brickyard which was sold by James Burnham to Elisha Brown.

John Fawn's Lot.
No. 24 on Diagram.

Beyond the Candlewood road, John Fawn, one of the earliest settlers, who owned the property and built the oldest part of the house, now owned by the Ipswich Historical Society, received a grant of some 25 acres. John Webster of Newbury sold to Robert Kinsman, "that farm which John Webster his father bought of the assignees of John Fane as by a bill of sale under their hands 25 acres at a place called Chebacco," having the land of Thomas Bishop southwest, a creek, southeast, Samuel Symonds and Nathaniel Rogers north, William Story northwest, Nov. 10, 1652 (Ips. Deeds 1: 182). William Story is not mentioned in the grant to John Tuttle as an abuttor and probably bought part of the John Fawn land, which was acquired by Robert Kinsman.

Mr. Kinsman played a famous part in the resistance to Gov. Andros in 1687,[2] and was one of that noted group which suffered so severely for their patriotic action. He was appointed Quartermaster in 1684 and had seen active service in the Narragansett campaign. He had a seat appointed to him "at the table" in the meeting house in 1700. As he was but twenty-three years old, when he purchased the farm, it is probable that at this time he married Mary Boreman, though the date of the marriage is not known. No mention of buildings on the farm is

[1] The school house formerly stood in what is now the orchard of Geo. A. Whipple's farm, a little south of the dwelling. A small lot, 36 ft. front, 40 ft. deep was bought of Hervey Whipple by the Town and a school house erected, facing the Essex road (846: 136. Feb. 5, 1872.) The building has been removed within a few years to Manning St. On the triangular lot in front of this school house lot, a blacksmith shop formerly stood.
[2] See Ipswich in the Mass. Bay Colony. Chapter XIV.

made in the deed of sale and the young couple may have established their home in a new house, planned and built to their mind. Here they spent their lives. Five daughters and four sons were born here and here the Quartermaster died, Feb. 19, 1712 at the age of eighty three. He conveyed to his son, Joseph, "his now dwelling house," and the 14 acre home lot, bounded on one end by the Common, on another by the highway to Chebacco and 20 acres of pasture land adjoining, March 21, 1698 (13: 128). He was a glazier by trade and in his will he bequeathed to his sons, Joseph and Robert, "all my Glazeing Tools, Husbandry and Carpenter Tools, of all sorts." He further specified,

"I give to my daughter, Sarah Perkins, who stayed longest with me, my Bed in ye great chamber, with all ye furniture belonging to it."

"I give to my Daughter, Unice Burnam, my chest of draws."

"I give to my five daughters, Mary, Sarah, Joanna, Margarett & Unice, all my moveable estate of household goods . . . and all my quick stock of all sorts & kinds whatsoever, as cattle, sheep & horse kind . . . also my crane, tramells & hooks."

Item, I give unto my maid, Eliz^a Dingey, five good sheep if shee abide with mee till my decease, otherwise I give but three good sheep."

(Proved March 12, 1712. Pro. Rec. 310: 520-1.)

Joseph Kinsman was twenty-five years old when his father conveyed the farm to him and as his first child was born two years later, it is probable that he brought home his bride, Susanna Dutch, about the time the conveyance was made. She died on Nov. 9th, 1734, at the age of 60 years, and he married Sarah Peabody of Boxford, April 27, 1736. By his first marriage, there were eleven children, six daughters and five sons, all of whom grew to mature age and all were married, save Joseph, who died at the age of 23 years.

He died in the old homestead, no doubt, and by his will (proved May 25, 1741. Pro. Rec. 24: 232) he divided his estate:

"I give and bequeath to John Kinsman, my son, all ye land whereon the house and barn now standeth, with ye house and barn that's now in his possession,[1] with all ye land that I bought of my brother Robert Kinsman. That is to be understood, his homestead with all ye common rights adjoining to it, that did belong to a south eaight so called and allso a nine accor right lying in a pastor called Browns & Kinsmans pastor. The which right also belonged to a south eaight, and hes to enjoy ye same according to ye quiteclamies that wee^v alredy given to each other, and also all my righte and interst that I have in Wilderness hill pastor so called . . ."

To his sons, Pelatiah and Benjamin, he gave his "now dwelling house," his barns and lands, in equal division. To his son Nathaniel, he gave £250 in money. His household goods and £5 in money were given to his daughters, Susannah How, Eunice and Sarah Wells, Elizabeth Brown, Hannah Wallis and Martha Dennis.

[1] The property now owned and occupied by Mr. Charles G. Brown, in the same neighborhood.

Palatiah Kinsman bought his brother's interest and sold the old homestead and 38½ acres adjoining to John Wainwright, March 18, 1754 (101: 79), and the pasture land to his brother John. In the previous year, Feb. 1, 1753 (101: 28) he had bought the Col. Wainwright farm in Argilla and he probably removed to that neighborhood. His descendants still retain the Argilla farm. Col. Wainwright sold 17 acres on the east side of the farm to John Kinsman, Oct. 11, 1754 (101: 62). John Wise, the guardian of John Wainwright, the insane son of Col. John, who had inherited from his father, sold 12 acres to Isaac Procter, leaving the highway 2½ rods wide, Sept. 9, 1755 (103: 111) and 10 acres more to the same, bounded northwest by another way from Ipswich to Chebacco, Dec. 30, 1757 (108: 271). This completed the sale of the homestead and as no mention is made of the buildings, we may presume that they had disappeared. An old well is remembered by the older people, near a pair of bars, very near the road, a few rods from the corner of the Essex and Candlewood roads, which may indicate the approximate location of the ancient farm house.

Isaac Procter sold 22 acres to Elisha Brown, March 16, 1768 (125: 105). He sold an acre and a half on the corner to Nehemiah Brown, March 16, 1789 (161: 13), which the heirs of Nehemiah sold to Nehemiah, the son, July 17, 1821 (248: 157), he to James Brown, with 20 young fruit trees thereon standing and bearing, April 5, 1833 (270: 49), and the heirs of James to Hervey Whipple, July 3, 1852 (463: 116). His son, George Albert Whipple, inherited and still owns.

A larger lot, 8½ acres with a barn, was sold by Elisha to his son Joseph, March 16, 1789, the day on which he disposed of all his property, as we have remarked before[1] (157: 140). Joseph conveyed this to his son, Joseph Jr., Aug. 1, 1806 (191: 259) and it was inherited by Gardiner A. Brown, his son, whose heirs are still in possession. Elisha had sold 12½ acres on the south side of these lots to his son Benjamin, April 20, 1768 (158: 128). Benjamin bequeathed 2¾ acres on the Candlewood road to his son David and the remainder to Benjamin and Nathaniel (proved June 13, 1809. Pro. Rec. 365: 97). David included this in his bequest to the school district and when the Trustees sold the land, Mr. George A Whipple bought this lot, triangular in shape.

Thomas Manning, the executor of Nathaniel Brown, sold 4¼ acres to Elisha Brown, June 22, 1831 (286: 209). Benjamin Brown conveyed his half interest in the remainder to Thomas Brown, July 15, 1809 (194: 176). Both these lots are improved by E. Newton Brown, one of the heirs of Elisha.

John Kinsman and Samuel, heirs of Capt. John, sold 47 acres of upland and salt-marsh, opposite the dwelling of John Jr., extending to Haffield's Creek to Elisha Brown Jr. and Joseph Brown, April 24, 1783 (144: 85). Some division of the land was made, I presume, as in Elisha Brown's will, about 32 acres is distributed. He gave 7 acres to Daniel and Elisha, 20 acres upland and marsh to Daniel, and the Old Field, containing about 5 acres to the widow (proved May 1, 1809. Pro. Rec. 377: 530).

[1] Page 13.

Daniel sold the 20 acre lot to Theodore Andrews, Jan. 5, 1842 (328: 251) and he, to Joseph Brown, Jan. 31, 1842 (329: 154). It has descended to Gardiner A. Brown and his heirs. The 7 acre lot and the Old Field are still improved by the heirs of Elisha.

John Perkins Sr. and Thomas Howlett's lots.
Nos. 25 and 26 on Diagram.

The Candlewood road, leading toward Hamilton, affords an interesting study. Farms were granted on the east side of the road at the settlement of the Town. John Fawn, as we have seen, received 30 acres or more on the corner of the Chebacco road.[1]

"There was Granted to Thomas Howlett thirtie acres of upland and ten of meaddow at the head of Chebacko creeke the meaddow lyinge on both sides the Creeke and the upland on the West side of the meaddow." (Town Records.)

"Granted to John Perkins Senr thirtie acres of upland and ten of meaddow lying towards the head of Chebocky creeke havinge Thomas Howlett's Land on the Southwest." (Town Records.)

"Memorand, that John Perkins the Elder hath sould unto Thomas Howlett a psell of Land of forty acres more or less medow and upland lying at Chebocye Granted unto the sayde John Perkins in the year 1636 bounded on the Northeast by a pcell of Land formerly granted unto Mr. Faune now in the possession of John Webster and partly also on the same syde by the Land of Richard Haffield on the Southwest by a pcell of Land granted unto the sayde Thomas Howlett at the Northwest end thereof butting upon a highway leading to Chebacky at the southeast upon the common." Howlett gave in exchange two lots at the east end of the Town and £7 10s. "Entered the 23d day of the second month, 1638" (Town Records).

Mr. Howlett was now the proprietor of 80 acres, more or less, and it was probably considerably more as the same tract was reckoned at 100 acres, when Thomas Bishop gave deed of it. He was in possession of the farm as early as 1652. There is no trace of any buildings on the land when John Perkins sold to Howlett but one or both of these parties may have built on the lots, as the executor of Thomas Bishop conveyed to the administrator of Rev. Jonathan Mitchell of Cambridge, who held a mortgage, a farm of 100 acres, bounded south and west by common land, southeast by John Choate's land with two dwellings, two barns, etc., Dec. 13, 1677 (Ips. Deeds 4: 115).

Sarah Bishop of Weathersfield, widow of John, son of Thomas Bishop, certified that by his will, Feb. 6, 1670, Thomas bequeathed the farm to his sons, John and Thomas, and that an execution was levied by Mrs. Margaret Mitchell, who sold the farm to Francis Wainwright (Ips, Deeds 4: 449) Sarah conveyed her title to Anthony Checkley, Aug. 30, 1683 (Ips. Deeds 5:59). Thomas Bishop made similar conveyance, Jan.

[1] Page 22.

20, 1684 (Ips. Deeds 5: 68). Anthony Checkly and Thomas Bishop, late of Barbadoes, sold the farm in two lots, one of 66 acres with house, barn etc. to John Brown, and 36 acres with house and barn to Sergeant John Choate, bounded by Choate's own land partly on the south, Jan. 1, 1684 (Ips. Deeds 5: 57). Brown's title was contested by Bishop, and the 19 papers in the case, Bishop vs. Brown cover many pages in the old Court files. The Indenture by Francis Wainwright, leasing the farm to John Brown, April 8, 1682, is beautifully engrossed on parchment. (Vol. 40, leaf 140).

John Brown conveyed his farm to his sons, James and William. To James, he gave "one full third and another third except what I have given to my son William with 6 acres now given him, with my mansion, having Corporal Joseph Kinsman north and east," July 9, 1721 (39: 54). In the division, James received 39 acres 56 rods, March 14, 1727/8 (50: 176), and William, 27 acres 13 rods, south of James.

In 1736, this range of farms, Joseph Kinsman's, James and William Brown's and Samuel Choate's, whose farm was south of William Brown's, was enlarged by a singular instrument. The document begins, "Joseph Kinsman, James Brown, William Brown and Mr. Samuel Choate are the owners of a division of land known by the name of Kinsman's, Brown's and Choate's division in the South Eighth, the interest of ye sd Kinsman being one old right and half an old right, James Brown one old right 3 new rights etc. . . . and whereas they have chosen us the subscribers to set out to each of them according to their several proportionable parts,

We have set to Joseph Kinsman, about 7 acres 5 rods etc." This pasture measured 59¾ rods on the way leading to Chebacco pond (the Candlewood road) beginning at the corner of the way to Chebacco, the Essex road.

To James Brown, this committee set 6 acres 75 rods adjoining his homestead, measuring 53 rods on the highway, from the lot appointed to Kinsman; to William Brown, 3 acres 2 rods, having 30½ rods frontage; and to Samuel Choate, a lot, 42¼ rods on the road, 9 acres 133 rods, reserving a highway through the same to Chebacco (the present Choate Street).

The report was filed by the Committee, Francis Sayer, Thorndike Low, David Low and William Giddinge, Dec. 29, 1736 (84: 37). This may explain why the Gardiner A. Brown buildings are set so far from the road. They occupy the same site as the original, and the ancient buildings of the Joseph Kinsman and the William Brown farms are known to have been set about a similar distance. The front land was a common pasture and each house was approached by a lane. One deed contains an allusion to the Brown, Choate and Kinsman pasture, as including a part at least of the Geo. A. Whipple lot on the west side of the highway. It may be that the pasture lay wholly on the west side of the original thoroughfare and that after these pastures were annexed to the three farms, the highway was changed to its present location.

James Brown acquired a goodly estate which included houses and lands on North Main Street, as well as the farm. His inventory (filed June 29, 1741) contains interesting items

a silver hilted sword and belt	£14– 0–0
pistols and holster	3–10–0
17 oz. plate	23–16–0
a negro man called Kant	70– 0–0
a negro woman called Bett	80– 0–0
wearing apparel	17–10–0
saddle and bridle	60/–0
and the farm stock.	
5 cows £45–0–0, pr. oxen 24–0–0, 1 steer 8–0–0	77– 0–0
3 2 yr olds 15–0–0, 3 yr old & ½ 12–10–0	27–10–0
3 calves 6–2–6, 18 sheep & 13 lambs 23–5–0	29– 7–6
3 swine	10– 0–0
dwelling house, barn, at farm & 50 acres	1350– 0–0
23 acres Wilderness Hill in Chebacco side	330– 0–0
27 acres Gould's Pasture	555– 0–0
20 acres Wilderness Hill South 8	250– 0–0
Total	6530– 1–0

He bequeathed all his real estate on the south side the river to his son James, except a 6 acre lot in Lee's meadow; to his son Jonathan, all real estate on the north side the river and this 6 acres; to his son Francis, £600 passable money at the age of 21; a portion to his four daughters, Lucy, Eunice, Elizabeth and Sarah. His wife, Sarah, is to be executrix until James is twenty-one, when he shall be (proved June 1, 1741. Pro. Rec. 324:576).

James, the heir of the farm, died and Jonathan also, leaving a widow, Elizabeth, who married Samuel Sawyer. A family feud arose over the distribution of the estate and Mr. Sawyer cleared himself of any part or lot in the matter. He and his wife, Elizabeth, "to end all disputes between us and the surviving children of our Honored Father-in-Law, Mr. James Brown, shopkeeper, deceased, namely Eunice Brown and Sarah Brown, singlewomen, Elizabeth Perkins, wife of Robert Perkins, relating to the real estate of said James respecting the Title and Descent thereof on ye decease of James Brown, a minor and grandson to the said James and only son of Jonathan Brown (by the said Eliz. Sawyer) her former husband," in consideration of their relinquishing their right in certain part, quitclaim to Eunice, Sarah and Elizabeth their interest in the farm and the outlying pastures, March 12, 1760 (111: 94). Susanna and Elizabeth Sawyer, daughters of Samuel and Elizabeth, gave a similar quitclaim, Jan. 8, 1783 (159:13).

Capt. Robert Perkins, who had married Elizabeth Brown, July 19, 1753, occupied the farm apparently and his daughter, Elizabeth, became the wife of Joseph Brown, son of Elisha, Dec. 3, 1779. They began their housekeeping probably in the west half of the old Joseph Marshall house, as we have said,[1] but Joseph bought the interest of the heirs, James Perkins

[1] Page 13.

of Nobleborough, John Perkins of Dresden, Robert Perkins of Woolwich, Sarah Perkins of Ipswich, ½ of the estate, Oct. 31, 1797 (167: 265). He built the present dwelling and occupied it until his death. He made conveyance of the west half of the dwelling and 4 acres, north of the way to the house, to his son Joseph Jr., April 18, 1839 (312: 287). Joseph Jr. inherited the estate and enlarged it by the purchase of 15 acres adjoining the farm on the south, from the original William Brown estate, Jan. 31, 1842 (329: 154). His sons, Joseph P. and Gardiner A. Brown, succeeded to the ownership and the latter acquired a complete title by purchase from the heirs of his brother, Oct. 12, 1858 (578: 98, 99). He bequeathed it to his son, A. Story Brown.

William Brown, son of John, bought 8 acres of upland of Samuel Choate, son of John Choate, March 29, 1707 (20: 202). He was a weaver by trade and had already built a house for himself on his father's land. On April 18, 1707, John Brown Sen., farmer, conveyed to William, "for his encouragement and towards his settlement . . . two acres of my land, being part of my farm, whereon ye dwelling house of ye sd son now stands" (28: 19). In the division of his father's estate, 27 acres 13 rods were laid out to him and 1 acre 10 rods in Gould's pasture to make his full portion, March 14, 1727/8 (50: 176). His farm comprised therefore some 37 acres, with other land on the west side of the highway, which will be considered later.

In the division of his estate, he gave to his son, William, the land on the other side the road and also "as long as he shall keep a blacksmith shop thereon a piece of land where his shop stands, south on ye yard fence before the shop, west on the highway, north on ye lane that leads up to my dwelling house." The remainder of his estate was given to Stephen and Elisha. His son, Thomas, received money, Benjamin, his right in Ipswich Canada. The children of Nehemiah and his daughter, Dorothy Burnham, were remembered (will proved April 2, 1753. Pro. Rec. 331: 243). A negro boy was valued at £20 among his goods and chattels and 2 horses at 15–10–0 (331: 296).

Elisha Brown quitclaimed his interest in his father's homestead, the dwelling and southern part of the land, to Stephen, Feb. 22, 1754, (117: 95) and June 26, 1762(117: 96), and sold his half of 15 acres upland and marsh to his son, Elisha Jr., Feb. 6, 1772 (292: 77).

The widow of Elisha Jr. received this lot under his will (proved July 1, 1799. Pro. Rec. 367: 19) (division Pro. Rec. 377: 530). In the division of her estate, it fell to Daniel, June 26, 1821 (Pro. Rec. 399: 500), who sold to Theodore Andrews, Jan. 5, 1842 (328: 251) and he, to Joseph Brown, Jan. 31, 1842 (329:154). The lot was called "the Close" and did not include an acre and a half in one corner which is still owned by the heirs of Elisha. The engine house stands on this small lot.

Stephen Brown sold a small lot, 1¼ acres, to Timothy Tibbets, a bricklayer, "beginning at the corner of the lane that leads to the house," measuring 16 rods on the road, prior to 1800 (239: 16) and the remainder of the ¹and that came to him from his father, 13 acres, to Josiah Brown, April 14,

THE RESIDENCE OF MR. A. STORY BROWN
The farm was bought by John Brown² in 1684.

1807 (180: 123). No mention of the old William Brown dwelling is made and it had probably disappeared. Timothy Tibbets sold the 1¼ acres he had bought of Stephen Brown to Ephraim Brown, Jan. 2, 1800 (239: 16) and, he, to Josiah, April 12, 1825 (238:75). The whole lot was inherited by his son, Manasseh Brown Jr., whose heirs still own. Eliza Brown, executrix of James Brown, of Adams Co., Illinois, who died on May 15th, 1864, conveyed to Manasseh Jr. all the right James had in several parcels (recorded Pro. Rec. 119: 35), Dec. 4, 1865 (693: 265).

John Choate, we have observed,[1] bought 36 acres with a house and barn of Anthony Checkley and Thomas Bishop, Jan. 1, 1684. He had previously bought a house and land, "earable and meadow," 12 acres, of Thomas Willson, July 8, 1665 (Ips. Deeds 3: 17). He conveyed to his son John Jr. "a parcel of upland on which the dwelling house of sd Choate Jun. now stands," bounded by his own land toward the north west, May 1, 1692 (Ips. Deeds 5: 505).

His son, Samuel Choate, received or bought the remainder of the John Choate property, with the dwelling bought from Bishop. He sold 8 acres, before mentioned, to William Brown, his next neighbor, Mar. 29, 1707 (20: 202). Samuel Choate sold 43 acres with the house and barn to Thomas Boardman, reserving a road that is laid out through said premises leading to Chebacco, April 16, 1762 (110: 134). Boardman sold 40 acres with one old building, bounded south by the road that leads to Ebenezer Choate's to William Brown, April 13, 1772 (130: 159). William Brown conveyed his homestead on the corner of Fellows Lane to his son, James, and 25 acres of the Choate land, June 15, 1786 (145: 185) and the remaining 15 acres, July 1, 1786 (145: 200). It was included in the gift by will to Josiah, son of James (proved Feb. 7, 1826. Pro. Rec. 405: 224) and by similar conveyance to Manasseh Jr., whose heirs still own.

Gould's Pasture.
No. 27 on Diagram.

The great tract of land, now owned by E. Newton Brown, William G. Horton, Frederick G. Cross, John W. Mansfield, A. Story Brown, Geo. A. Whipple and the heirs of William H. Kinsman, extending from Choate Road to Red Root or Red Wood Hill, was included in the early part of the eighteenth century in two great pastures, known as Gould's Pasture and Wilderness Hill Pasture.

Gould's Pasture extended from Choate Road to the lot now owned by John W. Mansfield. Henry Gould improved a small lot here in 1728, as appears from the deed of Simon Wood, Thomas Wade and Jonathan Fellows, the Committee of Proprietors to James Brown of "half a certain piece of common land in the South 8th, now in possession of Henry Goold, 1¼ acres, as the fence now stands," May 8, 1728 (50: 175) and the deed of the same to Sarah and Hannah Goole, of half a lot then in possession of

[1] Page 26.

Henry Gould, "Gould to have improvement during his life, May 8, 1728 (50: 197). But he seems to have had no title to any portion and the whole pasture was included in the Common land.

In the deed of division of Kinsman's, Brown's and Choate's division in the South 8th, previously mentioned, the Committee proceeded to assign to each a lot in Gould's Pasture. To James Brown, they allotted 37 acres 48 rods, abutting on the way now known as Choate St. or Choate Road, reserving this way and Gould's lot of land, and on the way to Chebacco Pond, the present Candlewood road. This is almost identical with the lot owned and occupied by E. Newton Brown. To William Brown, brother of James, they assigned 14 acres 49 rods.

In the inventory of James Brown, the Gould's Pasture lot is mentioned, containing 27 acres, June 29, 1741 (Pro. Rec. 324: 576). A ten acre lot had apparently been sold, which is undoubtedly the lot which Thomas Boardman sold to Timothy Thornton and Robert Perkins, sons-in-law and heirs of James Brown, on the corner of Choate Road and Candlewood Road, Feb. 5, 1772 (130: 69, 131: 49).

In the following year, Thornton petitioned for a division of the Gould's pasture lot, which included about 38 acres, joining the lot already owned by Thornton and Perkins, "excepting about an acre and a quarter in the center thereof, incompassed, belonging to said Robert Perkins," Feb. 8, 1773 (131: 213). Perkins conveyed this small lot to Thornton, Feb. 11, 1773 (131: 50). In further settlement of the family dispute, previously alluded to,[1] Susanna and Elizabeth Sawyer, quitclaimed to Robert and Elizabeth Perkins and Timothy and Eunice Thornton, any interest they had in the 27 acres Gould's pasture, Jan. 8, 1783 (159: 13). Thornton evidently became sole owner of the whole tract. Prior to 1796, he sold a lot, presumably about 2 acres, to Elisha Brown. Mr. Brown erected a house and barn, which were occupied by his son, Ephraim. In his will, he bequeathed to Ephraim, "all the land I purchased of Mr. Thornton, with the buildings" (proved July 1, 1799. Pro. Rec. 367: 19).

On June 10, 1796, Thomas Gilbert Thornton of Pepperelboro, and James Brown Thornton of Ipswich, mariner, sold to Joseph and John How Boardman, 35 acres in Gould's pasture (163: 123). Joseph's interest was conveyed to Ephraim Brown, and by mutual agreement, John How Boardman received 20 acres, the southern part, and Brown, 17 acres on the north side of the lot, May 25, 1797 (239: 16). Ephraim Brown also became owner of the 9 acre lot, assigned to Joseph Kinsman, in Gould's pasture in 1736, which Kinsman sold to William Brown Jr., blacksmith, May 8, 1742 (84: 134). He sold 30 acres with the buildings, to Josiah Brown and Winthrop Boardman, April 12, 1825 (238: 97). The widow, Elizabeth Boardman, conveyed her half interest to Manasseh Brown Jr., July 7, 1845 (362: 243) and Josiah, father of Manasseh, conveyed his interest to him, Dec. 18, 1854 (506: 200). Manasseh Brown Jr., sold to E. Newton Brown, the present owner, Dec. 21, 1867 (850: 216).

John How Boardman sold his lot, said to contain 17 acres, to Win-

[1] Page 27.

throp Boardman, March 9, 1820 (223: 252). Ephraim Brown acquired it and it was later owned by Asa Brown, who held it in 1854. Joseph Kinsman owned it and his heirs, Lucy Cogswell of Essex and Aaron Cogswell, Joseph Kinsman, Asa Kinsman, John Brown and his wife, Eunice K., in her own right, sold to Obadiah and Joshua Lamson 22 acres, 30 rods, April 28, 1864 (666: 77). The Lamsons sold to Thomas P. Pingree, March 3, 1869 (770: 7), who sold to Joseph Huckins, May 1, 1876 (1012: 273). The Huckins heirs sold to William G. Horton, Feb. 26, 1889 (1243: 408).

William Brown, son of James, received 14 acres 49 rods in Gould's pasture, in the division of the common land, Dec. 29, 1736 (84: 37). He bequeathed the bulk of his real estate to his sons, Stephen and Elisha (proved April 2, 1753. Pro. Rec. 331: 243). But no mention of Gould's pasture occurs in the inventory (Pro. Rec. 331: 296), and he may have conveyed this lot to Elisha before his death. Elisha conveyed this lot to his brother, Stephen, Feb. 22, 1754 (117: 95). Stephen Brown sold the lot in two parts, one of 5 acres abutting on Candlewood road, to Samuel and Benjamin Patch, on Jan. 15, 1790 (151: 99) and the remainder, 9½ acres, to Nathan Fellows, "with liberty of a way one rod wide on the south side of land I sold to Samuel and Benjamin Patch," Jan. 15, 1790 (150: 248). John Patch sold this lot to Joshua Lamson, Feb. 7, 1842 (329: 192), Lamson to William H. Kinsman, land and building, Feb. 24, 1869 (766: 259). It was sold to Jacob Scanks, April 1, 1870 (793: 281), to William H. Kinsman, June 14, 1878 (1000: 241), to Eben Perkins, June 26, 1878 (1000: 242), and to Frederick G. Cross, the present owner, Sept. 23, 1887 (1205: 472). The 9 acre lot in the rear, was owned later by William H. Kinsman, who sold to Thomas P. Pingree, June 6, 1868 (749: 52), and was included in the later sales, already mentioned, to Huckins and Horton.

The Wilderness Hill Pasture.

No. 28 on Diagram.

The great pasture, called the Wilderness Hill pasture, on the slope of the noble hill, which was called by that name from the earliest times, was divided into lots, but no record of the division remains. The first in this series was owned by Elisha Brown, son of William, a 19 acre lot (inventory, 1799 Pro. Rec. 367: 225). The inventory of his son, Elisha Jr., mentions 21 acres on the hills, May 26, 1808 (Pro. Rec. 376: 456). This pasture, now said to contain 23½ acres, was sold to Ephraim and Daniel Brown, (380: 166). Daniel acquired Ephraim's interest and sold to Theodore Andrews, Jan. 5, 1842 (328: 251) who sold to Elisha Brown, Jan. 31, 1842 (329: 126). William T. Cross of Salem became the owner and sold to Joseph Rowell, Nov. 1, 1850 (436: 65). Rowell sold the land with a barn to William H. Kinsman, March 13, 1854 (491: 137). Mr. Kinsman built the house and sold to William T. Cross, April 28, 1856 (530: 117) His son, Frederick G. Cross, sold to John W. Mansfield, April 7, 1888 (1219: 455) and Mr. Mansfield still owns and occupies.

James Brown's inventory (Pro. Rec. 324: 576. June 1, 1741) contains the items, "23 acres Wilderness Hill on Chebacco side, 20 acres Wilderness Hill South 8th." Susanna and Elizabeth Sawyer quitclaimed their interest in these lots to the other heirs, Jan. 8, 1783 (159: 13). The heirs of Robert Perkins, who sold their interest in the farm to Joseph Brown, included $\frac{4}{9}$ of 22 acres on Wilderness Hill, Oct. 31, 1797 (167 265). Joseph Brown Jr. inherited, and his son, Gardiner A., bought the interest of the heirs of his brother, Joseph P. in 28 acres, the Hill pasture, bounded north by William Cross, east, land late of Ephraim Brown and Elizabeth Boardman, south by Hervey Whipple, west, by the highway, and about 12 acres near the Hill pasture, bounded west by the road, east, by Isaac Knowlton, south by William H. Kinsman, Oct. 12, 1858 (578: 99). The heirs of Gardiner A. Brown still own the larger lot, but he sold the 12½ acre pasture to William Henry Kinsman, May 5, 1859 (594: 100). Mr. Kinsman owned large tracts on the hills adjoining, some of which had been in possession of the family for generations.

Fuller's Pasture.
No. 29 on Diagram.

On the west side of the Candlewood road, the George A. Whipple farm has been traced already in the narrative of the old Chebacco road.[1]

Sergeant William Brown and Lieut. Joseph Kinsman bought about 10 acres of William, John, Ebenezer and Jacob Fuller, May 21, 1733 (70: 130). They had bought previously of James Fuller, about 10 acres, south of the above mentioned purchase, "at a place known as Fuller's Pasture in the Inner Common," April 4, 1732 (66: 32). Mr. Kinsman disposed of his interest, as all subsequent conveyances are in the William Brown line. Elisha and Stephen, sons of William, inherited the residue of the estate, including this lot which is called Link-horn or Lincoln Hill in the inventory and a half acre in Lincoln or Link-horn swamp (will proved April 2, 1753, Pro. Rec. 331: 243) and Elisha probably built the house and buildings, the last traces of which disappeared only a few years since. The cellar still remains.

Elisha Brown Jr. bought a half acre of James Burnham, Dec. 17, 1791 (151: 166) on which he established a brickyard. In his will, he is styled "Gentleman," and his inventory mentions a blue coat, waist coat and breeches, $9.50, a hat and wig, $4, a fustian suit, $4, loom and weaving harness, $5, 2 wheels, $1. His estate included the homestead, 14 acres and buildings and the brickyard, 13 acres upland and marsh with a barn, 19 acres in Wilderness Hill, 5 acres with a house and ⅔ barn (the T. M. Norman place) and the land he had purchased of Mr. Thornton. The Thornton property, he gave to his son Ephraim; to the widow, the 14 acre lot, (called 13 acres in inventory) the Old Field, 5 acres, the orchard, ½ acre, near the house, and the east end of the dwelling; to Daniel, the brick yard, 20 acres on the Gloucester road, known as Kinsman's land, the west end of house and 7 acres on the north side of the lot. Daniel and Elisha received

[1] Pages 21 and 22.

the 23 acre pasture in common (proved July 1, 1799. Pro. Rec. 367: 19). Benjamin also occupied part of the house.

His son, Elisha, (Capt. Elisha) died a few years after and there was set off to his widow, Martha, his interest in the dwelling and land south of the house, May 1, 1809 (Pro. Rec. 377: 534–5). The disposition of several of the lots has been traced already. The homestead has continued in the ownership of the heirs. Winthrop Low of Essex quitclaimed to Charlotte, wife of Elisha Brown, son of Capt. Elisha, interest in 7 acres on the north side of the lot, half the house and the half acre, called the clay pit, the old brick-kiln, June 20, 1851 (446: 285). Eliza Brown conveyed to E. Newton Brown, her right in the homestead and lands, March 8, 1871 (850: 216).

William Brown Jr., the blacksmith,[1] bought 7 acres in the Fuller Pasture of Nathaniel Fuller, March 28, 1732 (65: 264), on which he built a dwelling. His father had received 3 acres in the division of the Brown, Kinsman and Choate pasture already quoted, on the corner "of the lane leading to Joseph Fellows," and the way to Chebacco Pond, Dec. 29, 1736 (84: 37). He conveyed to his son William Jr., "2 acres 30 rods upland, adjoining my said son's dwelling," measuring 10 rods on the road to Chebacco Pond and 17 rods 2 ft. on the Lane, March 3, 1736–7 (84: 127).

The house must have been quite a little north of the present Manasseh Brown homestead. Benjamin Kinsman, son of Joseph Kinsman, sold to Brown, the 5 acres on the lane adjoining his property, which had been assigned to his father in the division of the Brown, Kinsman, and Choate pasture, May 25, 1742 (84: 135).

William Brown Sen., bequeathed to his son, about ¾ of an acre, which still remained in his possession, with a reserve of privilege of crossing the land for watering, in his will abovesaid, quoted, April 2, 1753 (Pro. 331: 243). William Brown Jr. conveyed to his son, James, his homestead and 16 acres and 25 acres on the east side of the Candlewood road, June 15, 1786 (145: 185) and 15 acres adjoining the latter lot, July 1, 1786 (145: 200). James Brown conveyed to his son, Josiah, all his real estate, Feb. 7, 1826 (405: 224) which was inherited by his son, Manasseh Brown Jr. Eliza Brown, executrix of James, brother of Manasseh, conveyed to Manasseh all his right in various lots, Dec. 4, 1865 (693: 265). The present dwelling was built early in the last century, probably by James Brown.

John Andrews's Farm.

No. 30 on Diagram.

John Andrews was the first owner of the farm, now owned in the main by Mr. Benjamin R. Horton. Andrews sold to William Fellows, "my farm on the south side the river bounded with the brook called Mile Brook towards the west· the lot of Mr. Saltonstall called the forty acres toward the northwest upon the Common toward the northeast and southeast upon land of John Fuller toward the South in part and on a swamp called Walkers

[1] Page 28.

Swamp toward the south in part with all houses barns etc., Feb. 7, 1659 (Ips. Deeds 1: 236). Mr. Fellows gave a deed to Richard Jacobs, whose house was on the south side of Mile River, of an acre, which Jacobs had bought of John Andrews, the former owner of the farm, in the southwest corner of the farm, abutting on the river, Walker's Swamp and William Fellows's land, 1665 (Ips. Deeds 4: 242).

The will of William Fellows provided for his widow, "a quarter acre of good land yearly to sow flax on," and directed "my son, Isaac, shall have the marsh at Hog Island beside what I have given him already," and that his sons, Ephraim, Samuel and Joseph should have the other half of the farm with the buildings and stock (proved March 27, 1677, filed in Pro. Office in Salem). The inventory mentions 38 acres of upland at home, "foure rod of ground on the meting house hill where ye old house stood" (near the Methodist Meeting House).

A quitclaim agreement was made, which confirmed Isaac in the possession of his portion and Ephraim in the posssesion of land and the buildings on the corner of the two ways, and 8 acres by Mile Brook, March 30, 1702 (Pro. Rec. 308: 24–6).

The parts assigned to Samuel and Joseph will be considered in our survey of Fellows's Lane. Ephraim Fellows sold to Robert Kinsman Jr. The line was "north as the fence runs (*i. e.*, on Candlewood road) till you come to a square with the back of the old dwelling house sd Ephraim now lives in, also the work house standing below said dwelling house," May 30, 1704 (16: 145). This locates the Andrews-Fellows house on the line of Fellows Lane and probably on the open common, which was made when the New Road, so called, was laid out through the Horton farm. It faced the south, and the rear side or leanto abutted on the lane. No mention of this property is made in Quartermaster Kinsman's will, and he had probably conveyed it to his son, Joseph, whose son, Pelatiah, sold to his brother, Benjamin, 23 acres, March 8, 1741 (84: 66). No mention is made of the old dwelling and it had probably been destroyed.

Isaac Fellows, son of William, conveyed to his son, Jonathan, "my farm, lately in the tenure and occupation of William Durgey, excepting 5 acres," about 50 acres, dwelling etc., reserving the use of the premises during his life, March 31, 1705 (18: 214). Jonathan sold to Benjamin Kinsman, April 28, 1742 (82: 103). Kinsman sold both farms, the Isaac Fellows 50 acres and the 18 acres[1] he had purchased of Palatiah, Kinsman, with all the buildings, to Capt. John Boardman, Dec. 21, 1747 (90: 207). Captain Boardman devised to his son Thomas, "all the residue of the real estate I bought of Benjamin Kinsman, that I have not given him before," a further portion to his son, John, and shares to his daughters, Abigail Prime, Sarah and Mary (proved Oct. 13, 1760. Pro. Rec. 337: 352).

The Boardmans or Boarmans were originally located on East St. and by the Labor-in-vain Creek, but they were now well established in this neighborhood. Thomas Boardman was succeeded by his son, Thomas, who

---

[1] 23 acres in original deed.

THE JEREMIAH KISSMAN HOUSE
built in 1756.

See Pages 36 and 61.

conveyed to his sons, Joseph and John How Boardman, "my interest in all real estate, whereof my honored father, Thomas Bordman, Gent. died seized of, excepting that part set off to my honored mother, Elizabeth as her dower," May 28, 1779 (205: 76). John How Boardman conveyed to Winthrop Boardman the homestead of John H. and Joseph, March 9, 1820 (223: 252) and Elizabeth, the widow of Winthrop, sold to Joseph Horton, about 90 acres and buildings, March 26, 1846 (365: 127). His son, Benjamin R. Horton inherited. The house was built either by Capt. John, the first, or Thomas, we may presume.

John Fuller's Farm.
No. 31 on Diagram.

John Fuller owned the next farm to the south in 1659. But Robert Kinsman Sen., the Quartermaster, conveyed to his grandsons, Stephen and Thomas, sons of Thomas deceased, in consideration that Thomas pay to his eldest sister, Elizabeth £20 at or before 3 years have expired after he is 21, and Thomas pay to the youngest sister, Mary, £20 on same terms, a house and 24 acres bounded north and west by Isaac Fellows, southeast by the Common, south by land Thomas above sd bought of Town of Ipswich, to be equally divided when they become of age, April 15, 1701 (14: 117). Thomas, the son of Robert, had acquired the lot alluded to a few years before.

"The Committee impowered to look after Incroachments and to sell land for ye payment of ye Town debt have for to Reimburse money payd to Mr. John Rogers for part of his hundred acres of land sold unto Thomas Kinsman of Ipswich for his conveniency for ye setting up his fence on better ground an angle of land adjoining to his land near Walkers Swamp Island so called bordering all ye way upon his own land in all about two acres and a half, etc."

June 29, 1694 (33: 5)   Thomas Wade
James Fuller
Joseph Quilter

Thomas Kinsman, mariner, conveyed to his brother, Steven Sen., "the tenement of housing and land given me by my grandfather, Robert, and part my father, Thomas, bought of the Town of Ipswich," Jan. 3, 1714 (33: 5) and the heirs of Thomas quitclaimed to Stephen, Dec. 19, 1729 (56: 277).

Walker's Swamp Island.
No. 32 on Diagram.

Stephen Kinsman gradually acquired a large tract in what was called Walker's Swamp, or Walker's Swamp Island, which had been apportioned on the basis of old and new rights as the larger Inner Common of the South Eighth. He bought of Abraham Fitts, ¼ of No. 4, May 7, 1730 (56: 276) and ½ and ⅛ of No. 4, Nov. 22, 1731 (67: 256); of Jacob Perkins, ½ of No. 2 laid out to Jacob and his brother, John, 8 acres, April 12, 1733 (67: 257); of Moses Wells, ½ of No. 3, 9 acres, Jan. 18, 1734 (75: 31); of Nathaniel

Wells, ½ an old lot, 9 acres, "reserving the privilege of a winter way across the premises as it was voted by the proprietors," Jan. 18, 1734: (75: 32); of Abraham Tilton, ¼ of an old right, 4 acres, Oct. 25, 1740 (81: 91); of Thomas Staniford, ⅛ of 16 acres, July 4, 1741 (85: 68) and of Daniel Staniford, ⅛ of an old lot, 2⅔ acres, Oct. 27, 1749 (96: 14).

His dwelling was on the original farm, but he had built a house on Walker's Island which was occupied probably by his son, Jeremiah. He bequeathed to his wife, Lydia, the parlor end of his dwelling and garden, on the foreside of his mansion house; to his son, Stephen, "that part of the dwelling he now lives in, with the old barn and shop, with all my looms and weaving tackling, etc.;" to Jeremiah, "all my lands in Walker's Swamp with the dwelling house and buildings thereon" (proved Dec. 27, 1756. Pro. Rec. 334: 189). His estate was inventoried, a house, barn and 60 acres in Walker's Island, dwelling, barn, and shop and 47 acres (Pro. Rec. 334: 224). Stephen Kinsman and his wife, Elizabeth (Russell), brought up a family of twelve children and dwelt in the old homestead until 1767, when he sold his farm, 47 acres and buildings, to Samuel Patch, Oct. 23, 1767 (151: 98). John Patch Jr. inherited and built the present house about 1800, it is said. The old dwelling, which was burned, stood in the field, northwest of the later site.

John Patch Jr. sold to Joshua Lamson, Feb. 7, 1842, (329: 193) 48 acres, also 12 acres 32 rods, south of the homestead, "conveyed to me by Jeremiah Kinsman," April 6, 1819, Feb. 7, 1842 (329: 192). This lot reverted to the Kinsman ownership as Joshua Lamson sold 47 acres and buildings to William H. Kinsman, Feb. 24, 1869 (766: 259); he to Jacob Scanks, April 1, 1870 (793: 281) who sold back to W. H. Kinsman, June 14, 1878 (1000: 241). He sold again to Eben Perkins, June 26, 1878 (1000: 242), Perkins to Frederick G. Cross, 44 acres and house, Sept. 23, 1887 (1205: 472), who still occupies.

Jeremiah Kinsman was living in the house built by his father on Walker's Island in 1756. A family tradition affirms that it was erected in 1752. He died there in 1818 and bequeathed the Walker's Island farm to his sons, Jeremiah and William, in equal parts, but William was to have all the farming tools and stock (proved June 2, 1818. Pro. Rec. 393: 139). The "cottage," as the lower house is called, was probably built by Jeremiah, Kinsman or his son, William. William Kinsman bequeathed all his real estate to his son, William Jr. (proved Nov. 7, 1843. Pro. Rec. 412: 227). He had a large family, all of whom disposed of their interests to William H. Kinsman, whose daughter, Rhoda F. Kinsman, still owns and occupies.

John Brown's Farm.
No. 33 on Diagram.

The first farm we shall consider on Fellows's Lane is that of John Brown's heirs, which has descended in an unbroken family line from the original John Brown, who cleared the forest and built his house before 1660. An ancient Court document is of great interest in this connection.

"THE COTTAGE."
The residence of Miss Rhoda F. Kinsman.

See Pages 36 and 68.

"The Deposition of Thomas Burnum of Ipswich and Martha Thorne of Ipswich Both of full age Testifies and says That Abowe Seventy Years Agoe They knew Old Mr. John Brown Live in a House in Ipswich Town Near the House of the Reverend Mr. William Hubbards And that before the Year one Thousand Six Hundred & Sixty the said John Brown built a House att the Farme and Liv'd in said House he built att the Farme till after the Year of our Lord One Thousand Six Hundred and Sixty four as Witness our Hands this 30th Day of March 1723

Sworne in Court by both
in Court at Ipswich March 26, 1723.

"The above is a copy of a paper filed in action of John Brown Jr. and William Brown against the proprietors of the Commons in Ipswich to recover a common right belonging to their grandfather John above named who left a son and only heir John, who, May 26, 1714, deeded the said common right to the plaintiffs, sons of the 2d John.

At Court at Ipswich last Tuesday Mar., 1723.
The inventory of John Brown Sen. included

House, barn and Commonage	£65
13 acres of land belonging to the dwelling	£65
a dwelling (in Heart-break Road)	£30

presented by his son John, Sept. 13, 1677 (Ips. Deeds 4: 183).[1]

In the whole area of the great Inner Common of the South Eighth, this is the first lot, which was granted to an individual and improved by the erection of a dwelling, of which record remains. John Brown Jr. bought of Col. Francis Wainwright, the 20 acres which he had bought of Samuel Ayers, brother-in-law of Samuel Fellows, March 5, 1702 (26: 101). He conveyed this lot, under the name John Brown Sen., carpenter, to his sons, John, the 3d of the name, and Nathaniel, May 26, 1714 (27: 28). He conveyed lands to his son William on April 18, 1707 (28: 19) and May 26, 1714 (27: 28). On June 2, 1721, the surviving children, heirs of their brother Nathaniel, then deceased, quitclaimed their interest in his estate to their father "to be at his free dispose to and among whom he shall think fit." (313:308). Eventually this farm came to John.

The John Ross Farm.
No. 34 on Diagram.

John Brown, son of John Jr., sold a small lot to Joseph Fellows, June 13, 1732 (67: 113) and enlarged his farm by the purchase of another adjoining, of John Ross, "a certain old lot about 20 acres in the South Eighth with dwelling," bounded south by the land of said John, and west by his

---

[1]The complete Inventory with other documents are printed in full in the Genealogy of John Brown, in this volume.

land and that of the widow of James Burnam, Nov. 22, 1737 (125: 42). This is easily and surely identified with the farm known later as the Nathan Brown farm, to which entrance is gained by a way through the John Brown farm. The cellar of the ancient dwelling still remains.

In his will, John Brown, cordwainer, gave to his wife, Mary, the use of his goods; portions of his estate to his grandson, Samuel, son of John, late of Ipswich; to grandson Abel, to granddaughters, Hepzibah and Mary, and to his daughter, Sarah Brown. He gave to his daughter, Mary Lufkin, his negro child, Luie and negro woman Phillis, after his wife's decease. The residue was given to his sons, Joseph and Nathan (proved May 28, 1759. Pro. Rec. 336: 241). John Brown Jr. had conveyed to his son, John Brown 3d, 2 acres in the Inner Common, with dwelling and other buildings, Jan. 20, 1745. This lot we have already traced. It is included in the T. M. Norman land, now owned by William J. Cameron, on the road to Essex. Joseph and Nathan quitclaimed to Joseph and Benjamin Fellows their title to the west side of a tract of land called Woods or South Pasture, Oct. 12, 1742 (84: 178) and Joseph and Benjamin Fellows quitclaimed to Joseph and Nathan Brown their interest in the east side of the same, Oct. 12, 1742 (87: 211).

Joseph Brown conveyed to Nathan a half of about 18 acres of upland and meadow, May 2, 1760 (109: 155). Nathan seems to have acquired the whole of Joseph's portion and owned the original John Brown farm and the John Ross farm. He distributed his estate by a will, assigning her part to his wife, Elizabeth; rooms in the house to his daughters, Susanna and Hannah Boardman; to his sons, Jeremiah, Nathan and Abraham, each a quarter of his real estate and to his son, John, "half the dwelling I now live in (the John Brown house) half the barn and a quarter of the land" (proved June 2, 1794. Pro. Rec. 363: 235).

John and Abraham, in consideration of a deed of quittance from Nathan, quitclaimed to him, 40 acres upland and meadow in the north part of the homestead with dwelling, barn, etc., now in occupation of sd Nathan, June 11, 1794 (232: 283). Abraham Brown also conveyed to Nathan his interest in the Wainwright lot and the west half of the homestead, June 6, 1815 (206: 275).

John and Nathan died within a few years of each other. The Inventory of John (approved Apr. 14, 1817. Pro. Rec. 391: 402) included about 13 acres, and buildings, the ancestral home lot, the Hill Field or Ringe Pasture, 13 acres, the Old Field 16 acres, which he bought of Isaac Fellows, Oct. 28, 1807 (184: 1) one half of the Kinsman meadow and pastures in Redwood Hill. His widow, Hannah, asked for a division of her third and the Committee reported that they had set off to the widow, the house and 13 acres and 4 acres in Kinsman's meadow, Dec. 2, 1817 (Pro. Rec. 390: 486). Theodore Gibbs of Essex who had married Lucy Brown, daughter of John and Hannah, conveyed to Hannah, his wife's interest in the farm, June 28, 1831 (278: 193).

Nathan Brown's will (proved May 4, 1823. Pro. Rec. 401: 78) distributed his belongings to his wife, Abigail; to his sons, Nathan, Langley

THE JOHN BROWN HOMESTEAD

on Fellows's Lane. It probably occupies the site of the original dwelling.

See Pages 36, 40, 89-92.

and Francis, ⅔ of the real estate and the remaining third to Francis. Nathan and Langley sold to Francis, Feb. 4, 1823 (232: 285). Nathan conveyed to Langley the 20 acres (Wainwright) and west half of the house he had bought of Abraham, May 5, 1823 (232: 284). Francis conveyed to Langley an undivided half of his father's estate, half of all he devised him by will and half of all his mother, Abigail Brown, and brothers had conveyed to him since her decease, the homestead and buildings and the Hill Pasture about 30 acres, May 5, 1823 (233: 290). Langley and Francis sold to John P. Lakeman the Wainwright lot and west half of the house, Dec. 25, 1826 (245: 75). An execution was levied on Lakeman and his estate was sold to John Brown Jr., May 11, 1836 (289: 56). He was son of John Brown Jr. whose will was probated, April 14, 1817. His sister, Sarah, conveyed to him, styled John Brown 2d, her interest in the homestead, "with all rights of reversion in the dower of our mother Hannah, and all rights I have as heir to my sisters, Clarissa Brown, Lois Brown and Abigail Brown deceased," July 11, 1834 (277: 162). By the purchase of the John P. Lakeman interest he became owner of the whole dwelling and the original 13 acres, the Ringe Pasture, the old field, the Wainwright land and half the Kinsman meadow. His heirs still own and it is one of the few instances in which there has been no departure from the original line of descent and the same family has dwelt upon and tilled the same land from a date prior to 1664 to the present year. The original dwelling was replaced a century or more ago by the present mansion, which contains some timbers of the ancient house.

To follow the fortunes of the old John Ross or Nathan Brown farm in the midst of woods and swamps, Langley and Francis Brown sold to Oliver Appleton Jr. a farm and all buildings, Oct. 20, 1823 (236: 145); Appleton to Ebenezer Cogswell and John Dane, 54 acres and buildings, March 16, 1825 (237: 285). Mr. Cogswell sold 3 acres to Capt. Joseph Gardiner, owner of the adjoining estate, Jan. 4, 1837 (296: 294). John Dane sold to George Dane, the 30 acre field north of the ancient house lot, Oct. 19, 1842 (469: 133), Dane to Ezekiel Merrill, Jan. 8, 1853 (473: 252), he, to Alonzo B. Fellows, Oct. 22, 1857 (560: 276) and Mr. Fellows to Joseph A. Brown, son of John Brown 2d, May 3, 1883 (1107: 249).

The old house lot, in which the cellar alone remained at that time, was sold by John Dane and Ebenezer Cogswell to John Tuttle, Tristram Appleton and Humphrey Lakeman, 12 acres, reserving the cartway on the east side of the old cellar, April 16, 1835 (312: 53). Lakeman conveyed his interest to Appleton, June 13, 1836 (291: 50) and Tuttle conveyed, Feb. 28, 1839 (312: 53). Mr. Appleton sold the lot to Thomas and John Roberts, who owned the adjoining estate, April 10, 1861 (620: 297) and it was included in the subsequent sales to Samuel M. Haskell, June 11, 1890 (1283: 514) and to the mortgagees, Alphonso M. Knowlton and Frank C. Richardson, April 10, 1901 (1637: 279).

Returning now to the William Fellows farm, Samuel Fellows Sen., late of Ipswich, now of Newbury, in consideration of many and great kindnesses from his loving brother-in-law, Samuel Ayres Sen. of Newbury, "having for many years living with him & have been provided for by him as also for & in consideration of an obligation that he hath this day with his two sons Samuel Jun. and John," conveyed to Samuel Ayres Sen., "all my housing and land, upland and meadow which were given to me by my father William, ⅓ of ½ of his farm, ⅓ of the building," May 23, 1701 (14: 34). Isaac Fellows and others, executors of Joseph, quitclaimed to Samuel Ayres, assignee to Samuel Fellows, a small tract, March 30, 1702 (15: 151). Samuel Ayres Sen. sold to Francis Wainwright, 20 acres upland and swamp Dec. 29, 1702 (18: 5) and Col. Wainwright sold to "farmer" John Brown, March 5, 1702 (26: 101). The subsequent history of this lot has already been traced in connection with the John Brown farm.

Joseph Fellows,[2] son of William,[1] as has been mentioned[1] received by the will of his father a third of a half of the farm. His brother Ephraim received in addition to the homestead, 8 acres on the present Fellows Lane, which was set off to him in the division of the property (Pro. Rec. 308: 24, 25, 26). He conveyed this to Joseph, bounded by other land of Joseph's on the northwest and the land of Ephraim and Samuel, southeast, in 1687 (Ips. Deeds 5: 578). It appears from this that Joseph's share of the William Fellows farm and this 8 acre lot, were west of the 20 acre lot, which was conveyed by his brother Samuel to Samuel Ayres and which we have identified with the 20 acre field now owned by Mr. John H. Brown. Joseph's farm, therefore, is included in the estate of Mr. James H. Proctor.

The Saltonstall Forty Acres and Thomas Firman's Farm.

Nos. 35 and 36 on Diagram.

The William Fellows farm was bounded on the northwest by the lot of Mr. Saltonstall, called the forty acres, and this lot, called the ox pasture in later deeds, was the northwest bound of Joseph's original estate. He began at once to enlarge his domain. His first purchase apparently was a three acre lot, which is alluded to as in his possession, April 18, 1681, in a deed of exchange between John Low and himself. John Low was then the owner of a tract of upland and meadow bounded by the Mile Brook, the Saltonstall pasture and the "common ground," which Thomas Firman had sold to Thomas Low and Edward Bragg, Oct. 27, 1647 (Ips. Deeds 1: 35) and which had been conveyed or bequeathed by Thomas to John, his son. The deed of exchange conveyed to Joseph Fellows, 8 acres, bounded southeast by the Saltonstall 40 acres and the 3 acres he had bought of Low, southwest by Mile Brook and northwest by Low's other land in consideration of a transfer by Fellows of an 8 acre lot, farther west (10: 7).

In 1683, April 3d, Fellows bought a lot of Nathaniel Jacobs which Jacobs describes, "all my land on the north side of Mile Brook and on ye North side of ye bridge bounded with Mr. Saltonstall's 40 acres on the northwest

[1] Page 34.

running down to the brook and bridge on the southeast the land of Joseph Fellows southwest and northeast reserving the right for highway to Town through the aforesaid as he hath through Mr. Saltonstall's 40 acres, 1½ rods wide" (10: 7).

Richard Jacobs received a grant of 40 acres, more or less, of upland and meadow on the other side of Mile Brook which was recorded in the Town book, Aug. 20, 1638. In this secluded spot, he built his dwelling. The most direct way to Town lay over Mile River and through the pastures to the way now known as Fellows's Lane. He built a bridge prior to 1658 and on Dec. 6, 1658 it was "Ordered that George Giddings and Edward Bragg are appoynted to lay out a highway through Mr. Saltingstalls 40 acres and a pt. of John Andrews his farm to the Bridge over the River to Richard Jacob's House a rod and a half wide." Jacobs desired full control of the land on both sides of the River, perhaps to facilitate the erection or maintainance of the approaches to the bridge which were still in good condition, when Mr. Proctor, the present owner, built the beautiful bridge which spans the River at the same point. He bought, therefore, an acre of land of Mr. Andrews, the deed of which was given by William Fellows in 1665 (Ips. Deeds 4: 242) but as Andrews sold in Feb. 7, 1659, he probably bargained for the land immediately upon the official lay-out. Richard Jacobs bequeathed his lands to his brother Nathaniel, in 1676 (Ips. Deeds 4: 86.) The purchase of this small piece gave Mr. Fellows access to this very convenient way through the Saltonstall land. Thomas Jacobs, the administrator of the Joseph Jacobs estate, sold the farm with dwelling and other buildings, to Samuel Chapman, Nov. 1, 1701[1] . . .

"leaving ye highway and causeway to ye river for equall improvement of Samuel Chapman Thomas Jacobs and the heirs of said Joseph Jacobs . . . also part of said 65 acres is granted sd Samuel Chapman for a highway on ye easterly side of the river to ye Common which is set out on y^t side ye River two rods wide opposite to an old causeway on ye westerly side of ye river which highway goes through ye land that said Jacobs purchased of William Fellows and sd Jacobs own land granted by ye Town of Ipswich allso sd Thomas confirmeth to sd Samuel Chapman the privilege of horse and foot way from ye slue through the widow Fellows land and Major Salton-

---

[1] The heirs of William Fellows went to law with the executor of Richard Jacobs's estate to settle the title to a 3 acre lot near the bridge and another lot in Sept and Nov. 1678. In Vol. XXIX of the Court Papers twelve original documents in the case, Fellows et al. admrs. v. Jacob Exec. of Richard Jacob, Sept., 1678 and twenty-six papers in the case, Fellows et al. in Rev. v. Jacobs Execr. of Richard Jacobs, Nov., 1678, are filed. They show that the original owner Corporal John Andrews leased the farm to John Choate and Samuel Ingalls before he sold to William Fellows, and the quitclaim of Sarah, widow of John Andrews, declares that he was resident in Lynn when he died. This was executed April 4, 1663.

Choate and Ingalls quarreled with the Jacobs's over their claim to ownership of certain lots, and cut down the bridge, and at a later period Ephraim Fellows repeated it.

stall's land to ye Common sd Thomas reserving right of horse and foot way to ye slue bridge, . . ." Nov. 1, 1701 (14: 256).

Chapman sold to John Annable Sen., March 18, 1701-2 (15: 56).

Joseph Fellows bought a 9 acre lot of John Low, which may have been the same he exchanged with him, Feb., 1685 (Ips. Deeds 5: 437) and a ten acre upland lot with growing timber of John Low Sen. and Dorcas, his wife, Jan. 1, 1689 (10: 8). He had bought 30 acres altogether of the John Low land. His inventory included house, barn and homestead lot of 26 acres, and 30 acres bought of John Low which extended from the Saltonstall lot to Abraham Tilton Jr. (the Ebenezer Fall farm) 1693 (Pro. Rec. 303: 159). One item is of special interest, a pigeon net 10', suggesting the great flights of wild pigeons which Cooper describes in the Leather Stocking tales.

His wife Ruth, as the deeds reveal her, was a woman of uncommon energy. She had built an addition to the homestead, as his will specifies that the widow shall have rooms in the dwelling "the part of the house y^t said Ruth built." His son Joseph consented that his brother William should enjoy their mother's dowry. His portion was two thirds of the house, barn and 24 acre lot, 1 acre orchard and 8½ acres of upland in the 30 acres bought of John Low. William had the residue (proved June 17, 1703. Pro. Rec. 310: 22, 23). The widow bought 4 acres adjoining the estate of John Low Jr., carpenter, who had bought the residue of his father's estate, Dec. 7, 1693 (10: 5).

Joseph,[3] son of Joseph,[2] by successive purchases, greatly enlarged the farm he had inherited. He acquired the interest of his mother and brother in the homestead apparently and made his home there. In consideration of upland and marsh received from his brother William, he conveyed to him, one acre of upland, which he had bought of the Town, "lying by ye widow Fellows house, bounded northwest on Thomas Manning's land, northeast on Town Common, south on widow Fellows land," Nov. 19, 1714 (69: 151). He bought lots in the Inner Common, which abutted on Fellows's Lane, opposite his farm, ⅔ of ½ of a New Common right in the farther division of the South Eighth of John Brown, June 11, 1724 (50: 217) and a 5 acre lot of William Hunt in the Ringe pasture, May 31, 1727 (50: 216). Four years later, he secured the great Saltonstall pasture from the heirs, May 12, 1731 (67: 121). It was always called the 40 acre lot, but the deed specifies 52 acres. It joined his homestead on the west, but seems to have extended across the way now known as Fellows's Lane. The cartway which still runs toward the River is undoubtedly the way laid out in 1658 and the Saltonstall lot may be identified with certainty by this. Another purchase from John Brown was made in 1732, June 13 (67: 113) and a 4½ acre lot in the south end of the South Pasture, abutting on his land on the south, was bought of Daniel Ringe et al., May 4, 1733 (67: 113). He also bought of Samuel Ayers a 9 acre lot, which abutted on the Essex road, as it is now called, March 8, 1738 (88: 142) but sold to Joseph Manning, June 27, 1740 (88: 132). This is included in the Willard H. Kinsman farm, as has already been noted in the study of that locality. He made

CANDLEWOOD. 43

an exchange with Manning and secured an acre lot near "Proctor's brook, so called," which intersects Ward's meadow, June 27, 1740 (88: 142) and with his son, Benjamin, bought an interest in the west side of Woods or South Pasture, of Joseph and Nathan Brown, Oct. 12, 1742 (84: 78). Joseph Fellows, now called Senior, sold to Benjamin, his son, a piece of woodland, 5 or 6 acres, "not far from my dwelling house," etc., Feb. 20, 1750 (97: 35). By his will, he provided for the distribution of his goodly farm. To his wife, Mary, he assigned the use of a third; to Benjamin, "all I have quit to him before, also a piece of fresh meadow at the west end of homestead, about 5 acres including, Ash Island; to his son, Joseph Jr. ¼ of the residue. He had previously sold him 1 acre in the homestead and another acre, bounded on the northeast by land in the possession of Nathan Brown, the line running through a pond to other land of Joseph Jr., March, 1756 (101: 279).

To his grandson, Nathan, he gave a fourth and the great chamber in the east side of the dwelling and a new building adjoining the east corner of said house; to Jacob and Sarah, some portions and the rest and residue to his son, Daniel, "as he is in measure bereft of his reason" (proved Oct. 4, 1762. Pro. Rec. 340: 26). The inventory mentioned house, barn and 115 acres of land (340: 67).

In the division of the estate, Joseph Jr. received the 2 acres and 36 poles previously deeded to him, and 19 acres 20 poles in the northwest part of the farm on Mile River. Nathan's portion was 14 acres 95 poles in the homestall, abutting on Fellows's Lane apparently, and "the way leading to the house," Nov. 15, 1762 (Pro. Rec. 344: 460). The widow's thirds were apportioned after her death to Daniel, 12 acres, the line running east by Mile River to a stake near the old bridge; to Nathan, about 9 acres, bounded south by the river, west by Daniel's land, April 1, 1776 (Pro. Rec. 351: 320, 321).

William,[3] son of Joseph,[2] and brother of Joseph,[3] as was noted,[1] received ⅔ of the dwelling of his father, 22 acres in the Low 30 acre lot, and by agreement, his mother's dowry. The widow, Ruth, bought 4 acres of John Low Jr. She built a house, barn and other buildings on her estate, mentioned in Joseph's deed to William, in 1714 (69: 151) and William in all probability, made his home with her. This new dwelling, is probably the ancient dwelling, part of which is yet owned and occupied by the Fellows heirs, and the main building, removed and remodelled, is owned by the heirs of Daniel W. Appleton. She bequeathed to Joseph Jr. 5 shillings, to her daughters each a sum and to William, the house, barn, stock, etc. (proved May 13, 1729 Pro. Rec. 316: 347). Samuel Waite et al. conveyed to William Fellows that part of the estate of Joseph set off to our mother, Ruth, for her thirds, "excepting title in 1 acre of land laid off to her, adjoining the river, above ye old sluce bridge, bounded by our brother, Joseph's land," Dec. 2, 1733 (69: 151). William Fellows conveyed to Joseph Jr.,

[1] Page 42.

his brother, 13 acres on Mile River, 26 acres bounded northwest on the Saltonstall lot, and 5 acres laid out for Joseph's common right, Dec. 20, 1733 (67: 113). He bequeathed his whole estate to his wife, Deborah. (Proved April 8, 1754. Pro. Rec. 332: 186). The estate contained house, barn and 34 acres adjoining (Inventory filed, April 15, 1754 Pro. Rec. 332: 191). The widow, Deborah, conveyed her interest in ⅔ of William's estate to Joseph, John Brown Jr. and his wife, Mary, Samuel Waite and his wife, Ruth, Thomas Low and his wife, Abigail, and Sary Harnden, in consideration of a deed of conveyance of ⅓ of real estate of William, April 3, 1754 (100: 203). Samuel Waite and Ruth conveyed ⅕ of 22 acres and ⅖ of ⅔ of the buildings to Benjamin Fellows, Nov. 12, 1755 (115: 96). The widow, Deborah, conveyed her remaining interest to him, April 1, 1756 (104: 5), Joseph Fellows Jr., Thomas Low and Abigail, their interest, ⅖ of ⅔ of 23 acres, May 14, 1756 (123: 279), Mary, widow of John Brown, her interest in the "upland of the homestead that belonged to my brother, William Fellows, deceased," Jan. 18, 1760 (115: 59), Joseph and Nathan Brown her sons, their interest, Nov. 24, 1764.

The sons of Joseph,[3] we have noted, were Benjamin, Joseph, Jacob and Daniel, to each of whom he bequeathed a portion of his real estate.

Joseph Whipple's Lot and others.
No. 37 on Diagram.

Benjamin Fellows,[4] son of Joseph,[2] had acquired some landed property before his father's death. On July 1, 1728, Joseph Whipple, executed a deed to Thomas Wade,
"in South 8 on the south side of highway laid out from ye saw mill to Braggs hill about seven acres bounded west on Thomas Manning south land laid out to William Fellows east land laid out to Thomas and Jonathan Wade north from a stake by corner of sd Thomas and Jonathan Wade standing on the south side of highway aforesaid on a strait line to the corner of Mr. Mannings land . . . reserving to myself so much of the land bounded as shall be at any time hereafter laid out for a way to William Fellows" July 1, 1728 (58: 194).

Timothy Wade sold to Benjamin Fellows, two lots, one now said to contain 11 acres, bounded south by William Fellows, north, the Hamlet road, east by Dr. Joseph Manning and west by John Manning, the other containing 8 acres, bounded south and east by Joseph Fellows, west by Joseph Manning and north by the Hamlet road, "reserving out of the first piece a way 1½ rod wide, from ye gate next ye road leading from ye saw mill to Chebacco, to William Fellows land," Nov. 24, 1740 (89: 119). The intervening lot, then owned by Dr. Manning, was also acquired by him. On these lots, Benjamin built his dwelling, which still stands on Lakeman's Lane, though the old chimney has been removed and the outer appearance changed by Mr. William J. Cameron, the present owner. The old road from the present Lakeman's Lane turned in east of the house originally. It was used apparently in 1728 but in 1740, it was well defined and a gate

CANDLEWOOD. 45

was hung across it, as was common with many ways. As has been stated,[1] he purchased the interests of most of the heirs of his uncle William's farm.

He bought from his brother, Joseph Jr., 3 acres, near a dwelling house in the possession of Abner Tarbox, March 27, 1756 (104: 75). His name cannot be found in the records of the Registries, and I am at a loss to know where he was located. Probably he was a tenant in one of the Fellows houses. He sold to Joseph, 8 acres upland and meadow, bounded by Mile River and the highway, July 12, 1757 (105: 206) and bought from him, his right in 17 acres, excepting a highway 2 rods wide through it from land he bought of his father, bounded by the river, Low's island and John Manning, July 20, 1757 (135: 204). Joseph Jr. and Susanna sold him 3⅓ acres of upland, Nov. 18, 1763 (135: 205). His inheritance from his father has already been noted.[2] He bought of Nathan, his nephew, 2 acres 26 rods, "beginning at the great gate which hangs across the road leading from Benjamin's to Isaac's," March 15, 1765 (135: 205). As guardian of his lunatic brother, Daniel, he had sold 4½ acres, beginning at the great gate by the road, southeast about 76 rods, to the lane that leads to the spring on the north side of the highway to Nathan, 1765 (135: 249). In like fashion he sold 3 acres of Daniel's land on Mile River, to John Jones (133: 61), which Jones sold to him the same day, May 12, 1772, (135: 206) and 4 acres near the great spring abutting on the river, to Barnabas Dodge March 28, 1777 (135: 136) which Dodge sold to him on April 4, (135: 136). By purchase from the heirs of William, he seems to have secured much of the real estate, but slight title in the dwelling.

He died in Nov., 1794, and devised his estate; to his widow, Rebecca, no real estate; to his son, Ephraim, the landing place which came to him from his father, "and that which fell to me from my brother, Daniel;" to his son, John, 2 acres of the homestead; all the remainder to John and Ephraim, equally, but Ephraim to have the dwelling, (proved Dec. 21, 1794 Pro. Rec. 363: 434, 5). The inventory included house, barn and other buildings with about 44 acres on the east side of the way, about 24 acres, called the Cow Pasture, Old field and Low's Island, about 16 acres called the further meadow and upland, about 4 acres of upland adjoining Nathan and Isaac (363: 449).

In the division, John Fellows received 20¼ acres on Mile brook, called the further meadow, 3¼ acres which came from Daniel, 13¼ acres called Shoemake Island, upland (on the east side of the way from Lakeman's Lane to Daniel W. Appleton's) and 12 acres of pasture, including William's orchard so called. Ephraim received the dwelling and 30¾ acres about it ("exclusive of the proprietor's way, which we consider and allow to be 1½ rods wide from John's land to said Ephraim's garden, from thence one rod wide to the highway") and 16½ acres bounded by Mile River, Manning's land and the proprietors way (Pro. Rec. 363: 536).

Joseph Fellows,[4] son of Joseph,[3] a tailor, known as Joseph Jr., received from his father, by gift or purchase, 2½ acres, bounded southeast and

[1] Page 44.
[2] Page 45.

northeast on John Brown, west and south on the homestead, "always reserving a cart path through the premises," Dec. 12, 1734 (72: 258). His father conveyed him an acre adjoining and another acre near the sheep pasture, March, 1756 (101: 279).

He built his house on this spot, a small, low dwelling, still standing and owned in recent years by Thomas Roberts and Samuel M. Haskell. Deborah Fellows, widow of his uncle William, conveyed to him a third of William's homestead, April 1, 1756 (103: 71) and he bought 8 acres already mentioned of his brother Benjamin, July 12, 1757 (105: 206). By his will (proved May 10, 1764. Pro. Rec. 341: 387) he devised to his widow, Susanna, the use of a third; gifts to his son, William, and to daughters, Sarah Potter, and Deborah Goodhue; to Susanna, one half of the west end of the dwelling while single, half of the looms, half of the slays, and the same to Abigail; to his son, Isaac, the remainder, including all the real estate. The estate comprised house, barn and cow house, 4 acres adjoining, and 26 acres adjoining Benjamin Fellows, (filed Oct. 8, 1764. Pro. Rec. 341: 412).

Isaac Fellows,[5] son of Joseph,[4] sold 9¾ acres, part of the 26 acres, Cow Pasture, to Nathan Fellows Jr., Feb. 23, 1816 (210: 108). Nathan Fellows sold to Ebenezer Cogswell, Sept. 15, 1827 (246: 108) who sold to Daniel Appleton, Feb. 2, 1844 (342: 152) whose heirs still own. It is bounded by the highway, is crossed by the old cart-way and is undoubtedly part of the original Saltonstall 40 acre lot. Isaac sold the balance of the Cow Pasture, 16 acres 4 poles to John Brown, Oct. 28, 1807 (184: 1) and it has passed by inheritance through successive generations to Mr. John H. Brown its present owner. This also was undoubtedly part of the Saltonstall lot. Isaac sold the homestead with 8 acres to his son, William, a cordwainer, Nov. 20, 1821 (229: 197). William Fellows,[6] son of Isaac,[5] sold to Capt. Joseph Gardiner of Boston, Oct. 27, 1832 (268: 14). Capt. Gardiner bought 3 acres adjoining of Ebenezer Cogswell, part of the old Nathan Brown farm, Jan. 4, 1737 (296: 294). Capt. Gardiner sold the house and 11 acres to Thomas Roberts, of Gloucester, shoemaker, Aug. 26, 1837 (302: 91.) Thomas and John Roberts bought of Tristram Appleton, 10 acres, part of the old Nathan Brown farm, including the cellar of the ancient dwelling, April 10, 1861 (620: 297). John Roberts and Sally sold to Samuel M Haskell, June 11, 1890 (1283: 514). It was sold under foreclosure of mortgage to John H. Brown, April 9, 1901 (1637: 277) who conveyed to Alphonso M. Knowlton and Frank C. Richardson, April 10, 1901 (1637: 279).

Daniel Fellows,[4] son of Joseph,[3] a man of unsound mind, received from his father, as has been stated,[1] the residue of his estate. Guardianship of Daniel was granted to his brother, Benjamin, Oct., 19, 1762 (Pro Rec. 340: 65). His home was in the homestead. After his death, division of his estate was made. The house, barn and 2½ acres adjoining were assigned to Nathan, his nephew, 3¾ acres near the river to his brother, Jacob, the same to his sister, Sarah Dodge, and 4½ acres to the heirs of Joseph, (filed May 4, 1779. 353: 453,4).

[1] Page 43.

CANDLEWOOD. 47

Returning to the heirs of Benjamin,[4] the eldest son of Joseph,[3] John Fellows,[5] son of Benjamin,[4] received half of the farm at his father's death. The lots have already been specified.[1] No mention was made of the dwelling formerly William's, in Benjamin's will, but he had acquired an interest in it by purchase from the other heirs. John was in possession at his father's death and had acquired title, though no record of purchase remains. He conveyed the west half of the dwelling, with a small lot and a small piece opposite, 5 rods by 3, to Nathan Fellows Jr., June 9, 1807 (201: 71) and another lot, 12 rods by 5, to the same, Dec. 15, 1815 (214: 167). To Joseph, cordwainer, he conveyed the east half of the house and about 10 acres, 9 acres on the opposite side of the road with a chaise house and 35 acres of pasture and tillage, Dec. 31, 1823 (234: 105). Deferring consideration of the farm of Ephraim for a little, the estates of Nathan and Joseph may now be traced to completion.

Nathan Fellows,[5] son of Nathan,[4] Joseph,[3] by the will of his grandfather, received ¼ of his farm, containing 115 acres, and part of the dwelling.[2] A 14 acre lot in the homestall was set off to him and a strip of land 10 ft. wide at the north and east end of the house, and in the division of the widow's dower 9 acres more were assigned him. His uncle, Benjamin, guardian of his father, sold him 4½ acres on the opposite side of Fellows Lane, two acres of which he retained.[3] His aunt, Sarah Dodge, sold him the 3¾ acres, allotted her in the division of the estate, March 8, 1783 (140: 177).

Nathan Fellows sold the farm, the house and 35 acres and 2 acres on the opposite side of the road to Nathan Fellows 3d, Oct. 17, 1835 (286: 219). Nathan Fellows 3d, who had now taken a middle initial W., sold the same to Simon Brown, April 3d, 1845 (353: 71), and it was sold by him to Simon Kinsman, April 3d, 1845 (352: 201). He bought an acre of Elisha Brown, part of the original estate, Nov. 3, 1847 (428: 33) and sold the whole farm to Ezekiel Merrill, May 4, 1850 (428: 33). He sold to Alonzo B. Fellows,[7] son of Joseph,[6] Oct. 22, 1857 (560: 276) who sold to James H. Proctor, the present owner, January 30, 1899 (1568: 464).

Nathan Fellows Jr., received from John Fellows, the west half of his dwelling and several lots.[4] He bought of Isaac Fellows, 9¾ acres, part of the cow pasture on Fellows Lane, Feb. 23, 1816 (210: 108). He sold his whole estate to Ebenezer Cogswell, Sept. 15, 1827 (246: 108) who sold to Simon Kinsman the half house and an acre opposite, April 1, 1830 (257: 10.) Mr. Kinsman sold back to Mr. Cogswell, Aug. 9, 1830 (257: 213) who sold then to Joseph B. Fellows, Sept. 6, 1830 (257: 214). But he was then deeply involved in financial difficulties. Suit had already been brought against him by Ammi Brown and by an execution, possession had been given Brown of the east half of the house and 15 acres 20 rods adjoining and the 13 acre pasture lot on the other side of the highway, July 12, 1830

[1] Page 45.
[2] Page 43.
[3] Page 45.
[4] See above.

(Ex. No. 6: 35), and on the same day, Grover Dodge, having secured judgment against Nathan and Joseph Fellows attained possession of a 2½ acre lot and a small piece containing 48 sq. rods near the house (Ex. No. 6: 33, 34). Judgment was made against Joseph, Nathan and Ephraim Fellows and 8¾ acres were set off to him, Sept. 28, 1830 (Exec. No. 6: 33, 34). Mary Fellows, the widow of John Fellows, gained judgment against Joseph and 13¼ acres were set off to her and 9 acres were set off to Judith Manning, both lots abutting on the river, July 12, 1830 (Ex. No. 6: 36, 37). The west half of the house and the lots he had bought from Nathan were all that was left to Joseph. Ammi Brown sold his holdings, the east half of the dwelling and lands to Daniel Appleton Jr. of Beverly, Jan. 16, 1832 (263: 63). He married Mehitable K. Cleaves of Beverly, April 10, 1832 and they made their home on the newly bought farm. Mr. Appleton cut the old dwelling in halves, moved his part, which was the main dwelling, a few rods away and enlarged and remodelled it. Parker Dodge et al. heirs of Grover Dodge sold his lots to Appleton, Feb. 21, 1837 (333: 265). He bought the 10 acre lot opposite of Ebenezer Cogswell, who had purchased it from Nathan Fellows Jr. in 1827, Feb. 2, 1844 (342: 152).

The widow, Mary Fellows, devised her land to her nephews, Levi and George Willett. To Levi, she gave a 10 acre lot, and 4 acres to George. Levi sold to Alonzo B. Fellows, June 3, 1852 (461: 197) and when Mr. Fellows sold his farm to James H. Proctor, he sold this lot as well, Jan. 30, 1899 (1568: 464). George Willett sold his 4 acres to Rev. Daniel Fitz, Pastor of the South Church, April 24, 1849. Dr. Fitz sold this to John Brown, also a piece of pasture land adjoining, called Fellows Hill, containing 6 acres, "being the same which Lucy Brown, administratrix of James Brown conveyed to me, May 16, 1849, excepting and reserving ½ an acre thereof, with a right of way which I have sold to the Town of Ipswich," June 5, 1851 (1568: 467). John H. Brown et al. heirs of John Brown sold this to Mr. Proctor, Jan. 28, 1899 (1568: 469). The Town established a gravel pit, which was used for many years. It was sold by the Town to Mr. Proctor, May 27, 1901 (1664: 367).

Sarah J. Fellows, Henry H. Wall and Frances, Elijah Emerson and Mary, of Cambridge, sold their interest in a 11 acre lot, between John H. Brown's "old field," and the river, part of the estate of their father, Joseph, conveyed to him by John, Dec. 31, 1823 (234: 106) to their brother Alonzo B. Fellows, Jan. 30, 1899 (1568: 462) who sold to James H. Proctor, the same day, Jan. 30, 1899 (1568: 464). Daniel W. Appleton inherited his father's estate and sold the 13 acre pasture, bought by his father of Ammi Brown to Mr. Proctor, Jan. 30, 1899 (1568: 466). On this lot, Mr. Proctor built his stately mansion, and the bare pasture has been transformed into beautiful lawns and gardens. A little more than 75 acres were secured by Mr. Proctor in these purchases. A part of this was included in the original John Andrews farm, sold to William Fellows, part in the Saltonstall 40 acre pasture and part, perhaps, in the John Lowe land. Mr. Proctor also purchased 34 acres on the other side of Mile River, in the Town of Hamilton.

MR. JAMES H. PROCTOR'S HOUSE.

Ephraim Fellows,[5] son of Benjaimn,[4] as was stated,[1] received his father's homestead at his death and half the farm, in 1796. He bought of Hannah Swasey, the 9 acre birch pasture, originally owned by the innkeeper, Increase How, and inherited by his descendants, on the north side of Lakeman's Lane, March 31, 1797 (173: 88). He divided his estate by will between his widow Eunice and his children.

To his widow he gave the northeast end of the dwelling and land adjoining, and 2½ acres in the birch lot, also the orchard west of the house, and wood land in Low's Island.

To Eunice, land in Low's Island.
To Oliver, the east field, 7½ acres.
To Lucy Brown, the low ground, 12¼ acres.
To Ephraim, the cow pasture, 5¾ acres, adjoining the Manning farm.
To George, 9 acres in the birch pasture.
To Elizabeth, the southwest half of the dwelling and land.
To Susanna Dennis, the river meadow at Low's Island.
    will proved, April 3, 1810 (Pro. Rec, 379: 174)
    division filed April 2, 1825 (Pro. Rec. 404: 593).

Elizabeth Fellows,[6] married John P.Lakeman. Execution was granted Oliver Underhill and possession was given him of all that she inherited from her father, Feb. 14, 1863 (Exec. No. 12: 15) and Aug. 13, 1863 (Exec- No. 12:36). The widow's third was owned then by Aaron F. Brown, who sold her portion and also the east field, assigned to Oliver, to Oliver Appleton, April 17, 1849 (410: 253). Appleton apparently sold the half house to Mr. Underhill. Catherine P. Underhill sold the house and land about it to Aaron Lord, June 15, 1878 (1000: 102). He sold to Jacob Scanks, June 17, 1878 (1000: 103), who sold to Daniel W. Appleton, Feb. 2, 1882 (1075: 216). Mr. Appleton sold the buildings and 5 acres of land to William J. Cameron, Oct. 28, 1885 (1161: 236). It was built, as has been said[2], by Benjamin Fellows, about 1740. The old chimney has been torn out and a general look of newness has dispelled all signs of its venerable age.

Oliver Appleton sold the East Field to Willard B. Kinsman, May, 1856 (531: 83) and his heirs sold to William J. Cameron. The orchard lot, sold by Aaron F. Brown to Oliver Appleton, was sold by him to Alonzo B. Fellows, May 7, 1856 (531: 82). He sold to Silas Henry Goodwin, Nov. 15, 1870 (811: 52) who built the house on the lot. He sold the house and lot to his brother-in-law, William J. Cameron.

George Fellows,[6] sold his part of the birch pasture to William Manning, Jan. 8, 1833, (270: 38) and the widow's 2 acres were secured at a later date. Manning owned the adjoining lot, the Smith lot, and his heirs sold his whole estate to George Fellows, Sept. 7, 1860 (612: 246). It is now included in the estate of Charles A. Campbell.[3]

The low ground, bequeathed to Lucy Brown, was sold by her administrator to Daniel Appleton, April 30, 1852 (506: 298), who also bought a

[1] Page 45.
[2] Page 44.
[3] No. XV. Pub. of Ips. Historical Society, p. 17.

small half acre lot at the bridge of Aaron F. Brown, Aug. 10, 1853 (506: 299). Ephraim,[6] sold the cow-pasture to Oliver Underhill, Dec. 13, 1826 (244: 1) who sold to John Manning, April 2, 1827 (350: 108). It is still included in the Ebenezer Fall farm.

Lucy Brown, the administratrix of James Brown, sold the 7 acres in Low's Island, given to Eunice Fellows, to Rev. Daniel Fitz, March 28, 1849 (492: 133) and Susanna Dennis sold her 2 acres to the same, March 11, 1854 (492: 134). His son, Daniel F. Fitz, sold both lots, deeded to him, July 5, 1861, to Daniel W. Appleton, Aug. 26, 1870 (807: 32).

This long series of wills, inventories and conveyances reveals many interesting secrets of the life of this little community. It was wonderfully self-sufficient. These farmers cultivated only a few acres. Their farm stock was limited and their "utensils of husbandry," as they are styled in one ancient inventory, were few and simple. Despite the fact that all the farm labor was done by hand, they had opportunity and necessity, no doubt, to turn to other employments, to complete the round of their activities. So we find few men, who are styled yeomen or farmers and many who tilled their lands, but added to their yeomanry the trades of the house carpenter, glazier, brickmaker and blacksmith, of the cordwainer, weaver and tailor, and by these trades they were known.

Hence the community had little need of help from without. When a new house was required, the noble oaks and pines were felled on their own wood lots, the great beams were fashioned with the axe, and the neighboring sawmill of Major Samuel Appleton on Mile River, converted the great logs into boards and smaller timber, shingles and clapboards. The brickmaker supplied the bricks, the blacksmith, nails, hinges and latches, and the carpenter and glazier did the rest.

The individual household was likewise an economic unit. Its food supplies were almost entirely derived from the Indian corn and rye, the beef, pork and poultry, the milk and eggs, butter and cheese, raised on the farm, while from their barley, malted at the Rogers malt house, they made their home brewed beer. Every family had its flock of sheep and a field was always sown with flax. Then the tireless and ingenious women of the household with deft touch spun and wove and bleached, provided table and bed linen and made the beautiful bed quilts, which are prized still for their splendid handiwork, cut and fashioned garments, knit stockings and mittens. Happily William Brown, the professional weaver, could help in the production of the heavier fabrics and the neighborhood tailor could fashion the more elaborate overcoats and fine dress coats, which the wealthier men needed. The cordwainers made the shoes. The wood lots at Chebacco and the great peat meadow, close at hand, provided fuel for the huge fireplaces. Home-made candles and smoky "betty lamps," or smokier pitch pine strips gave a feeble light.

All of these old farm houses were comfortably furnished and some inventories give evidence of luxury. There were neighborhood aristocrats, James Burnham, with his two negro slaves, his houses and lands; James Brown, the town shopkeeper who also had his Candlewood farm and his

CANDLEWOOD.   51

black slaves, Kant and Bett; and the cordwainer, John Brown, whose Luie and Phillis made the housework lighter. Clad in his velvet coat and short clothes, with wig and silver buckles and buttons, the Candlewood gentleman made a brave appearance. Some traces of the oldest houses remain in the cellars of two of the present dwellings at least, where the ancient oak summers still support the hearths of the fire places. The bevelled edges indicate well finished dwellings, resembling the old Whipple house, now owned by the Historical Society

In the great social necessities of life the old nieghborhood proved adequate to its own needs as well. A study of the genealogies appended makes it plain that in the large proportion of marriages, both bride and groom were from this group of houses. Playmates and schoolmates, these Browns and Fellowses and Kinsmans and the Appletons, a little farther removed, finally became partners for life. Frequently they spent their lives in the same dwelling in which they were born, and never went far enough afield to lose sight of the smoke from the chimnies or the smell of the peat reak of the old neighborhood. This passion for home has descended to the present generation and in thirteen of the comfortable dwellings of today, either husband or wife was born and bred on Candlewood soil.

Children came into these old homes in glad profusion, and it rarely happened that the first born son did not bear his father's name. Some names were loved so well that they passed from generation to generation, and in one case, John Brown of the Hamlet in Revolutionary times was enrolled as John Brown 7th. In the very beginning of our town, there were three John Browns, distinguished as Senior, the farmer and the glazier, and in a land lawsuit, the John Brown in possession based his defence in part, upon the fact that the writ did not specify which John Brown he was, as there were several of the name in the town.

Numerous as their children were, the parents were never at a loss for names. Praise God, Hate Evil and other Puritan names of that ilk, were never in vogue with them. The Bible furnished an inexhaustible series of noble and significant names and beginning with Adam and righteous Abel, the names of the patriarchs and prophets, the soldiers and sages of the Hebrew Word, the evangelists and apostles of later times, and of the holy women of Bible story, were given to their offspring.

The families themselves were patriarchal. Ten and twelve children were not unusual and sometimes the numbers swelled to heroic proportions. Nathan Fellows by his first marriage had twelve children, none of whom survived the age of seven. Marrying again and choosing apparently a woman of greater physical power, he had the pleasure of seeing thirteen children grow to manhood and womanhood. Stephen Kinsman had an even dozen, Moses had ten, and William Kinsman counted thirteen children around his daily board. One daughter, married in the best room and removed to another neighborhood, but returned fifty years later, with sons and daughters to celebrate her golden wedding in the old parlor. William and Elizabeth Brown rejoiced in thirteen children, Lieut. Nehemiah had eleven, John and Hannah Brown gathered thirteen about the great fire places in the farm house on Fellows Lane. Stephen Brown had eleven and James Brown's house was made merry and noisy by twelve. No wonder Sabbath day congregations were large in those good old days, when church going was the rule and whole families were found in the family pew, though the meeting house was cold and cheerless. The Candlewood school, now abandoned under modern methods of centralization, enrolled sixty pupils in the childhood of some who are still living.

The ability to bear the burden which was put upon the mothers of these old families, passes our comprehension. The mere clothing of her household, from husband to the babe, never absent from the cradle, when few fabrics were bought and everything was made by hand, the providing of the daily food with the primitive conveniences of the fire place, the butter and cheese making, the manufacture of the household linen, the endless anxieties, were too much for flesh and blood, as we think it. Sometimes dreadful epidemics caused terror in every home. In the family of Mark and Hepzibah Howe, in another parish of the town, a throat distemper, as it was called, caused the death of their daughter, Lucy, on Nov. 5, 1736, Mary followed on Nov. 15th, Hannah and Aaron on Nov. 18th, Abijah on the 21st, Mark on the 24th, Moses on the 28th, and Love on the 28th, eight deaths in twenty-three days. The great white plague was always claiming its victims. Scarlet fever was regarded as unavoidable and of no great significance. A lady, who died some fourteen years ago, taught school in her early womanhood and she went to her work as usual, after watching all night with a child suffering with this fever.

The house mother's care for her own was always increased by her readiness to minister to her neighbor's family in every critical hour. All modern rules for mothers and babes were habitually violated. Modern remedies and modern nursing were alike unknown. Yet they lived and reached a ripe old age. William Kinsman died in his old homestead in 1866 aged ninety, his father and mother both had reached the age of ninety-one, his grand-father had lived to be ninety-three and his sister was ninety-six when she died. Capt. Elisha Brown died in 1808 leaving his widow with six children under age, including a babe of ten months. That marvellous woman brought up her family and lived fifty-seven years a widow, dying in 1865 at the great age of one hundred and one years and two months.

Under such circumstances, it might be imagined that the lot of the children was as hard as that of their mothers, and that they must have suffered much from neglect. It is a fact that they were not dressed according to Paris fashions. They had less school privilege than the law demands for children today. But those children were taught diligently in the Bible and the catechism and the great hymns of the church. They learned to read and write, and sew and knit. The crowning glory of the girl's education was the sampler, cleverly wrought on the homespun canvass. The alphabet, in capitals and small letters, was generally followed by some genealogical record or by a mournful verse. One sampler, preserved in the collection of the Historical Society, bears the lugubrious sentiment:

CANDLEWOOD.

"When I am dead and in my grave
And all my bones are rotten,
When this you see remember me
That I mayn't be forgotten."

Happily the little maid who wrought that sampler was accustomed to these painful moralizings and all her playmates shared her dismal experience. Nevertheless her education prepared her well on the whole for her prospective cares and responsibilities. No doubt the joys of Thanksgiving, the excitements of the frequent weddings and the common home pleasures offset the dullness and straitness of child life in very satisfactory fashion.

The ancient neighborhood had its days of darkness and fear. John Brown Senior's inventory in 1677 contains the item,

"axes, sithes, sawes and other utensells of husbandry with some Armor £3–12s. –0."

The dread of Indian assault was always with them and when night settled down upon those scattered farm houses and the wolves howled in the forests, many a brave heart trembled at some unusual sound. When King Philip's war at last broke out, Ephraim Fellows was a trooper with Captain Paige and then with our Ipswich soldier, Captain John Whipple; Isaac Fellows was in Captain Willard's Co. Joseph Fellows and John Brown were also enrolled. James Burnham was a trooper in Major Appleton's Co. in the Narragansett campaign. Quarter master Robert Kinsman was a sufferer in the Gov. Andros episode and John Ross went to Quebec with Phipps. The witchcraft persecution carried consternation to every household and intense interest and sympathy were roused by the arrest of their old neighbors, John Proctor and his wife, in the Chebacco parish and the petition of Rev. John Wise and thirty-one men of his parish, all of whom were friends of the men of Candlewood, for their release. When the news of the march of the British regulars on April 19th arrived, many of the young men hurried to Lexington, in Capt. Robert Perkins's company of horse, or the several companies of minute men. The three or four days of their absence were a trying time to the neighborhood. Some of them served in the war and William Kinsman was in the battle of Bunker Hill. The allurements of the gold fever in '49 attracted a number of the young men to California. They never returned and no one knew the story of their lives.

While the love of home has been the conspicuous trait of the neighborhood life, in all these generations, there have been many migrations elsewhere. Capt. Jonathan Fellows long ago removed to Gloucester, and from him has descended a conspicuous line of merchants and wealthy and prominent citizens in Boston and New York. Fellows Athenaeum in Roxbury, now used by the Boston Public Library, was built and endowed by Caleb Fellows of this family line. From John Choate has sprung that illustrious Rufus Choate, whose fame is as wide as the world, and Joseph

H. Choate, the famous lawyer and Ambassador to England. Judge Edward Brown of the Appellate Court of Illinois and Bishop Kinsman of Delaware rejoice in their Candlewood forbears. Multitudes of worthy and lovable men and women have gone far and wide, and through these sons and daughters, the fathers and the mothers who lived their simple and hard lives so well, are handing on their stalwart virtues, their love of toil, their broad and sympathetic good neighborliness to the generations that are to come.

THE GENEALOGY
— OF —
ROBERT KINSMAN
— OF —
IPSWICH, MASS.

EDITORIAL NOTE.—In the year 1876, the Kinsman Family Record was published, entitled "Genealogical Record of the descendants of Robert Kinsman of Ipswich, Mass., From 1634 to 1875. Compiled for Frederick Kinsman by Lucy W. Stickney." I have copied all the Ipswich material and made careful comparison of this work with the original record. A few mistakes have been noted and corrected. The Ipswich families have been completed to the present year, and a careful study of locations has been made. I have made no attempt at tracing the lines of those who have emigrated from Ipswich, but have made constant reference to the printed Genealogy in the foot-notes for this portion of the work. I am greatly indebted to this admirable family history for this very material assistance.—T. F. W.

GENEALOGICAL RECORD OF THE DESCENDANTS
OF
ROBERT KINSMAN OF IPSWICH, MASS.

1. ROBERT KINSMAN,[1] the immigrant, a glazier by trade, received a grant of an acre of land on the south side of the way now known as Green St., near the corner of County St. He probably built his house here in the year 1635, though the record of the grant was not made until 1637. He died Jan. 28, 1664 and his will proved Mar. 28, 1665 (Pro. Rec. 1:213) gave his dwelling to Tabitha, his only unmarried daughter. His wife had probably died before this date as no mention of her is made in the will. His children were:

2 ROBERT,[2] born 1629. See No. 2.
3 MARY,[2] married 1st, Daniel Ringe; 2nd, Usual or Uzall Wardell.
4 SARAH,[2] married Samuel Younglove, Aug. 1, 1660.
5 HANNAH,[2] married William Danford, Mar. 20, 1670; died Oct. 18, 1678.
6 MARTHA,[2] married Jacob Foster, Jan. 12, 1658.
7 TABITHA.[2]

The new homes of the daughters were near the homestead. Mary, the eldest, lived on Turkey Shore Road, on the lot now owned by Mr. Arthur W. Dow. Sarah's husband, Thomas Younglove Jr., bought the houselot of Thomas Wells on County St., within the houselot of Mrs. John Heard in the rear of the South Church, Mar. 26, 1659, a few months before their marriage, and retained the ownership until 1696. Hannah's husband, William Danford, was not a resident of Ipswich apparently. Jacob Foster, who married Martha, lived within a few rods of the Kinsman houselot, at the time of his marriage and their wedded life was spent in the immediate neighborhood. Robert alone made a little farther remove.

2. ROBERT KINSMAN,[2] born in 1629, followed his father's trade. He married Mary Boreman, daughter of Thomas, whose dwelling was in East St. As he purchased his Candlewood farm in 1652, his marriage occurred probably about that time. The Quartermaster died on February 19, 1712 and was buried in the old High Street Burying Ground, where his gravestone still stands. Their children were:

8 MARY,[3] born Dec. 21, 1657.
9 SARAH,[3] born March 19, 1659; married Jacob Perkins.
10 THOMAS,[3] born April 15, 1662. See No. 10.
11 JOANNA,[3] born April 25, 1665; married Nathaniel Rust Jr., Feb. 22, 1684.

12 MARGARET,³ born July 24, 1668.
13 EUNICE,³ born Jan. 24, 1670; married Nathaniel Burnham.
14 JOSEPH,³ born Dec. 20, 1673. See No. 14.
15 ROBERT,³ born May 21, 1677. See No. 15.
16 PELATIAH,³ born Nov. 10, 1680. See No. 16.

10. THOMAS KINSMAN,³ born in 1652, married Elizabeth Burnham, July 12, 1687, and lived on the farm now owned and occupied by Mr. Fred. G. Cross, less than a mile from his birthplace. He died July 15, 1696, and his widow married Isaac Ringe of Ipswich (pub. July 27, 1700). Their children were:

17 STEPHEN,⁴ born about 1688. See No. 17.
18 ELIZABETH,⁴ born about 1690; married Jacob Perkins, son of Jacob and Sarah (Kinsman) Perkins (pub. Mar. 6, 1713).
19 THOMAS,⁴ born April 3, 1693.
20 MARY,⁴ born Oct. 14, 1695; married Thomas Waite Jr. (pub. Dec. 14, 1717).

Thomas forsook the land for the sea. He was styled "mariner" in his deed of conveyance of his share in the homestead to his brother in 1714. His heirs quitclaimed to Stephen, Dec. 19, 1729 (56: 277).

14. JOSEPH KINSMAN³ was born Dec. 20, 1673 in the Candlewood home. He married first Susanna Dutch of Ipswich. Her gravestone in the old High St. Ground bears the inscription. "Here lyes Buried the Body of Mrs. Susanna Kinsman, wife to Lieut. Joseph Kinsman, who departed this life, Nov' 9th Ann° Dom' 1734." He married second, Sarah Peabody¹ of Boxford, April 27, 1736. It has been noted already² that his father conveyed his dwelling to him with the adjacent land, March 21, 1698, about the time of his first marriage. His children, all by the first marriage, were.

21 SUSANNA,⁴ born Feb. 16, 1700; married 1st, Increase How (pub. Aug. 10, 1723); married 2d, John Smith, Jan. 28, 1762.
22 JOSEPH,⁴ born Sept. 15, 1701; died Nov. 18, 1724.
23 EUNICE,⁴ born June 23, 1705; married Moses Wells (pub. Nov. 20, 1724).
24 SARAH,⁴ born June 23, 1705; married Nathaniel Wells (pub. July 7, 1723).
25 ELIZABETH,⁴ born Nov. 11, 1707; married William Browne Jr. (pub. Jan. 1, 1726).
26 JOHN,⁴ born Nov. 21, 1709. See No. 26.
27 HANNAH,⁴ born Nov. 21, 1709; married Robert Wallis Jr. (pub. Sept. 20, 1735).
28 MARTHA,⁴ born July 13, 1712; married Thomas Dennis (pub. Mar. 25, 1732).

¹ Lieut. Joseph Kinsman, pub. Sarah Peabody of Boxford, Mar. 27, 1736.
² Page 23.

29   NATHANIEL,[4] baptized July 10, 1714; married 1st, Anna Robinson, 1741; married 2nd, Dorcas Parsons, 1787; lived in Gloucester.[1]
30   PELATIAH,[4] baptized July 12, 1715.   See No. 30.
31   BENJAMIN,[4] baptized April 26, 1719.   See No. 31.

Increase How, housewright, the husband of Susanna, bought the corner lot, now owned and occupied by Dr. William E. Tucker, "with a good mansion house," of Joseph Whipple, Dec. 28, 1724. He became an inn-keeper and his hostelry enjoyed wide renown. By the will of her husband, the wife was allowed the use of the east half of the inn in 1754, but she married Capt. John Smith, Jan. 28, 1762. He bought the Burley mansion on Green St. in 1760 and there his wife, of long experience in the fine art of tavern-keeping, resumed her vocation. This old inn still stands, with promise of many years of usefulness.

The twin daughters, Eunice and Sarah, married brothers, the sons of Nathaniel Wells, a farmer in the Argilla neighborhood. Moses Wells and Eunice lived for many years in the old house which was known in its last days as the Molly Martin house on East St. Capt. Nathaniel Wells and Sarah spent their lives on the Argilla farm of his ancestors, where thirteen children were born to them. Elizabeth, Hannah and Martha, married Ipswich men and became the mothers of large families. Of the sons, Joseph died in early manhood, Nathaniel removed to Gloucester, where all his children were born. Benjamin Kinsman inherited half the parental homestead, but sold to his brother, Pelatiah, and bought the Jonathan Fellows farm, now owned by Benjamin R. Horton, on the Candlewood road, a half mile from his birthplace, in 1742, two years after his marriage, and made his home there until 1747 when he sold to Capt. John Boardman. In 1760 he removed to Cornwallis, Nova Scotia. John and Pelatiah were content to dwell in their ancestral town.[2]

15   ROBERT KINSMAN,[3] born May 21, 1677, married Lydia More or Moore of Boston, April 3, 1700 and for a second wife, Rebecca Burley, daughter of Cornet Andrew Burley, June 28, 1705. His deed of sale to his brother Joseph (40: 17) Feb. 18, 1720–21, shows that he made his home in the Fellows homestead on the corner of Candlewood Road and Fellows Road. A deed dated Oct, 28, 1721 (73: 25) gives his residence as Norwich, Conn. He died there June 7, 1761, his widow Rebecca, surviving until Nov. 11, 1775.[3] The children of Robert and Rebecca, all born in Ipswich, were:

32   REBECCA,[4] born Aug. 15, 1706; died Dec. 17, 1719.   Gravestone in High St. Burying Ground.

[1] The Kinsman Family, p. 68.
[2] See The Kinsman Family for the families of the daughters and other interesting matter.
[3] The will of Robert Kinsman is given in The Kinsman Family, p. 59, and his family is also traced.

33 MARY,[4] born Jan. 20, 1707-8.
34 JOANNA,[4] born July 11, 1710.
35 ROBERT,[4] baptized May 3, 1713.
36 MARGARET,[4] baptized May 25, 1718.
37 JEREMY,[4] baptized Feb. 28, 1719.

16. PELATIAH KINSMAN,[3] born Nov. 10, 1680, chose the life of a sailor and was sailing master of the ship "Hopewell" in 1706. He married Sarah Combey, July 1, 1708, in Boston, where he made his home. His will was proved in 1727.[1]

17. STEPHEN KINSMAN,[4] born about 1688, with his brother Thomas received from their grandfather Quartermaster Robert, the title of their father's farm. He bought his brother's interest and eventually acquired a considerable landed estate, though by trade he was a weaver. He married first, Lucy Kimball, daughter of Caleb and Lucy Kimball of High St. (pub. Nov. 24, 1711) who died Feb. 22, 1715-16, at the age of 23 years; second, Lydia Kimball, daughter of Richard and Lydia Kimball (pub. Nov. 19, 1716). He died in the home of his birth, Dec. 8, 1756. His children by the first marriage were:

38 STEPHEN,[5] born March 15, 1713; died in infancy.
39 THOMAS,[5] born Feb. 13, 1715; married Mary Tilton (pub. April 25, 1745). He made his home in Hamilton, where he died April 7, 1779.

By the second marriage:

40 STEPHEN,[5] baptized March 30, 1718. See No. 40.
41 DANIEL,[5] baptized Oct. 32, 1720. See No. 41.
42 JEREMIAH,[5] baptized May 3, 1724. See No. 42.
43 LYDIA,[5] baptized Aug. 10, 1729; married Ephraim Adams, April 6, 1749.

26. JOHN KINSMAN,[4] born Nov. 21, 1709, by the will of his father, in 1741, received the land with the house and barn he then occupied on the site of Mr. Chas. G. Brown's dwelling. He married, first, Hannah Burnham, daughter of James and Sarah (Rogers) Burnham, Jan. 31, 1733, who died May 31, 1753. It has been stated[2] that he bought the interest of the other heirs in the Burnham estate and acquired a large tract of fine farm land and dwellings. Captain John, as he was called, married second, Elizabeth (Fellows) Perkins, the widow of Joseph Perkins (pub. Dec. 9, 1753). He probably built the large mansion, on Heart Break Road, recently owned by Aretas D. Wallace. His children, all by his first marriage, were:

44 HANNAH,[5] baptized June 1, 1735; died April 20, 1737.
45 JOHN,[5] baptized Aug. 21, 1737. See No. 45.

[1] The Kinsman Family, p. 62.
[2] Page 35.
[3] Page 8.

46 JAMES,⁵ baptized May 13, 1739. See No. 46.
47 HANNAH,⁵ baptized June 27, 1741; married James Perkins, Oct. 28, 1762.
48 JOSEPH,⁵ baptized May 22, 1743; died Nov. 6, 1762.
49 SARAH,⁵ baptized Oct. 20, 1745; married William Appleton (pub. April 21, 1764).
50 SAMUEL,⁵ baptized July 19, 1747. See No. 50.
51 JONATHAN,⁵ baptized Jan. 7, 1749. See No. 51.
52 MARTHA,⁵ baptized Jan. 19, 1752; married Samuel Gilman Jr. of Exeter, Sept. 16, 1779.

James Perkins and William Appleton were substantial citizens of Ipswich. Capt. Samuel Gilman was a resident of Exeter. Three sons, John, James and Samuel lived out their days in Ipswich.

30. PELATIAH KINSMAN,⁴ baptized July 12, 1715, as has been said,[1] inherited a half interest in the homestead of his father and grandfather and bought his brother Benjamin's half. He married Jane Farley, daughter of Michael Farley, and for the first years of their married life, they lived undoubtedly in the homestead. But on Feb. 1, 1753, he bought the Col. Wainwright farm in the Argilla neighborbood, two miles perhaps from the old home, removed there and disposed of the Candlewood home in 1754. [2] Five of their great family of thirteen children were born in the old house. Mrs. Kinsman died April 2, 1791, aged 64, the husband died Oct. 4, 1796. Their children were:

53 MICHAEL,⁵ baptized April 6, 1746. See No. 53.
54 NATHANIEL,⁵ baptized March 20, 1747. See No 54.
55 JANE,⁵ baptized March 11, 1749; married Lieut. Mark Haskell (pub. March 3, 1798.)
56 SUSANNA,⁵ baptized July 7, 1751; married David Dennis, of Newcastle, July 1, 1779.
57 EUNICE,⁵ baptized Sept, 17, 1752; died unmarried, Sept.17,1832.
58 MOSES,⁵ baptized July 7, 1754. See No. 58.
59 AARON,⁵ baptized July 7, 1754. See No. 59.
60 ISRAEL,⁵ baptized Aug. 15, 1756; mariner unmarried.
61 LUCY,⁵ baptized March 26, 1758; married Richard D. Jewett, Dec. 25, 1791.
62 PELATIAH,⁵ baptized May 18, 1760; died in infancy.
63 HANNAH,⁵ baptized Aug. 25, 1764; died Oct. 9, 1786.
64 PELATIAH,⁵ baptized Nov. 2, 1766; died Oct. 4, 1776.
65 MERCY,⁵ baptized Nov. 2, 1766; died unmarried Sept. 22, 1836.

So far as known, none of this great family ever removed from Ipswich.

31. BENJAMIN KINSMAN,⁴ baptized April 26, 1719; married Elizabeth Perkins (pub. Dec. 27, 1740). Their children born in Ipswich were:[3]

[1] Pages 23. 24.
[2] Page 24.
[3] The Kinsman Family, p. 70 gives marriages.

66 ELIZABETH,[5] born Oct. 20, 1741.
67 BENJAMIN,[5] born Nov. 3, 1743.
68 NATHANIEL,[5] born Aug. 13, 1745.
69 ROBERT,[5] born May 27, 1747.
70 EBENEZER,[5] born June 2, 1750; died June 17, 1750.
71 EBENEZER,[5] born Aug. 10, 1751.
72 SUSANNA,[5] born June 17, 1753.

The Kinsman Family, p. 70, states that he removed to Cornwallis, Nova Scotia, in 1760, where were born:

73 JOSEPH,[5] born Dec. 16, 1760.
74 MARY,[5] born Aug. 13, 1763.

40. STEPHEN KINSMAN,[4] born March 30, 1718; married Elizabeth Russell, April 10, 1739. His father's will, proved in 1756, bestowed on him, "that part of the dwelling (i. e., his grandfather's house[1]) he now lives in with the old barn and shop, with all my looms, and weaving tackling etc." "The parlor end" of the dwelling was given to Lydia, his widow. Stephen sold his farm to Samuel Patch in 1767.[1] During their residence in the old farm house twelve sons and daughters were born:

75 STEPHEN,[6] baptized March 23, 1739; married Elizabeth Caryl, 1762.
76 NATHAN,[6] baptized Oct. 4, 1741; married 1st, Mercy Wheeler; married 2nd, Elizabeth Shattuck, 1772.
77 AARON,[6] baptized Aug. 21, 1743; married 1st, Rose Burnham, Dec. 5, 1765 and son Aaron[7] was baptized Oct. 12, 1766 in Ipswich; married 2nd, Mary Hall, of Medford, 1775.
77a
78 ISAAC,[6] baptized Dec. 15, 1745.
79 ELIZABETH,[6] baptized April 10, 1748.
80 LYDIA,[6] baptized June 24, 1750; married Francis Knight of Manchester, Jan. 21, 1768.
81 EBENEZER,[6] baptized May 24, 1752; died in infancy.
82 EUNICE,[6] baptized Dec. 22, 1754.
83 EBENEZER,[6] baptized Feb. 19, 1758; probably Baptist clergyman.
84 EPHRAIM,[6] baptized Jan. 11, 1761; married Mary Hall.
85 SARAH,[6] baptized Jan. 16, 1763.
86 ABIGAIL,[6] baptized Jan. 16, 1763.

In extreme contrast with the children of Pelatiah who clung without exception to their native soil, not a single child of the family of Stephen so far as known remained in Ipswich.[2] Stephen became a prominent citizen of Hopkinton, Nathan lived for years in Concord, N. H., but spent the latter portion of his life in Landaff. Aaron removed to Concord, N. H. about 1770, was Captain in Col. Stark's regiment at Bunker Hill and lived later in Hanover. Ephraim removed to Springfield, N. H. and later to

[1] Page 36.
[2] The Kinsman Family, p. 76.

Williamstown, Vt. Ebenezer is identified by the author of "The Kinsman Family,"[1] with the Baptist clergyman of the name, who was pastor in Limerick, Me., 1796–1807.

41 DANIEL KINSMAN,[5] baptized Oct. 23, 1720; married Mary Perkins, Jan. 23, 1740 and made his home in Ipswich, it is believed. He died March 11, 1746 and his widow married Abraham Carter of Gloucester (pub. June 30, 1750). Their children were:

    87 DANIEL,[6] baptized Sept. 20, 1741; died July 28, 1742.
    88 DANIEL,[6] baptized May 13, 1744; married Abigail Morse, April 7, 1768. He married in Hopkinton, lived for many years in Hubbardston, but spent his last days in Shrewsbury.
    89 LUCY,[6] baptized Aug. 24, 1746; married Ebenezer Trask of Gloucester (pub. April 6, 1768).

42. JEREMIAH KINSMAN,[5] baptized May 3, 1724; received from his father, by his will, all the land he owned in Walker's Swamp,[2] "with the dwelling house and buildings thereon," 1756. He had married Sarah Harris(pub.Jan.21,1743)and the goodly house,which still stands was probably built for their abode. A family tradition affirms that it was built in 1752. It was repaired and largely rebuilt by the late William H. Kinsman. The good wife died Sept. 19, 1805 at the age of 79 years. The husband survived until March 3, 1818. Their children were:

    90 SARAH,[6] married Capt. John Andrews, Dec. 18, 1766, lived and died in North Yarmouth, Me.
    91 DOROTHY,[6] baptized (adult), May 4, 1764; married Joseph Adams of Gloucester Sept. 19, 1774.
    92 JEREMIAH,[6] born Oct. 6, 1748; baptized May 4, 1764. See No. 92.
    93 WILLIAM,[6] born Aug. 27, 1752; baptized May 4, 1764. See No.93.
    94 MEHETABLE,[6] born about 1757; baptized May 4, 1764; married John Burnham, Nov. 23, 1780 and removed to Enfield, N. H.

The daughters of this group of children migrated and Jeremiah; but William clung to the farm.

45. JOHN KINSMAN,[5] was baptized Aug. 21, 1737. We went for his wife to the Argilla neighborhood, where the other group of the Kinsman name was growing up, and married Abigail Wells, daughter of Ensign Nathaniel and Sarah Kinsman on Feb. 9, 1758. In 1759, he bought a 3½ acre pasture lot of his father and built a dwelling, on the site now occupied by the house of Mr. Charles G. Brown in Candlewood, a few rods from the ancient dwelling place of Quarter master Robert. He sold the house and lot to Moses Kinsman in 1784. He had married, second, Margaret Appleton, June 3, 1773. Their children by the first marriage were:

    95 JOHN,[6] born Nov. 7, 1762.
    96 JAMES,[6] born July 22, 1764.

[1] Page 76.
[2] Page 36.

46. JAMES KINSMAN,⁵ baptized May 13, 1739, married Mary Boardman Nov. 6, 1760. Three weeks before, Oct. 18, 1760, his father had conveyed to him three fourths of a dwelling and land, a part of his large estate on the Essex road and the young couple established themselves under shadow of the young bridegroom's home.¹ The husband died in 1762 and the widow sold part of the land to Capt. Kinsman.

97 Their daughter, MARY,⁶ born Dec. 18, 1761, married James Remmick, Sept. 10, 1782, in Dover, N. H., where her mother lived, having married Samuel Bragg (pub. Aug. 17, 1765) who removed to Dover and sold his Ipswich farm in 1784. Mary Remmick had received a legacy from her grandfather, Capt. John Kinsman. She and her husband, then of Barrington, N. H., sold this interest to Asa Andrews in 1819.

50. SAMUEL KINSMAN,⁵ baptized July 19, 1747, inherited the homestead of Captain John. He married Martha Smith, Nov. 30, 1769. In 1784, he bought the farm near his father's house now owned by Mr. Carl Caverly and made his home there.² Their children were:

98 MARTHA,⁶ baptized June 23, 1771; married 1st, Stephen Boardman, June 2, 1791; married 2nd, Elias Haskell of Gloucester, Sept. 21, 1812.
99 BETSEY,⁶ baptized July 7, 1776; married John Wells Jr., Dec. 15, 1796.
100 SAMUEL,⁶ baptized Aug. 7, 1785; married Hannah Pearson, Nov. 5, 1809, who died Sept. 5, 1859, aged 75 yrs. 6 mos. He died April 8, 1860.

Mr. Kinsman died Dec. 29, 1806 aged 59 years and his widow Dec. 10, 1820, aged 70.

51. JONATHAN KINSMAN,⁵ baptized Jan. 7, 1749 was a student at Brown University and is the first of the long line who is known to have had a college education.³ He married first, his life long friend, Hannah Burnham, daughter of their neighbor, Isaac and Hannah Burnham. He became a prominent citizen of Parsonsfield, Me., where his wife died Sept. 4, 1795. He married second, Susanna Bemont, in 1796. He removed subsequently to Athens, Me., where he died, April 27, 1825. Two of their nine children were born in Ipswich:

101 HANNAH BURNHAM,⁶ baptized Feb. 27, 1774.
102 SALOME,⁶ baptized Sept. 10, 1775.

Their daughter, Mary,⁶ born in Saco, Me., Oct. 10, 1784⁴ became the wife of John Burnham Brown, the Candlewood farmer whose land holdings have already been traced,⁵ on April 2, 1818.

¹ Page 9.
² Page 6.
³ The Kinsman Family, p. 80.
⁴ The Kinsman Family, p. 98.
⁵ Page 11.

53. MICHAEL KINSMAN,⁵ baptized April 6, 1746, married first, Sarah Treadwell (pub. Nov. 19, 1768) and second Mary Knowlton, Dec. 15, 1783. He died Nov. 25, 1795. In the last year of his life, we find that he bought the house and lot, now owned and occupied by the widow of J. Farley Kinsman, April 21, 1795. The children by the first marriage were:[1]

103 BETSEY,⁶ married Aaron Blaney Jr.; resided in Bristol, Me.
104 PELATIAH,⁶ born Jan. 11, 1785; died April 18, 1807.
105 MARY,⁶ born June 16, 1787; married Henry Little Jr. of Newcastle, Me.
106 ISRAEL,⁶ born June 8, 1789; removed to Salem, Philadelphia and New York, where he became a prosperous merchant.
107 SARAH,⁶ born Oct. 5, 1792; married David Dennis Jr., lived in Nobleborough, Me.
108 MICHAEL,⁶ born Sept. 18, 1794; removed to Philadelphia.

The widow, Mary, married David Dennis, Esq. of Nobleborough, Me., pub. April 22, 1809 and her daughter Sarah, married David Dennis Jr.

54. NATHANIEL KINSMAN,⁵ baptized Mar. 20, 1747, married first, Priscilla Treadwell, March 12, 1772, who died Jan. 9, 1786; and second, Elizabeth Choate, Dec. 31, 1786, who died July 18, 1834. Capt. Nathaniel died July 1, 1807. His dwelling was on Summer St., now owned by Mrs. Philip E. Clarke. The children by the first marriage were:

109 PRISCILLA,⁶ born Oct. 6, 1773; married Thomas Hodgkins, Aug. 27, 1795; lived in Portland, Me.
110 NATHANIEL²,⁶ born Nov. 24, 1775; married Deborah Webb, a ship master, made his home in Salem.[2]
111 HANNAH,⁶ born Dec. 8, 1777; married John P. Bartlett of Portland Me., where she lived.
112 MICHAEL,⁶ born Aug. 9, 1780, died Dec. 12, 1781.
113 MICHAEL,⁶ born April 3, 1783, died at sea unmarried Feb. 11, 1800

Children by the second marriage:

114 JOHN CHOATE,⁶ born July 5, 1789,[3] a shipmaster, removed to Salem 1838. See No. 114.
115 ELIZABETH,⁶ born July, 1, 1791; died March 1, 1804.
116 MARY,⁶ born Jan. 7, 1795; died unmarried Aug. 6, 1820.
117 MARTHA,⁶ born Feb. 2, 1798; died Dec. 16, 1821.

58. MOSES KINSMAN,⁵ baptized July 7, 1754, was born on the Argilla farm. He married Lucy Cogswell, Sept. 28, 1780; and on May 7, 1784, bought of John Kinsman Jr. his dwelling in Candlewood, on the corner of the North Gate road, where he spent the remainder of his life. His wife died Nov. 29, 1804, at the age of 46 years and he married Susanna Cogswell,

---

[1] Kinsman Family, p. 83.
[2] Kinsman Family, p. 100
[3] Kinsman Family, p. 101.

Dec. 21, 1809. He died March 24, 1836; his widow, Jan. 10, 1841, aged 75 years. His children, all by the first marriage, were:

118 LUCY,⁶ born Oct. 14, 1781; married Aaron Cogswell, May 20, 1802.
119 JOSEPH,⁶ born March 14, 1783. See No. 119.
120 .... ⁶; died July 17, 1784.¹
121 MARY,⁶ born Dec. 13, 1785; married Bemsley Smith, Oct. 6, 1811.
122 HANNAH,⁶ born Oct. 14, 1787; married Ephraim Brown Jr. of Gloucester, Oct. 6, 1811.
123 ELIZABETH,⁶ born April 15, 1789; married Capt. Winthrop Boardman, Dec. 28, 1824; died Aug. 4, 1861.
124 FARLEY,⁶ born Nov. 18, 1790; married Jerusha Norwood of Gloucester, where they lived. He died Sept. 26, 1825.
125 SUSANNA ELWELL,⁶ born July 6, 1793; died Sept. 24, 1808.
126 ABIGAIL ELWELL,⁶ born Nov. 3, 1796; married Capt. Winthrop Boardman, Jan. 30, 1821, died June 8, 1823.
127 MOSES,⁶ born Oct. 17, 1798; married his cousin, Jane Kinsman, daughter of Aaron, Dec. 31, 1834. He acquired possession of the homestead and built a new dwelling on the same site where he lived until May 7, 1862. He left no children. His widow died Sept. 22, 1890, aged 91 years 2 months.

59. AARON KINSMAN,⁵ twin brother of Moses, was born July 6, 1754. He married Hannah Howe (pub. June 5, 1795), inherited or purchased the ancestral farm and lived there all his life. He died Oct. 13, 1836 but his widow survived until March 3, 1860, when she died at the age of 89 years 4 months. Their children were:

128 NATHANIEL,⁶ born Oct. 17, 1795. See No. 128.
129 HANNAH,⁶ born Dec. 31, 1796; died Dec. 14, 1869.
(Twins still-born were buried Mar. 24, 1798.)
130 JANE,⁶ born July 19, 1799; married her cousin Moses Kinsman Dec. 31, 1834; died Sept. 22, 1890. See No. 127.
131 CHARLOTTE,⁶ born March 29, 1801; married Elisha Brown, July 2, 1840, died March 29, 1860.
132 CLARISSA,⁶ born March 29, 1801; died, unmarried, Feb. 4, 1896.
133 AARON,⁶ born June 26, 1804; died Jan. 29, 1903.
——,⁶ born June 26, 1804; died June 26, 1804.

This whole family spent their days within a mile or two of their birthplace. Nathaniel bought and occupied the farm which is now owned by Joseph Marshall. Aaron never removed from the farm of his ancestors and never married. In his young manhood he was a member of the Ipswich Troop of horse, which met General Lafayette and escorted him into Ipswich, Aug. 31, 1824. A heavy rain marred the pleasure of the occasion and Lafayette desired the officer in charge to dismiss the troop as quickly as possible. The sword and horse pistol carried by Mr. Kinsman on this occasion are preserved in the collection of the Ipswich Historical Society.

¹ Town Record, "a child of Moses died July 17, 1784."

OF ROBERT KINSMAN 65

Jane married Moses, the son of Moses and Lucy, and lived her married life on the Moses Kinsman farm in Candlewood. Charlotte married Elisha Brown and found a home in the Elisha Brown dwelling on the Candlewood road. Hannah and Clarissa never married.

92. JEREMIAH KINSMAN[6] was born Oct. 6, 1748 and went to live in the new house, built by his father, when he was four years old. He married Martha Andrews, Nov. 16, 1769, who died April 11, 1810; and married second, in New Ipswich, N. H., Lydia Campbell, May 7, 1812 who died Sept. 24, 1757 at the great age of 98 years 8 months. He served in the Revolution and was credited with fifteen months and twenty-six days. After the war, he removed to Fitchburg. The Kinsman genealogy, page 95, gives his children, to whom should be added, the first born Jeremiah, baptized, Sept. 30, 1770, and died in infancy. Their children, all born in Ipswich, were:

134 JEREMIAH,[7] baptized Sept. 30, 1770;[1] died in infancy.
135 LYDIA,[7] born July 7, 1772.
136 JEREMIAH,[7] born Aug. 19, 1775.
137 DANIEL,[7] born March 30, 1778.
138 MARY,[7] born Feb. 2, 1781.
139 LUCY,[7] born Aug. 15, 1783
140 JOHN,[7] born April 24, 1786.
141 SALLY,[7] born April 7, 1790.[2]
142 ASA,[7] born March 30, 1793.

93. WILLIAM KINSMAN[6] was born Aug. 27, 1752; received a half, as his share of the farm, which probably included the lower house, now known as the cottage, where he spent his life. He married Anna Brown, daughter of Lieut. Jacob and Anna (Quarles) Brown of Hamilton, March 2, 1773. He died Sept. 30, 1843, aged 91 years and his widow died April 16, 1849 at the same age. He enlisted in Capt. Parker's Company of Newburyport and was in the battle of Bunker Hill. He was a Revolutionary pensioner for many years.[3] Their children were:

143 ANNA,[7] born May 27, 1773; married Benjamin Potter of Hamilton; April 8, 1794; died Dec. 28, 1869, aged 96.
144 WILLIAM,[7] born Sept. 4, 1776. See No. 144.
145 JACOB B.,[7] born April 9, 1779.[4] See No. 145.

114. JOHN CHOATE KINSMAN,[6] born July 5, 1789, married Anna Lord, daughter of Nathaniel and Lucy (Smith) Lord, May 10, 1810. He was a shipmaster in early life and his family occupied the homestead on Summer St., now owned by Mrs. Philip E. Clarke. He removed to Salem later. Their children,[5] all born in Ipswich, were:

[1] Ipswich Town Records. The name is not given in the Kinsman Family, p. 95.
[2] Name not given in Ipswich baptisms.
[3] The Kinsman Family, p. 96.
[4] The Kinsman Family, p. 137.
[5] The Kinsman Family, p. 101, gives marriages and later generation, but the Ipswich Town Record is John C. Wells m. Mary C., daughter of John Choate Kinsman, Sept. 30, 1851.

146 JOHN,[7] born Sept. 30, 1810.[1]
147 ELIZABETH,[7] born July 31, 1812; married James L. Wells of Salem, May 20, 1832.
148 LUCY ANN,[7] born Aug. 22, 1814.
149 SUSAN CHOATE,[7] born Jan. 5, 1817; married Israel Crafts, Oct. 19, 1834.
150 NATHANIEL,[7] born June 6, 1819.*
(A child of John and Anna Kinsman died Sept. 22, 1821, aged 3 weeks.)
151 MARY C.,[7] born Nov. 26, 1822.
152 MARTHA,[7] born May 14, 1829.

119. JOSEPH KINSMAN[6] was born in the old homestead on the corner of the North Gate Road, March 14, 1783. He married Eunice Brown, daughter of James and Jemima (Kinsman) Brown, May 18, 1809 and bought the Michael Kinsman farm on the Argilla Road, Jan. 21, 1821. The barn still standing bears the date, 1822, and he probably built a new dwelling at the same time. He died May 31, 1855 at the age of 72 years, his widow, July 17, of the same year, aged 81 years 6 months 21 days. Their children were:

153 JOSEPH,[7] born June 24, 1811. See No. 153.
154 ASA,[7] born Sept. 5, 1814; married Caroline A. Parsons, May 1, 1858. They dwelt for many years in the brick house on Fruit St., now owned by Sturgis Coffin Jr. where Mrs. Kinsman died Sept. 29, 1885, aged 72 years 11 months. He died Jan. 25, 1886. They had no children.
155 EUNICE,[7] born Sept. 3, 1818; married John Brown, Sept. 17, 1840, heir of the ancient John Brown farm on Fellows Lane, Sept. 10, 1840. She died Dec. 2, 1881.

128. NATHANIEL KINSMAN[6] was born on the Argilla farm of his forbears, Oct. 17, 1795. He bought the Nehemiah Brown farm in Candlewood,[2] April 10, 1828 and on December 16, 1828, he married his near neighbor in Argilla, Joanna Brown, daughter of Tristram and Joanna, who owned the farm lately sold by John B. Caverly. The young wife died July 28, 1832, at the age of 34, leaving two little children. Mr. Kinsman lived until July 18, 1864. Their children were:

156 JOANNA,[7] born Oct. 25, 1829; still living unmarried.
157 ABIGAIL,[7] born Oct. 9, 1831;[2] married Joseph Marshall, May 30, 1860 and still lives on the farm.

144 WILLIAM KINSMAN[7] was born in the "cottage" so called, now the residence of Miss Rhoda F. Kinsman, Sept. 4, 1776, married Sarah, daughter of Stephen and Elizabeth Brown of Hamilton, Nov. 4, 1802, and died

[1] The Kinsman Family, p. 144.
[2] Page 13.

in his life-long home, Nov. 12, 1866. His wife had died on March 11, 1860. He was ninety years old, his parents both attained the age of ninety-one, his grand-father was ninety-three and his only sister attained the age of ninety-six. Their children were:

158   BETSEY BROWN,[8] born June 24, 1803; died May 23, 1841.
159   LOUISA,[1],[8] born Feb. 12, 1805; married Capt. Henry S. Holmes, May 17, 1825, in the old homestead and fifty years later, they celebrated their golden wedding in the same room in which they were married, Captain Holmes died Jan., 1886, and his widow, Aug. 9, 1894.
160   SIMON BROWN,[8] born Jan. 26, 1807. See No. 160.
161   NANCY,[8] born April 1, 1809; married Stephen Blatchford, Aug. 14, 1834. Their home was in Hamilton,[2] where she died Mar. 6, 1882.
162   JACOB,[8] born March 29, 1811; married Abbie Staniford, Feb. 23, 1837. They removed to Topsfield[2] where he died Jan. 2, 1900.
163   SUSAN,[8] born April 17, 1813; died Aug. 3, 1831.
164   SARAH,[8] born July 5, 1815; married Oliver M. Whipple, May 15, 1844. They lived in Lowell,[3] where she died April 30, 1885.
165   WILLIAM HENRY,[8] born Feb. 1, 1818. See No. 165.
166   MARIA D.,[8] born April 15, 1820; married Lewis Emerson of Waltham, Nov. 27, 1844 where they made their home.[4] She died Oct. 11, 1891.
167   WILLARD BENAIAH,[8] born Feb. 3, 1822. See No. 167.
168   CHARLOTTE AUGUSTA,[8] born April 18, 1824; married Andrew Burnham 2d, of Essex, Nov. 24, 1844 and in Essex they made their home,[4] where she died Feb., 1861.
169   GEORGE,[8] born Jan. 26, 1826; married Elzina A. Tilton, Aug. 27 1865, who died in Waterford, Conn., July 23, 1872. He died Aug. 14, 1899.
170   DANIEL FITZ,[8] born Jan. 10, 1828; married Mattie A. Wood, June 13, 1855. Their home was in Colorado City, Colorado.[5] He died Jan. 16, 1888.

145.   JACOB BROWN KINSMAN[7] was born April 9, 1779, married Bethiah Dodge, of Hamilton, pub. April 10, 1802. He was a ship-master and died in Hispaniola, Jan. 27, 1811. His widow married Nicholas Woodbury of Hamilton, May 24, 1831 and died Jan. 24, 1861 aged 79. Their children were:[6]

171   CHARLOTTE,[8] born Sept. 24, 1803.
172   OLIVER DODGE,[8] born Sept. 26, 1805.

[1] The Kinsman Family, p. 194.
[2] The Kinsman Family, p. 195.
[3] The Kinsman Family, p. 196.
[4] The Kinsman Family, p. 197.
[5] The Kinsman Family, p. 198.
[6] The Kinsman Family, p. 137.

173   JACOB,⁸ born Jan. 20, 1808; died Oct. 8, 1810¹.
174   WILLIAM,⁸ born Oct. 18, 1809.   See No. 174.

153.   JOSEPH KINSMAN⁷ was born June 24, 1811. He acquired the homestead and lived there until his death, Mar. 27, 1886. He married, Mary E. Brown, daughter of Joseph and Rebecca (Appleton) Brown of Candlewood, Sept. 20, 1842. Their children were:

175   JOSEPH FARLEY,⁸ born April 23, 1844. He married Caroline, daughter of Aaron F. and Nabby Brown of the Argilla neighborhood, Oct. 1, 1873. He served in Co. D. 48th Reg. M. V. in the War of the Rebellion. At his father's death, he acquired possession of the homestead, where he died Aug. 31, 1906, leaving no children. His widow survives.
176   EDWARD,⁸ born   1845; died March 5, 1846 aged 6 mos.
177   GUSTAVUS,⁸ born Aug. 19, 1850. See No. 177.

Mrs. Kinsman died Feb. 20, 1861 and he married the second time, Hannah S. Pert of Manchester, Jan. 22 1863, who died Jan. 27, 1881. Mr. Kinsman died March 27, 1886.

160.   SIMON BROWN KINSMAN,⁸ born Jan. 26, 1807, married Elizabeth B. Stone of Hamilton (pub. June 6, 1829), died July 14, 1831. Their children were:

178   MARY ELIZABETH,⁹ born Jan. 21, 1830; died Mar. 1, 1844.
179   RHODA ELVIRA,⁹ born July 19, 1831; died Oct. 8, 1851.
180   LYDIA ANN,⁹ born June 19, 1834; married Charles A. Homans of Gloucester, March 20, 1856.²
181   MARTHA ELLEN,⁹ born June 5, 1839.
182   ELIZABETH,⁹ born Feb. 27, 1846; died Jan. 16, 1873.

He was a resident of Ipswich until after 1856 when he removed to Woburn.

164.   WILLIAM HENRY KINSMAN⁸ was born in the Kinsman "cottage," Feb. 1, 1818 and married Frances J. Lamson of Hamilton, Jan. 1, 1857. He acquired possession of his father's estate and spent his whole life on the farm, where he died Nov. 30, 1891. His widow survived until April 22, 1907, dying at the age of 81 years. Their children were:

183   MARY FRANCES,⁹ born Nov. 28, 1857; died Jan. 14, 1858.
184   ALICE FRANCES,⁹ born Dec. 12, 1858; died Oct. 6, 1859.
185   CHARLES HENRY,⁹ born Feb. 18, 1860; died Mar. 24, 1872.
186   ALICE FRANCES,⁹ born April 6, 1861; died Oct. 3, 1861.
187   RHODA FRANCES,⁹ born Sept. 30, 1862. She owns and occupies the ancestral farm.
188   ALICE AUGUSTA,⁹ born Sept. 23, 1864; died May 18, 1869.

*Ipswich Records. Child of Jacob Kinsman died Jan. 26, 1810.
†The Kinsman Family, p. 215.

189 ARTHUR DANIEL,[9] born June 8, 1866, married Mary Abby Gardner Smith, daughter of Francis and Caroline Smith, May 8, 1899. They live in Ipswich.

167 WILLARD BENAIAH KINSMAN,[8] was born in the ancient "cottage," Feb. 3, 1822. He married Harriet Manning, daughter of William and Mary Manning, Mar. 24, 1844. They made their home on the Essex Road, but later in the Manning homestead on County Road, where he died, Jan. 23, 1894. Mrs. Kinsman died Feb. 14, 1889, aged 66 years 9 months. Their children were:

- 190 SARAH MARIA,[9] born July 3, 1844; married Joseph A. Story, May 19, 1868.
- 191 ANNIE MANNING,[9] born Sept. 24, 1846; resides in Somerville.
- 192 HARRIET MANNING,[9] born Sept. 24, 1846; married Edward B. Wildes, May 26, 1870, who died Jan. 30, 1899, aged 52 years Her present residence is in Somerville.
- 193 MARY BROWN,[9] born March 9, 1848; married John F. Le Baron, Nov. 28, 1870; died Sept. 19, 1883.
- 194 WILLARD FRANCIS,[9] born Nov. 29, 1849. See No. 194.
- 195 RHODA E.,[9] born Sept. 6, 1854; died Oct. 13, 1859.
- 196 LOUISE EMMA,[9] born May 29, 1861; died Dec. 2, 1878.

174. WILLIAM KINSMAN,[8] born Oct. 18, 1809; married Nancy D. Green of Kensington, N. H.————. They lived for many years in the house on County Road, Ipswich, now owned by Mrs. Joseph R. Wilson, where Mrs. Kinsman died Nov. 20, 1886, aged 80 years 6 months 15 days, and Mr. Kinsman, Jan. 22, 1888. Their children were:

- 197 NICHOLAS W.,[9] born April 15, 1838; removed to San Francisco, where he married Margaret Miller, who died in 1889. He died in May, 1909.
- 198 BETHIAH D.,[9] born Feb. 18, 1841; resides in Ipswich; unmarried.

177. GUSTAVUS KINSMAN,[8] was born Aug. 19, 1850 in the dwelling on the Argilla Road. He married Susan M. Kimball of Hamilton, Nov. 24, 1875. Mr. Kinsman purchased the Capt. Ebenezer Caldwell estate, where he resides. Their children are:

- 199 MARY ELIZABETH,[9] born June 2, 1877; married Edwin W. Hawes of Swampscott, Oct. 7, 1908.
- 200 GRACE LILLIAN,[9] born Jan. 6, 1883; died Mar. 27, 1883.

194 WILLARD FRANCIS KINSMAN[9] was born Nov. 29, 1849. He studied in the Massachusetts Agricultural College, and married Mary A. Quincy of Rumney N. H., Sept. 24, 1876. They built the sightly buildings on the Essex Road[1] and have always resided there. Their children are:

[1] Page 17.

201   WILLARD QUINCY[10] born May 7, 1877.   See No. 201.
202   ELIZABETH GRACE,[10] born March 8, 1879; married Charles E. MacGlashan of Norwood, Mass., May 20, 1909.   They live in Norwood.

201.   WILLARD QUINCY KINSMAN,[10] was born in the new dwelling on Essex Road, May 7, 1877 and married Mary E. Nichelson of Cambridge, June 9, 1904.   They make their home in the homestead.   Their children are:

203   DOROTHY QUINCY,[11] born Nov. 7, 1904.
204   WILLARD QUINCY JR.,[11] born March 26, 1906.
205   JOHN EDWARDS,[11] born April 30, 1908.
206.   Walter Lewis,[11] born Aug. 23, 1909.

THE DESCENDANTS OF
WILLIAM FELLOWS
OF IPSWICH, MASS.

EDITORIAL NOTE.—Great assistance in the investigation of this line has been rendered by Miss Harriet Davis Fellows of Cornwall-on-Hudson, who furnished the data regarding the descendants of Capt. Jonathan Fellows of Gloucester. Mr. Horatio Davis of Boston has also contributed family notes. Mr. Joseph Davis has made a careful study of the Fellows line, from which he is descended, and is confident that the children of Cornelius Fellows and Sarah Williams, No. 53, were the first to write the name Fellowes. T. F. W.

GENEALOGICAL RECORD OF THE DESCENDANTS
OF
WILLIAM FELLOWS OF IPSWICH, MASS.

1. WILLIAM FELLOWS is known to us, first, as one of the Town cowherds. In the earliest contract with these officials mentioned in our Town Records, under the date of Sept., 1639, agreement was made with William Fellows to keep the herd of cows on the south side the river, from the 20th of April to the 20th of November. He was bound by his contract, "to drive them out to feed before the sunne be half an hour high and not to bring them home before half an hour before sunset." He was also required to drive the cattle, "coming over the River back over the River at night," and to take charge of them "as soon as they are put over the River in the morning." He was liable for any harm coming to the herd and was to receive 12 pence for each cow before he took them, a shilling and six pence fourteen day safter mid-summer and the rest at the end of the terms in corn or money, a total of £15. In 1640, he was associated with Mark Quilter and Symon Tompson as the cowkeepers on the north side of the river.

Twenty years later, he bought the John Andrews farm[1] and took up his residence in Candlewood. In 1664, when Richard Saltonstall conveyed the title in several lots to his son, Nathaniel of Haverhill, on the occasion of his marriage with Elizabeth, daughter of Rev. John Ward, he included in his gift a farm of 150 acres at "Chebacco," "now in the occupation of William and Isaac Fellows." This farm is now owned by the heirs of Asa P. Stone in Argilla. William Fellows was a "tenant to Richard Saltonstall," Sept., 1659. Mr. Fellows and his son were also lease holders of 15 acres of meadow near the land of Dep. Gov. Symonds. In 1666, with John Proctor Sen., he bought a four rod lot with a house an the west corner of Green St. and the Meeting House Green. The double ownership continued during his life but on Dec. 21, 1676 his executors bought the Proctor interest of Proctor's heirs.

His widow survived him and at his death five children were living:

2 ISAAC,[2] born about 1637. See No. 2.
3 EPHRAIM.[2] See No. 3.
4 SAMUEL.[2] See No. 4.
5 JOSEPH.[2] See No. 5.
6 SARAH,[2] born July 26, 1657; married John Rust, a widow in 1722.

[1] Page.

7 ABIGAIL,[2] married Samuel Ayres,[1] April 16, 1677.
8 MARY,[2]
9 ELIZABETH,[2] } added by a family genealogist.

2 ISAAC FELLOWS[2] served in Captain Willard's Company in King Philip's war, and was credited to the Town, July 24, 1676.[2] In 1678, he was one of the surveyors of highways. He was associated with his father in the lease of the Saltonstall farm in the Argilla neighborhood and other land. He bought of Henry Bennett a house on Wigwam Hill in 1680, and may have removed thither as in 1705, his conveyance of his farm to his son, Jonathan, mentions that it was then occupied by William Durgey.

He married Joanna Borm (contraction for Boardman), Jan. 29, 1672 Corporal Isaac died April 6, 1721 "upwards of 84," and his widow died March 22, 1732. Their children were:

10 ISAAC,[3] born Nov. 27, 1673. Isaac Fellows Jr., bought the Samuel Younglove house and land on South Main St. on June 16, 1694. Ephraim Fellows, his brother, presumably, sold the same to Dr. Samuel Wallis, Nov. 20, 1713.
11 SAMUEL,[3] born Feb. 8, 1676. See No. 11.
12 EPHRAIM,[3] born Sept. 3, 1679. See No. 12.
13 JONATHAN,[3] born Sept. 28, 1682. See No. 13.
14 DAVID,[3] born April 7, 1687.
15 JOANNA,[3] born Nov. 19, 1689.

3. EPHRAIM FELLOWS[2] received a permit from the Town in 1670 to fell timber for a house, 16 feet square. He was a trooper in the King Philip war, in 1675[2] and one of the road suryevors in 1678. He bought the interest of Younglove heirs in the estate of Isaac Fellows Jr., June 16, 1694, and in the deed he is called a locksmith. He conveyed the same to Dr. Wallis in 1713.[3] His wife, Mary, died Feb. 23, 1671. He married 2d, Ann ———. Their children were;

16 ELIZABETH,[3] born Sept. 14, 1685.
17 ANNA,[3] born Feb. 25, 1693–4.

4. SAMUEL FELLOWS[2] made his home for many years with his brother in-law Samuel Ayres Sen. and removed with him to Newbury. His children were:

18 Samuel Jr.[3]
19 JOHN,[3] married Rachel Varney at Chebacco, Oct. 14, 1692 and was living in that parish that year, as his name follows that of Thomas Varney in Rev. John Wise's petition.[4] A son,
19a VARNEY[4] was born March 25, 1694.

[1] Samuel Ayres Sen. was a resident of Newbury in 1701, when Samuel Fellows made conveyance to him of his share in the William Fellows farm.
[2] Ipswich in the Mass. Bay Colony, p. 220.
[3] Ipswich in the Mass. Bay Colony, p. 452.
[4] Ipswich in Mass. Bay Colony, p. 291.

5. JOSEPH FELLOWS[2] made his home on the farm which he acquired by inheritance and purchase. He served in the King Philip war as his wages were assigned to Ipswich in 1675–6.[1] He married Ruth Fraile, April 19, 1675. Mrs. Ruth Fellows an "antient widdo" died on April 14, 1729. He died before 1693. Their children were:

20 MARY,[3] born May 3, 1676; married John Brown Jr., who died before 1764, when she and her sons, Joseph and Nathan, sold the homestead to Benjamin.
21 JOSEPH.[3] See No. 21.
22 WILLIAM.[3] See No. 22.
23 SARAH,[3] born May 17, 1685; pub. Peter Harden of Bridgewater, Sept. 24, 1709; living in 1754.
24 RUTH,[3] married Samuel Waite, son of John and Katherine Waite, born Oct. 20, 1685 (pub. Nov. 9, 1717); living in 1754.
25 ABIGAIL,[3] pub. Thomas Low Jr., Sept. 30, 1721; living in 1756.

11. SAMUEL FELLOWS,[3] born Feb. 8, 1676, married Sarah Fuller, Jan. 5, 1731. She was born Nov. 8, 1713, daughter of James and Phebe Fuller. He died Aug. 25, 1735 (Ips. Records). (Widow Sarah Fellows pub. Nathaniel Killum, July 22, 1738. Widow Sarah Fellows married Nathaniel Low, Jan. 31, 1739.) Their child was:

26 SARAH,[4] baptized Oct. 15, 1732; pub. John Bennett Jr., Mar. 30, 1754.

12. EPHRAIM FELLOWS,[3] born Sept. 3, 1679, married Hannah Warner, daughter of the late Nathaniel Warner, May 19, 1703.
Their daughter was:

27 HANNAH,[4] baptized Aug. 12, 1705; pub. Samuel Ingalls, Feb. 29, 1723.

13. JONATHAN FELLOWS,[3] born Sept. 28, 1682, succeeded to his father's farm and retained it from 1705 to 1742. The Town Record mentions a publishment to Elizabeth Dutch, March 17, 1704. This may be a clerical error as he married 1st, Hannah Dutch, May 17, 1705. Their children were:

28 HANNAH,[4] born March 30, 1706.
29 JONATHAN,[4] born June 15, 1707. See No. 29.
30 ELIZABETH,[4] born Oct. 22, 1709; pub. 1st, Joseph Perkins, Nov. 2, 1728; pub. 2nd, Capt. John Kinsman, Dec. 9, 1753.

Mrs. Hannah Fellows died Jan. 28, 1710. He was published 2nd, to Sarah Day, Dec. 13, 1712. She was daughter of John and Sarah Day, born Jan. 9, 1692. Their children were:

31 ISAAC,[4] baptized May 9, 1714.
32 JOHN,[4] baptized April 28, 1716.

---

[1] Ipswich in Mass. Bay Colony, p. 220.

"The wife of Jonathan," died May 1, 1716. He was published 3rd, to the widow Sarah Rust, Dec. 29, 1716. Their children were:

33   SARAH,[4] baptized Dec. 22, 1717; pub. Samuel Knowlton, June 26, 1736.
34   ISAAC,[4] baptized May 17, 1719. See No. 34. (Fellows Record.)
35   ABNER,[4] baptized Dec. 4, 1720.
36   MARY,[4] baptized July 22, 1722; married Richard Tucker of Newburyport, Oct. 20, 1768.
37   JEREMIAH,[4] baptized April 5, 1724.[1]

Sarah, the wife of Sergeant Jonathan, died May 30, 1725.

Deacon Jonathan was published 4th, with Mrs. Deborah Tilton of Hampton, N. H., May 26, 1733. He was a deacon of the First church in Ipswich and died in 1736 (Town Record).

21.   JOSEPH FELLOWS[3] spent his life on the farm,[2] which he greatly increased in value. He married Sarah Kimball, Dec. 17, 1701. Their children were:

38   JOSEPH,[4] born April 20, 1703. See No. 38.
39   JACOB,[4] born Sept. 14, 1705; married Sarah Frail, Nov. 5, 1739.
40   BENJAMIN,[4] baptized Jan. 27, 1711. See No. 40.
41   DANIEL,[4] baptized Sept. 20, 1713. See No. 41.
42   NATHAN,[4] baptized Oct. 13, 1717. See No. 42.
43   SARAH,[4] married Moses Dodge of Beverly, Feb. 12, 1761.

Sarah, wife of Joseph, died April 1, 1738 aged 56 years 10 months 12 days. He married 2d, the widow Mary Story of Chebacco May 15, 1739, who died Jan. 12, 1776 aged 80 years. Their child was:

44   SARAH[4], baptized May 7, 1741.

Joseph Fellows, died Sept. 8, 1762.

22.   WILLIAM FELLOWS[3] married Elizabeth Rust, Dec. 7, 1693. On January 7, 1694, he bought the interest of the other heirs in the small lot on the corner of Green Street and Meeting House Green. By a deed of sale March 29, 1708, William Fellows, mariner, conveyed this lot.[3] Their children were:

45   NATHANIEL,[4] born April 24, 1696.
46   WILLIAM,[4] born Feb. 25, 1697.
47   ELIZABETH,[4] born April 29, 1700.
48   JOHN,[4] born March 30, 1702.

---

[1] The Fellows data, furnished by Miss Harriet D. Fellows, give the children of Jeremiah[4]—Jeremiah[5], b. June 12, 1749; Benjamin[5], b. Nov. 11, 1750; Jonathan[5], b. Jan 19, 1753; d. 1754; Ruth,[5] b. Oct. 21, 1754; Jonathan[5], Dec. 20, 1757. His residence is not given. His name does not appear on Ipswich records.

[2] Page 42.

[3] Ipswich in Mass. Bay, p. 336

49 MARY,⁴ born Oct. 11, 1705.
He was published 2nd, to Deborah Frail of Salem May 2, 1730, and devised his whole estate to her (will proved April 8, 1754). William Fellows died March 5, 1754.

29. JONATHAN FELLOWS JR.,⁴ born June 15, 1707, published with Abigail Gaines, Nov. 22, 1729, who died Jan. 30, 1730. Captain Jonathan Jr. married 2nd, on Aug. 14, 1735, Elizabeth Saunders of Boston, daughter of Caleb Norwood of Boston who had married, first, John Saunders. Babson (History of Gloucester, p. 323) says that he settled in Squam about 1740 and that his only public service was that of Captain of a Company in the campaign against the French in 1756. He died June 20, 1759. The only child by the first marriage was:

50 JONATHAN,⁵ baptized Jan. 24, 1730 at Ipswich.

The children by the second marriage were:

51 SAMUEL,⁵ born and baptized May 16, 1736 at Ipswich. See No. 51.
52 GUSTAVUS,⁵ born Sept. 18, 1737; baptized Sept., 1737 at Ipswich. See No. 52.
53 CORNELIUS,⁵ born Nov. 19, 1738 at Ipswich. See No. 53.
54 ELIZABETH,⁵ born June 22, 1740 at Gloucester; married Peter Cunningham of Pomfret, Conn.
55 NATHANIEL,⁵ born May 30, 1743 at Gloucester. See No. 55.
56 CALEB,⁵ baptized Nov. 11, 1744 at Gloucester, died in infancy.
57 CALEB,⁵ born April 19, 1746 at Gloucester.
58 ABIGAIL,⁵ born April 19, 1746 at Gloucester; married William Cunningham Oct. 16, 1766.

Jonathan Fellows of Gloucester, coaster, and Elizabeth, with other parties, refer the settlement of the will of Caleb Norwood of Boston, innholder, dated Nov. 9, 1735, which devised an house and 40 acres at Gloucester, the estate of his five daughters, Elizabeth, Abigail, Sarah, Deborah and Alice to referees, Jan. 6, 1747. (Essex Registry of Deeds 100:41).

34. ISAAC FELLOWS,⁴ born May 12, 1719, married widow Abigail Blake; died May 8, 1790.¹ Their children were:

59 ABIGAIL,⁵ born Dec. 27, 1759.
60 ELIZABETH,⁵ born June 3, 1762.
61 ISAAC,⁵ born July 25, 1764. See No. 61.
62 JESSE,⁵ born May 17, 1767.
63 SARAH,⁵ born Oct. 1, 1770.
64 JUDITH,⁵ born Aug. 10, 1773.

38. JOSEPH FELLOWS,⁴ baptized April 20, 1703, a tailor by trade, received from his father a small tract and built the house known later as

¹ The data concerning Isaac Fellows and family have been furnished by Miss Harriet D. Fellows of Cornwall-on-Hudson. His residence was not in Ipswich.

the Sally Roberts house on the north side of Fellows Lane.[1] He was published with Susanna Giddings, Jan. 1, 1731. His will was proved May 10, 1764. His widow married Dea. Joseph Hale of Boxford, Nov. 25, 1771. Their children were:

65 WILLIAM,[5] baptized May 12, 1734; married Mary Crafts, Jan. 3, 1760. He died July 16, 1785, his widow Dec. 8, 1816, aged 82.
66 SARAH,[5] baptized April 25, 1736; married Moses Potter,[2] June 1, 1757.
67 DEBORAH,[5] baptized May 28, 1738; married Jonathan Goodhue of Gloucester, April 27, 1758.
68 JOSEPH,[5] baptized Aug. 3, 1740; died Aug., 1764.
69 ISAAC,[5] baptized May 27, 1744. See No. 69.
70 SUSANNA,[5] baptized July 2, 1749; married Nehemiah Knowlton, Oct. 11, 1771.
71 ABIGAIL,[5] baptized Oct. 27, 1751; married Josiah Haskell of Gloucester, Feb. 13, 1772.

40. BENJAMIN FELLOWS,[4] baptized Jan. 27, 1711, built for his home the house later occupied by his son, Ephraim, and grandson Ephraim, now owned by Mr. William J. Cameron, on Lakeman's Lane.[3] He married Eunice Dodge of Beverly, Dec. 1, 1736. Their children were:

72 EUNICE,[5] baptized Dec. 4, 1737; married John Wood of Newbury, July 6, 1758.
73 LYDIA,[5] baptized Aug. 19, 1739; married William Alford of Newburyport, Sept. 19, 1765.
74 ISRAEL,[5] baptized Jan. 4, 1740–1.
75 EPHRAIM,[5] baptized June 14, 1747; died early.

Eunice, the wife of Benjamin, died July 19, 1747. He married the widow Sarah Elwell of Gloucester, March 29, 1749. Their children[4] were:

76 JOHN,[5] baptized Sept. 5, 1751. See No. 76.
77 EPHRAIM,[5] baptized Jan. 20, 1754. See No. 77.
78 BENJAMIN,[5] baptized June 29, 1760. See No. 78.

He was published with Mrs. Rebecca Souther, March 20, 1778. He died Nov., 1794 and his will devised his property to widow Rebecca, John and Ephraim. (Proved Dec. 2, 1794). The widow Rebecca died May 8, 1802.

41. DANIEL FELLOWS,[4] baptized Sept. 20, 1713; was "in a measure bereft of his reason," when his father died in 1762. Guardianship of Daniel

[1] Page 46.
[2] Page 4.
[3] Page 44.
[4] The Town Record mentions Jemima Fellows, daughter of Benjamin and Jemima, who was bapt. Jan. 14, 1749, and married John Dane of Salem, Jan. 21, 1773.

as a person non compos mentis, was granted to his brother, Benjamin, Oct. 19, 1762 (Pro. Rec. 340:65).

42. NATHAN FELLOWS,[4] baptized Oct. 13, 1717; was published with Anne Start, Feb. 5, 1742. He was drowned March 15, 1743, while crossing Mile Brook with a loaded team. His widow Anne was published with Stephen Brown, Aug. 10, 1746. Their child was:

79 NATHAN,[5] baptized Feb. 26, 1743. See No. 79.

51. SAMUEL FELLOWS,[5] born May 16, 1736 at Ipswich, removed to Gloucester, where he married Mercy Treadwell (pub. April 15, 1763). He was Ensign in Capt. Jonathan Fellows's Co. in 1755. Their children were:

80 NATHANIEL TREADWELL,[6] baptized at 5th Church Feb. 5, 1764, and on the same at day the 3d Church.
81 SAMUEL,[6] baptized at the 4th church, Aug. 4, 1765.

52. GUSTAVUS FELLOWS,[5] born Sept. 18, 1737, at Ipswich, removed with his father's family to Gloucester. He married 1st, Hannah Peirpoint of Boston, daughter of Robert, Feb. 17, 1761. It is believed that he removed to Boston in 1774, where he had a distillery on Harvard St. He married 2nd, Sarah Pierpont, daughter of James Pierpont and Sarah (Dow). He died Aug. 5, 1816 and his widow April 12, 1828 aged 78 years.[1] Their children were:

82 HANNAH,[6] died in infancy.
83 ABIGAIL CUNNINGHAM,[6] married Perrin May of Boston, Nov. 10, 1789.
84 ELIZABETH,[6] married 1st, Isaac Davis of Boston, married 2nd, Aiden Ayres.
85 SARAH,[6] married Joseph Warren Chase of Boston.
86 GUSTAVUS,[6] married Abigail Kelly of Maine.
87 JAMES PIERPONT,[6] died at age of eighteen on a voyage to Calcutta.
88 SOPHIA,[6] married 1st, Phillip Clark; married 2nd, L. F. De Les Dernier of Maine. Their daughter, Emily de Les Dernier, an authoress, wrote a novel, "Fanny Jt. John."
89 FRANCES,[6] married Jeremiah Plummer of Alden, Me.
90 HANNAH PIERPONT,[6] married Joseph Bancroft.
91 JONATHAN,[6] served on the Great Lakes under McDonough, and was wounded. He died unmarried.

53. CORNELIUS FELLOWS,[5] born Nov. 19, 1738, married 1st, Sarah Williams of Roxbury, daughter of John and Elizabeth Williams, Nov. 29, 1763.[2] She was born Dec. 8, 1741 and died April 11, 1789 aged 47 years 4 months. Captain Fellows married 2nd, Hannah Parker of Roxbury, Dec. 30, 1794[3]. He died at Guadaloupe, W. I. in July, 1795. Their early home

---
[1] Records of Hollis St. Ch., Boston.
[2] Gloucester records.
[3] Roxbury records.

was in Gloucester, where Nathaniel Low sold to Cornelius Fellows of Gloucester, trader, land and salt marsh by Rings Mill Pond, March 6, 1773 (131: 184). Joseph Somes sold to Cornelius Fellows, a house and an acre of land on the northwest side of the highway from "Anna-Squam meeting house," to Halibut Point, bounded north-east on Hodgkin's Cove, west on the burying ground, south on the highway, Feb. 23, 1774 (133: 52). He was a selectman that year. He removed to Boston as early as 1778, as his son Cornelius was baptized in the First Church, Aug. 2, 1778. Their children were:[1]

92 JONATHAN,[6] born Dec. 26, 1765; died young.
93 ELIZABETH,[6] born May 7, 1768; baptized May 17, 1768 at the 3d Church, Gloucester; married David W. Bradley of Boston, Nov. 4, 1788; died May 20, 1791.
94 HANNAH PIERPOINT,[6] born May 7, 1768; baptized May 22, 1768 at the 4th Church, Gloucester; died Jan. 30, 1796 unmarried.
95 JONATHAN,[6] born Jan. 8, 1770; baptized Jan. 18, 1770 at the 3d church. See No. 95.
96 CALEB,[6] born July 9, 1771. See No. 96.
97 JONATHAN WILLIAMS,[6] born March 8, 1773; baptized March 21, 1773 at the 3d church, Gloucester; married Sarah Dudley, March 29, 1795; died Oct. 18, 1800 at Havana.
98 CORNELIUS,[6] born 27–29 Oct. 1774; died in infancy.
99 SARAH,[6] born June 22, 1776; married Capt. Nathaniel Ruggles of Roxbury, Aug. 25, 1786.
100 CORNELIUS,[6] born July 25, 1778; baptized in First Church, Boston, Aug. 2, 1778; lost at sea.
101 NATHANIEL,[6] born Jan. 22, 1780; baptized in First Church, Boston, Jan. 30, 1780. See No. 101.
102 ELSY DONNELL,[6] born Feb. 4, 1781; married Joseph Davis.
103 HARRIET,[6] born Feb. 5, 1782 at Boston; baptized in First Church, Boston, Feb. 10, 1782; married Charles Davis of Roxbury, Sept. 8, 1799.
104 NANCY,[6] born June 3, 1783; baptized in First Church, Boston; June 6, 1784; married 1st, Charles Hunt; married 2nd, Jonn Shirley Williams; died at Roxbury, Aug. 7, 1853.

55. NATHANIEL FELLLOWS,[5] born in Gloucester, May 30, 1743, removed to Boston in 1774, where he married Lydia Stanton of Charlestown, daughter of Capt. John and Joanna (Ball) Stanton, Jan. 3, 1774 (Boston Records). His residence stood where the old Tremont House was afterwards built. He engaged in the dry goods business with his brother, Cornelius, until the partnership was dissolved, Dec. 28, 1780. He continued the same business at 70 Cornhill, 1783–1785. Their child was:

105 LYDIA[6], married Jonathan Amory Jr. of Boston, Oct. 21, 1794.

[1] The names and dates of the children were furnished by Miss Harriet D. Fellows of Cornwall-on-the-Hudson.

61. ISAAC FELLOWS,⁵ born July 25, 1764, married 1st, Jane Burnham who died April 20, 1801 aged 35 years; married 2nd, widow Rebecca Hurlburt, in May, 1804 who died in Dec., 1818 aged 45 years. The children by the first marriage[1] were:

106   JANE,⁶ born March 23, 1795; died Nov. 14, 1848.
107   ISAAC,⁶ born June 24, 1797. See No. 107.
108   IRA,⁶ born Nov. 12, 1799. See No. 108.

The children by the second marriage were:

109   LYMAN,⁶ born May 16, 1805.
110   REBECCA,⁶ born Nov. 14, 1806; died May 17, 1843.
111   ELIJAH,⁶ born April 1, 1809; died March 6, 1826.
112   FANNY,⁶ born March 15, 1812.
113   MARY,⁶ born May 12, 1814; died July, 1815.
114   ALVA,⁶ born June 28, 1817.

69. ISAAC FELLOWS,⁵ baptized May 27, 1744, inherited from his father and occupied the house known as the Sally Roberts house. He married Mary Roberts in Essex, Sept. 4, 1764, who died Feb. 26, 1818. He died Nov. 12, 1826 aged 83. He was a private in Capt. Thomas Burnham's Co. which marched on the alarm of April 19, 1775 and served three days. Their children were:

115   MARY,⁶ baptized April 20, 1766; died unmarried May, 1856.
116   JOSEPH,⁶ baptized March 11, 1770.
117   ISAAC,⁶ baptized April 26, 1772. See No. 117.
118   WILLIAM,⁶ baptized Feb. 14, 1780. See No. 118.

76. JOHN FELLOWS,⁵ baptized Sept. 5, 1751, owned and occupied the Williams Fellows house and sold the west half to Nathan Fellows Jr. in 1807, the east half to Joseph, 1823.[2] He spent his last years in the house, occupied later by Mrs. Calvin Batchelder and Miss Lydia Caldwell. He was a private in Capt. Thomas Burnham's Co. which marched on the alarm of April 19, 1775 and served three days. He married Martha Shatswell, Dec. 8, 1772, who died Nov. 4, 1803 aged 44. Their children were:

119   SARAH,⁶ baptized June 26, 1774; married Ammi Brown of Gloucester, July 15, 1798.
120   HANNAH,⁶ married John Lane of Ipswich, Jan. 7, 1798.
121   EUNICE,⁶ baptized March 3, 1776; married Daniel Potter Jr., Nov. 15, 1796.
122   MARTHA,⁶ baptized Sept. 12, 1779; married Moses Willett, May 24, 1804.
123   JOHN,⁶ baptized July 29, 1781; married Molly Willett, June 10, 1804. They lived in Cambridge. He died March 31, 1824, his widow Oct. 10, 1843 aged 79 years. They had no children.
124   NATHAN,⁶ baptized Aug. 24, 1783. See No. 124.

[1] These data were furnished by Miss Harriet D. Fellows.
[2] Page 47.

77. EPHRAIM FELLOWS,[5] baptized Jan. 20, 1754, inherited the homestead of his father Benjamin and at his death bequeathed it to his heirs.[1] He was a private in Capt. Thomas Burnham's Co. which marched on the alarm of April 19, 1775. He saw further service probably from Dec. 9 1777 to Feb. 3, 1778. He married Eunice Appleton, daughter of Lieut. Nathaniel and Susanna Appleton, Nov. 24, 1778, who died May 7, 1838 aged 77. He died Feb. 5, 1810. Their children were:

125 EPHRAIM,[6] baptized Nov. 28, 1779. See No. 125.
126 SUSANNA,[6] baptized Aug. 17, 1783; married Capt. Joseph Dennis, Sept. 14, 1809.
127 OLIVER,[6] born May 10, 1785. See No. 127.
128 EUNICE,[6] baptized Aug. 23, 1789; died unmarried Dec. 12, 1863.
129 AARON,[6] born April 10, 1795; died Sept. 27, 1812.
130 ELIZABETH,[6] born July 4, 1798; married John P. Lakeman, Sept. 23, 1830.
131 GEORGE,[6] born May 13, 1800; died Nov. 13, 1806, from a kick by a horse.
132 LUCY,[6] baptized July 24, 1791; married James Brown Jr.,[2] July 2, 1812.
133 SALLY WINN,[6] died March 24, 1804.
134 GEORGE,[6] born March 17, 1807. See No. 134.

78. BENJAMIN FELLOWS JR.,[5] baptized June 29, 1760, married Anna Webber of Gloucester (pub. April 24, 1784). John Lovett of Beverly sold to Benjamin Fellows of Beverly, joiner, land in the School House Lane, Sept. 8, 1786 (146:242.) Anna, the wife of Benjamin, was buried in Beverly, Dec. 21, 1794 aged 31 years. Their children, born in Beverly, were:

135 NANCY WEBBER,[6] born Aug. 29, 1785.
136 SALLY,[6] baptized Dec. 16, 1787; died Oct. 10, 1796 aged 8 years, 10 months.
137 BETSEY,[6] born Oct. 15, 1789.

(Anstice, who died in Beverly Oct. 29, 1866, aged 75 years 5 months 14 days, may have been of this family.)

79. NATHAN FELLOWS,[5] baptized Feb. 26, 1743, lived in the dwelling now divided and owned by the Fellows heirs and Daniel Appleton heirs. He married 1st, Betty Dodge. Their child was:

137a. NATHAN[6], born Jan. 3, 1768.

(Mr. Alonzo B. Fellows, grandson of Nathan,[6] remembers that his father, Joseph, son of Nathan by a second marriage, said that there were seven children by this marriage, none of whom lived to be seven years old. Miss Mary Willett Fellows, now in her ninety third year, is sure there were twelve children by this marriage, and thirteen by the second.)

[1] Page 49.
[2] See Brown Genealogy in same volume.

He married 2nd, Hannah Brown (pub. Aug. 20, 1785) who died June 1, 1835. He died Feb. 28, 1837 aged 93. Their children were:

138 BETSEY,[6] born March 24, 1786; married Benjamin B. Day of Gloucester, July 14, 1811.
139 HANNAH,[6] born April 13, 1787; married Joseph Chapman of Gloucester, Nov. 28, 1805.
140 ANNA,[6] born Dec. 26, 1788; married Robert Tuck of Beverly, Oct. 25, 1810; died Feb. 16, 1842.
141 SARAH,[6] born Oct. 16, 1790; married Olphert Tuttle of Beverly, June 13, 1820.
142 OLIVE,[6] born Aug. 28, 1792; married Moses Lane of Gloucester, Feb. 23, 1819. She died Feb. 12, 1823, aged 31, and her husband married her sister Mary.
143 SUSANNA,[6] born April 16, 1794; married Jonathan Dennison of Gloucester, April 3, 1821; died Oct. 27, 1861.
144 JOSEPH BROWN,[6] born Jan. 6, 1796. See No. 144.
145 MARY,[6] born Dec. 7, 1797; married Moses Lane, Jan. 30, 1828; died April 19, 1880, at Annisquam.
146 ANSTICE,[6] born May 15, 1800; with her sister Eunice she published "The Orphan's Advocate" in Boston for many years. She died unmarried, Oct. 29, 1873.
147 EUNICE,[6] born Feb. 27, 1802. She took the middle initial C.; edited "The Orphan's Advocate," with her sister, Anstice; died unmarried Sept. 27, 1883.
148 NATHAN,[6] born Oct. 18, 1803. He took a middle initial W.; died unmarried Dec. 10, 1887 at Annisquam, by a fall from a bridge.
149 SIMON,[6] born Oct. 28, 1805. See No. 149.
150 DANIEL,[6] born March 8, 1808; died at Baton Rouge, Sept. 16, 1839.

Mr. Nathan Fellows was a private in Capt. Thomas Burnham's Co. which marched on the alarm of April 19, 1775 and served three days. He enlisted Sept. 30, 1777 in Capt. David Low's Co. of volunteers, 3d Essex Co. Reg. and was discharged Nov. 7, 1777 at Cambridge. He also served forty days in the regiment which guarded General Burgoyne's captive army to Prospect Hill.

95. JONATHAN FELLOWS,[6] born Jan. 8, 1770 in Gloucester, removed with the family to Boston; married 1st, Eunice Franklin Oliver, Dec. 22, 1792, who was born Aug. 30, 1759 and died Nov. 30, 1799.

He married 2nd, Elizabeth Pugh Burney, April 20, 1801, who was born Sept. 8, 1766 in Pitt Co., N. C.; died March 4, 1850. He died Oct. 13, 1847, at Mount Pleasant, Henderson, Kentucky. Their chlidren were:

151 Infant daughter,[7] died Oct., 17, 1804.
152 WILLIAM,[7] See No. 152.
153. CORNELIUS,[7] died Dec. 18, 1871 at New Orleans.
154 ELIZA Burney,[7] born Sept. 14, 1808; died July 20, 1815.

82   GENEALOGICAL RECORD OF THE DESCENDANTS

96.   CALEB FELLOWS,[6] born July 9, 1771, married Mrs. Sarah Carver of Philadelphia and settled in Roxbury in 1816. His career was extraordinary and romantic. Sailing from Boston as mate of the ship, Fair American, for some unknown reason, he was set adrift in an open boat in mid-ocean. He was picked up by a ship bound to the East Indies, where he commanded various vessels engaged in river commerce and gained a fortune. Under the name of Captain Williams, he married a native woman, but no children were born to them.

He died on Nov. 8, 1852 and bequeathed $40,000 to erect a building similar to the Philadelphia Athenaeum, within half a mile of Rev. Mr. Putnam's meeting house in Roxbury. The residue was to be safely invested and the income to be devoted to the purchase of books and periodicals. The fund had increased to $54,000 in 1872, when the building, known as Fellows Athenaeum, was begun. It was formally dedicated early in July and opened for public use in July 16, 1873. It is now a branch of the Boston Public Library.[1]

101.   NATHANIEL FELLOWS JR.,[6] married 1st, Julia Hixon in Boston, May 8, 1803; married 2nd, A. L. A. H. Graton de Chambellan. Their children were:

155   ELSY,[7] married Joseph Saul.
156   CLARA RAFAELA.[7]
157   NATHANIEL.[7]
158   PAULINE.[7]
159   MATHILDA,[7] married M. Gaillardet and lived in Paris.
160   LOUIS.[7]

He married 3rd, Lucy Lambert, daughter of William Lambert, who died in Roxbury in 1829 aged 35 years. Their children were:

161   LOUISE.[7]
162   CHARLOTTE.[7]
163   SUSAN,[7] married Geo. F. Williams of Boston. She resides at No. 314 Beacon St.

Mr. Fellows had a large sugar plantation in Cuba and some, if not all, of his children, were born there. Some of them lived in Cuba and some in France. Mrs. Williams is the only surviving child.

107.   ISAAC FELLOWS,[6] born June 24, 1797, married 1st, Annie T. Perley, Dec. 9, 1823, who died Oct. 26, 1848 aged 45 years. Their children were:

164   MARY JANE,[7] born Sept. 22, 1825; died Aug. 14, 1827.
165   MARY JANE,[7] March 6, 1828.
166   ELIZA ANN,[7] born April 16, 1830; died Aug. 13, 1847.
167   CAROLINE PERLEY,[7] born Sept. 3, 1832.
168   ISAAC,[7] born July 8, 1835.

[1] See Pro. Rec. Dedham, and Drake's History of Roxbury, 1878. Page 359.

169 WILLIAM HENRY.[7]
170 LUCY EVELINE,[7] born May 20, 1841.
171 ELLEN MARIA,[7] born March 4, 1844.
172 INFANT SON,[7] born May 31, 1848; died June 1, 1848.

He married 2nd, Urvilla Loomer, Feb. 26, 1852.

108. IRA FELLOWS,[6] born Nov. 12, 1799, married Abigail Wright, Sept. 18, 1827. Their children[1] were:

173 HARRIET ELIZA,[7] born Jan. 15, 1829.
174 JULIA PIERCE,[7] born April 8, 1831.
175 SUSAN CELINDA,[7] born July 27, 1832.
176 LUCINDA MYNETT,[7] born March 15, 1835; died July 31, 1841.
177 ASA WRIGHT,[7] born June 6, 1836.
178 MARINDA MALVINA,[7] born Oct. 28, 1837.
179 IRA PAYSON,[7] born Jan. 6, 1840.

117. ISAAC FELLOWS JR.,[6] baptized April 26, 1772, married 1st, Joanna Butman of Beverly, Dec. 17, 1795. Richard Craft of Beverly sold to Isaac Fellows of Beverly, mariner, his right and title in the estate of the late William Butman, a house and 2½ acres near the Training Field, Dec 13, 1803 (174: 1). Their children were:

180 WILLIAM,[7] born June 6, 1797 in Beverly.
181 JOANNA,[7] born Jan. 17, 1799 in Beverly .

Joanna died when the baby Joanna was born, Jan. 17, 1799 aged 28 years 3 months. He married 2nd, Betsey Butman, Jan. 16, 1801, who outlived him and married Jonathan Smith Esq. of Beverly, Nov. 12, 1834. Their children were:

182 SUSANNA,[7] born Oct. 23, 1802; died Aug. 7, 1843.
183 CHILD,[7] born   ; buried July 14, 1804.

118. WILLIAM,[6] baptized Feb. 14, 1780, inherited the house known as the Sally Roberts house from his father.[2] He sold it to Captain Gardner in 1832 and died July 11, 1861. He married Sally P. Haskell of Gloucester, Nov. 13, 1823 who died June 30, 1837. Their children were:

184 ISAAC,[7] baptized July 28, 1833; died March 5, 1835 aged 10 years.
185 JAMES HASKELL,[7] baptized July 28, 1833; died in Rockport.
186 WINTHROP,[7] baptized July 28, 1833; died unmarried.
187 DAVID BRAINERD,[7] baptized Sept. 6, 1835.

124. NATHAN FELLOWS,[6] baptized Aug. 24, 1783, called Jr., a cordwainer, married Dorothy Foster of Rowley, pub. Sept. 27, 1807 and bought in the same year the western half of the John Fellows house now occupied

---

[1] Miss Harriet D. Fellows furnished the data of Ira Fellows, and his brother, Isaac. Neither resided in Ipswich.
[2] Page 46.

by Mr. Harry Wall. He sold his estate to Ebenezer Cogswell in 1827, removed to the house now owned by Isaac F. Dobson, and finally to the gambrel roofed cottage owned subsequently by Mr. Alfrey and since torn down for the extension of the South Cemetery. Dorothy died Sept 20, 1839 aged 55, he died Aug. 23, 1848. Their children were:

188 JESSE,[7] born Aug. 19, 1809; died in Boston unmarried, Nov. 11, 1856.
189 ELIZABETH ANN,[7] born April 20, 1811; married George Chapman of Beverly, mariner, Jan. 20, 1846; lived in Beverly; died at age of 80. They had no children.
190 DOLLY PINGREE,[7] born May 25, 1813; married Joseph Moody, of Newburyport, Sept. 11, 1838; died Dec. 16, 1842.
191 MARY WILLETT,[7] born March 18, 1815; still living in Newburyport.
192 DANIEL FOSTER,[7] born Oct. 11, 1816; married and lived in Worcester where he died.
193 MEHITABLE PINGREE,[7] born Feb. 3, 1819; married 1st, Joseph Moody of Newburyport, Dec. 7, 1843; married 2nd, Ebenezer Rolfe of Newburyport, April 6, 1853, who died Nov., 1902.
194 MELICENT FOSTER,[7] born Oct. 19, 1820; married in Boston, Benjamin Trefethan; died in 1851.
195 MARTHA SHATSWELL,[7] born May 1, 1822; married Isaac G. Johnson of Newburyport July 18, 1842; died in East Cambridge, aged 28 years.
196 NATHAN,[7] born May 24, 1832.

He married 2nd, Mrs. Bestey Dodge, March 2, 1840. He died Aug. 23, 1848, his widow Betsey, April 18, 1859 aged 70.

125. EPHRAIM FELLOWS,[6] baptized Nov. 28, 1779; married Charlotte Lakeman, daughter of James F. and Mary Lakeman (pub. Nov. 8, 1806). He bought the Treadwell house on the way to "Old England" in 1814[1] and spent the rest of his life there. He died Feb. 4, 1842, his widow, Feb., 1857 aged 70. Their children were:

197 TWIN,[7] died May 12, 1808.
198 TWIN,[7] died June, 1808.
199 CHARLOTTE[7], born Nov. 19, 1809.
200 EPHRAIM,[7] born July 17, 1811. See No. 200.
201 ISRAEL,[7] born Aug. 28, 1814. See No. 201.
202 LAVINIA,[7] born Sept. 18, 1816; married George W. Dike of Stoneham, Feb. 10, 1848.
203 ALFRED,[7] born May 9, 1818. See No. 203.
204 THOMAS BROWN,[7] born Feb. 26, 1820; died Oct. 28, 1839.

127. OLIVER FELLOWS,[6] born May 10, 1785, called Captain; married Sally Foster of Newburyport, daughter of Samuel and Mary (Wells) Foster (pub. Nov. 6, 1813). Oliver Fellows, caulker, died in Salem Dec. 5, 1859

---

[1] Ipswich in Mass. Bay Colony, p. 487.

aged 73 years 6 months. His widow died in Chelsea, Jan. 21, 1877 aged 91 years 4 months 25 days. Their children were:

   205 JOHN FOSTER,[7] born Jan. 8, 1815. John F. Fellows of Boston married Mary L. Sprague of Salem, Dec. 24, 1843.
   206 CAROLINE A.,[7] married Noah Brooks of Salem, May 29, 1856.

134. GEORGE FELLOWS,[6] born in Ipswich, March 17, 1807; spent his early life in Salem as a ship carpenter but removed to Ipswich and bought the Manning farm on County Road[1] where he died Jan. 27, 1883 aged 75 years 10 months 10 days. He married 1st, Margaret Adams of Maine, May 5, 1833. Their child, born in Salem was:

   207 ELLEN,[7] born 1835; died Nov. 9, 1908, aged 73 years.

He married 2nd, Sarah E. Stanwood of Ipswich Dec. 28, 1847, who survived him and died Sept. 5, 1893 aged 76 years 8 months. Their children, born in Salem, were:

   208 SARAH,[7] born Dec. 6, 1849; married Charles R. Lord of Ipswich, March 23, 1873.
   209 EUNICE,[7] born Feb. 27, 1852; died Oct. 7, 1897; unmarried.
   210 JOSEPH DENNIS,[7] born Nov. 13, 1854; died before July 29, 1856.[2]
   211 JOSEPH DENNIS,[7] born July 29, 1856; drowned Aug. 26, 1874.
   212 LAURA,[7] born July 29, 1856; living in Ipswich unmarried.

144. JOSEPH BROWN FELLOWS,[6] born Jan. 26, 1796; married Elizabeth A. Dennison of Gloucester, May 22, 1821 and bought the east half of the John Fellows house in 1823.[3] Their children were:

   213 ELIZABETH DENNISON,[7] born March 31, 1822; died Sept. 21, 1843.
   214 SARAH JANE,[7] born May 5, 1824; died April 16, 1906, unmarried.
   215 FRANCES DANE,[7] born March 14, 1827; married 1st, William C. Cassell of Charlestown, June 15, 1861; married 2nd, Henry Haskell Wall, Sept. 4, 1889.
   216 ALONZO BROWN,[7] born Nov. 25, 1829. See No. 216.
   217 MARY A.,[7] born Oct. 29, 1831; married Elijah Emerson, Sept. 12, 1854.
   218 JOSEPH EDWARD,[7] born March 12, 1835; died June 10, 1838.
   219 JULIA MARIA,[7] born March 8, 1840; died May 24, 1842.

149. SIMON FELLOWS,[6] born Oct. 28, 1805; married Rebecca S. Graves Dec. 29, 1833, who died Jan. 28, 1899 aged 82. Mr. Fellows died July 24, 1880. Their children were:

   220 MARY ELIZABETH,[7] born Jan. 27, 1835; married Philip E. Clarke, Nov. 29, 1860.

[1] The Old Bay Road. No. XV. Pub. of Ips. Historical Society, page 11.
[2] The Salem Records give Sept. 29, 1856 as date of death, but it is a family remembrance that he died before the second Joseph Dennis was born.
[3] Page 47.

221 MORINDA JOSEPHINE,[7] born Dec. 13, 1838; married Tyler Parrott Jr. of Lynn, June 29, 1859.
222 SARAH GRAVES,[7] born Nov. 25, 1839; married Daniel L. Hodgkins, Jan. 4, 1870; died Feb. 1903.
223 MOSES A.,[7] born July 29, 1843; lives with his sister, Abby M. on East St., Ipswich, unmarried.
224 ABBY MARIA,[7] born Nov. 25, 1846; makes her home with her brother Moses A., unmarried.
225 DANIEL H.,[7] born Feb. 13, 1851. See No. 225.

152. WILLIAM FELLOWS,[7] married Caroline Davis at Roxbury, June 9, 1829, who died May 27, 1852 at Louisville, Kentucky, of cholera. He died May 12, 1875 at his residence, No. 570 Fifth Ave., New York City. Their children were:

226 ELIZA BURNEY,[8] born April 22, 1830; married 1st, Thomas Rockhill Ingraham at New Orleans, Jan. 22, 1856, who died Oct. 24, 1860, at his plantation in Louisiana; married 2nd, I. M, Wardwell, Nov. 17, 1863; died Aug. 12, 1883 at Brooklyn, N. Y.
227 CAROLINE,[8] born Sept. 12, 1832 in Louisville; married D. P. Morgan, Sept. 30, 1858; died Jan. 24, 1886 at Sunny Lawn.
228 CLARA RAFAELA,[8] born June 20, 1834; married Oliver William Bird, Sept. 27, 1860 at Sunny Lawn, Clifton, who died Nov. 24, 1868 at No. 8 Fifth Ave., New York City. Mrs. Bird died Feb. 13, 1888 at Hempstead, L. I.
229 WILLIAM,[8] born June 8, 1836. See No. 229.
230 HARRIET DAVIS,[8] born Aug. 15, 1838 at Louisville, Kentucky, now living at Cornwall-on-the-Hudson.
231 CORNELIUS,[8] born March 8, 1840. See No. 231.
232 NANCY WILLIAMS,[8] died Nov. 21, 1860 at Sunny Lawn.
233 ALICE JOHNSON,[8] died Aug. 23, 1843, at Henderson.
234 ALICE,[8] born Aug. 18, 1844; married William Baylies Crocker June 6, 1866 at Sunny Lawn; died Aug. 15, 1892 at Carlsbad.
235 BURNEY.[8] See No. 235.

200. EPHRAIM FELLOWS,[7] born July 17, 1811, a carpenter by trade, inherited from his father the house on the way to Old England, where he died Oct. 31, 1894. He married Anstice Giddings, daughter of Major Joshua and Abigail Giddings, on July 2, 1846. She died Feb. 6, 1893 aged 83 years 11 months. Their marriage was childless.

201. ISRAEL FELLOWS,[7] born Aug. 28, 1814 in Ipswich, removed to Salem, where he married Catherine H. Goldsmith, June 14, 1838. He was a cabinet maker by trade and a dealer in furniture. He died March 7, 1881. Their children were:

236   CATHERINE E.,[8] married Benjamin T. Tilton, June 4, 1867.
237   THOMAS B.,[8] born Dec., 1846; died March 8, 1880 aged 33 years 3 months 5 days, unmarried.
238   SARAH E.,[8] born Jan. 18, 1850; married Charles W. Perkins, Oct. 6, 1875.
239   ANNIE,[8] born Nov. 17, 1855.
240   CARRIE E,[8] born   1856; died June 18, 1861 aged 5 years 6 months.

203.   ALFRED FELLOWS,[7] born May 9, 1818 in Ipswich, married Nancy Putnam of Danvers, Oct. 2, 1845, who died Sept. 14, 1900 aged 83 years lacking 8 days.   He died on Sept. 8, 1902.   Their children, all born in Danvers, were:

241   EMILY PUTNAM,[8] born July 28, 1846; married Edwin Reed, June 23, 1871, who died Oct. 14, 1908.
242   LOUISA JANE,[8] born Aug. 25, 1848; died Nov. 1, 1848.
243   EVELYN AUGUSTA,[8] born April 13, 1851;married Charles H. Masury March 1, 1877.
244   ANNE LAVINIA,[8] born Nov. 10, 1859; died Nov. 12, 1859.

216.   ALONZO BROWN FELLOWS,[7] born Nov. 25, 1829, bought the Nathan Fellows farm in 1857.   He married Henrietta Wheeler of Boston Nov. 15, 1876.   They lived on the ancestral farm until 1899 when he sold to James H. Proctor and bought the John Burnham Brown farm on the Essex Road,[1] in the same neighborhood, which is still his home.   Their children are:

245   ELVA A.,[8] born Oct. 1, 1877; married Clarence I. Sherwood of Portsmouth, N. H., Oct. 14, 1905.
246   JOSEPH E.,[8] born Jan. 19, 1882; married Jeannie M. Brown of Salem, Aug. 20, 1908.
247   IRENE F.,[8] born Feb. 20, 1884.
248   NATHAN WARREN,[8] born Jan. 15, 1887.
249   ELIZABETH D.,[8] born Sept. 11, 1888.
250   REGINALD A.,[8] born March 7, 1891.

225.   DANIEL H. FELLOWS,[7] born Feb. 13, 1851; married J. Augusta Archer, Jan. 21, 1866 and removed to Lynn, where the family has since resided.   He was a soldier in the War of the Rebellion in the 1st Mass. Heavy Artillery and was wounded at Petersburg, June 22, 1864.   He recovered and was commissioned Lieutenant. He died on Aug. 19, 1890. Their children are:

251   FREDERICK W.,[8] born April 19, 1868; married H. Maud Blois, May 14, 1902.
252   BERTHA AUGUSTA,[8] born Feb. 2, 1872.
253   SARAH SUTTON,[8] born March 31, 1874; married Frank H. Spencer of Lynn, May 9, 1900.
254   ADELIA ALTHEA,[8] born Nov. 6, 1876.
255   SUSAN ARCHER,[8] born Sept. 10, 1879.

[1] Page 11.

88   GENEALOGICAL RECORD OF THE DESCENDANTS, ETC.

229. WILLIAM FELLOWS,[8] born June 8, 1836 at Louisville, married Nannie Carter Eustace of Virginia, Aug. 12, 1874. Their child is:

256   HARRIET D.,[9] born Nov. 11, 1877 at Leamington, England.

231. CORNELIUS FELLOWS,[8] born March 8, 1840 at Louisville, Ky., married Caroline Suydan Whitney of New York, June 2, 1874. Their children are:

257   CORNELIUS,[9] born Jan. 1, 1879.
258   CAROLINE WHITNEY,[9] born April 24, 1882.

He was graduated from Columbia College and became a prominent figure in the social and club life of New York. He was one of the original members of the Coney Island Jockey Club organized in 1879, of which he was Secretary, and President of the National Horse Show. He was one of the oldest members of the Union Club. He died April 30, 1909.

235. BIRNEY FELLOWS,[8] married Henrietta Lonsdale of New Orleans, June 6, 1883.[1] Their children are:

259   LONSDALE,[9] born Oct., 1884 at New Orleans; died Sept., 1885 at New Orleans.
260   ALICE,[9] born Jan. 7, 1886 at New Orleans.
261   BIRNEY,[9] born Jan. 1, 1890 at Cannes, France.

[1] The more common spelling of his name has been Burney.

A GENEALOGY
OF THE DESCENDANTS OF
JOHN BROWN
— OF —
IPWSICH, MASS,

EDITORIAL NOTE.

This is not a complete genealogy. The tracing of all lines of descent in every generation would require an amount of research, and an expenditure of time and money, which makes it a task practically impossible for me and wholly beyond the scope of my original plan. My primary purpose has been to trace the Ipswich descendants and this plan has been adhered to in the main down to the year 1800. In constructing this portion of the work, I have made an independent personal study of all the Ipswich vital records. But Mr. Sidney Perley has already covered this ground in his monograph published in The Essex Antiquarian, vol. xii, No. 4. While I am not in complete agreement with his work, I have been glad to make frequent reference to it for families, which have migrated from Ipswich. His reputation for pains taking and accurate work is well known, and I have been glad to avail myself of his investigations, particularly in the Hamilton families of this line.

From the year 1800 or thereabout I have endeavored to make a fairly complete study of the male line of descent, following each family as far as possible. I have made special effort to connect the Ipswich families with their locations, and this is indicated in the footnotes, and in the Index. This will give vividness to the narrative and will be appreciated especially, I hope, by those who are familiar with Candlewood.—T. F. W.

GENEALOGICAL RECORD OF THE DESCENDANTS
OF
JOHN BROWN OF IPSWICH, MASS.

1. JOHN BROWN SENIOR, the earliest settler in the Candlewood region bearing the family name, is first mentioned in the Town Records in 1640. The Deposition of Thomas Burnum and Martha Thorne[1] affirmed that they knew that "Old Mr. John Brown live in a House in Ipswich Town near the house of the Rev. Mr. William Hubbard's" above seventy years ago, *i. e.*, about 1650. This has been identified already with a location on Heartbreak Road.[2] They affirmed further that before 1660, Mr. Brown, "built a house att the Farme and lived in said house he built att the farme till after the year of our Lord, One Thousand Six Hundred and Sixty four." This is identified as the farm now owned by John Henry Brown, on Fellows's Lane.

In the year 1670, John Brown sold John Andrews a mare. A law suit resulted in the following year and various depositions were made by the interested parties. John Brown Sen., affirmed that he sold the mare to John Andrews in August, 1670.

"I, Mary Brown, was present and heard my husband, John Brown Sen. sell the mare." Martha Brown, daughter of John Brown Sen. made deposition regarding her father's sale. John Brown also gave witness.

Court Papers, Vol. XVI. p. 142.

John Brown Sen. died on Sept. 13, 1677. The inventory of his estate is of especial interest, as it reveals the furnishing of each room in the ancient farm house and the complete equipment of the farm. The dwelling seems to have contained only two rooms and the chamber above.

"Inventory of all the goods and lands belonging to John Brown Sen. deceased this 13 of Sept. 1677 (Ips. Deeds 4: 183)

Imp^{rm} in money £2–6s.–9 }	
the Apparell of ye deceased £7–6s. }	09–12– 9
woollen & Linnen cloth	04–12– 0
	14–04– 9

IN THE HALL.

Imp^r. A feather bed with the appurtenances	07–00– 0
ye pewter 26s. ye Tinne ware 10s.	01–16– 0
It brass kettle skillet morter & warming pan	01–19– 0

[1] Page 37.
[2] Page 5. He was living there in 1648.

	three iron potts 25s. three p^r of pot hooks 5s.	01–10– 0
	Trammell friepan tongs slice tosting iron flesh fork etc.	01–06– 0
		13–11– 0
It	four chaires 8s. a table & two chests 16s.	01–04– 0
	pailes and other coopers ware	14– 0
		01–18– 0

THE PARLOR.

Imp^r	a bed with furniture	03–00– 0
	flax and yarne linnen and woollen	04–14– 0
	wheels & cardes	01–00– 0
		08–14– 0

IN THE CHAMBER.

Imp^r	Bed with the appurtenances	02–15– 0
	Hogsheads and other lumber	07– 0
	Kneading trough and hatchell 8s. woole 40s.	02–08– 0
	sheets 2lb. 10s. table cloths 20s.	03–10– 0
	napkins and pillow beers 27s. bridle and saddle 10s.	01–17– 0
		10–17– 0
Imp^r	thirteene acres of land belonging to the dwelling house	65–00– 0
	ye dwelling house barne & comonage	65–00– 0
	ye thirty acres of marsh with some islands of upland	120–00– 0
		250–00– 0
	Lands toward Wenham engaged to his younger son Nathaniel valued at 150 lb.	150–00– 0
It	two small peeces of marsh one at Plumb island the other at the Hundreds	20–00– 0
It	a dwelling house	30–00– 0
		200–00– 0
It	six loads of hay in the barne & eleven loads at the marsh all which	08–00– 0
	four acres of Barley in the barne	12–00– 0
	one acre of Rye in the barne	02–08– 0
	four acres of Indian corne	07–00– 0
	Indian Rye & malt in the house	03–16– 0
		25–04–

OF JOHN BROWN 91

Imp^r two oxen 10 lb 3 cows 10 lb 10s.		20-10- 0
It three 3 yeare old cattle		07-10- 0
It four 2 year old		08-00- 0
It three yeare old 3lb two calves 24s.		04-04- 0
Twenty three sheepe		08-10- 0
fifteene lambs		03-15- 0
eight swine 8lb thirteene shotes 3lb 5s.		11-05- 0
five horse kinde		04-00- 0
		67-14- 0
It plowes carts wheels slead yoke & chaines		03-05- 0
It Axes sithes sawes and other utensills of husbandry with some Armor		03-12- 0
		06-17- 0
	Sum Tot	606-19- 9

Aprized this 20th of Sept. 1677
 By Richard Hubbard
  John Whipple

DEBTS DUE FROM THE ESTATE.

To his daughter Martha as part of her portion	20-00- 0
funerall charges	05-00- 0
To Deacon Goodhue	05-00- 0
To Rates	03-00- 0
To worke done this summer	03-00- 0
To the maltsters	03-04- 0
	39-04- 0

John Browne in Court held at Ipswich the 25 of September 1677 upon oath delivered this to be a true Inventory of his father's estate to the best of his knowledge.

    as attest Robert Lord, Clerk.
 Court Records, Nov. 6, 1677.

"John Browne of Ipswich dyeing intestate power of administration Granted unto John Browne his eldest son by the Court, John Browne eldest son of John Brown deceased pduced an Inventory of the estate of his deceased father amounting to about 605^{lb} to wch he made oath, granted administration and disposed of the estate as followeth, first y^t besydes the 50lb apiece pay'd or designed to be given by the father to his two daughters, Jacob and Thorne, he shall within one year pay to each of them ten pound to his brother Nathaniell who hath already received upon his marriage 200lb we see not cause to allow more. The rest of the estate, of houses lands, cattells, goods etc we order to the said John Browne pvided the houses and lands stand bound to pay to his mother sixteene pounds to her content and a roome in the house with necessary furniture dureing her life and also pay such Legacies as she shall bequeath at her death to her children not exceeding the value of 21lbs."

On April 2, 1679, John Brown petitioned to be relieved from these terms of settlement. His brother Nathaniel, aged about 25 years testified, "not long before my father John Brown's death he spoke of the woman which is now my brother John's wife. My father said he was not willing he should marry with her. He said he would give to his son John all his living as he had already given to Sarah Martha and myself."

Court Papers, Vol. XXXI, pp. 17,18,19.

"Upon the considderation of the petition of the sd. John Browne and the testimony of Andrew Burdley, Nathaniel Browne and Mary Lambert the Court sees cause to take him off from paying the sd. sisters 10lb apiece and the 21lb to his mother for her disposal at her death."

Court Record, April 1, 1679.

These documents show that the wife's name was Mary and that the children were:

2 JOHN,[2] born about 1639. See No. 2.
3 MARTHA,[2] married Barnard Thorne between 1670 and 1679.
4 SARAH,[2] married Thomas Jacobs, Dec. 21, 1671 (Parish Record).
5 NATHANIEL,[2] born about 1652. See No. 5.

2. JOHN BROWN,[2] was born about 1639. Another John Brown called "the glazier" and "the drummer," of about the same age, a resident in Ipswich, has been confused with the John Brown, son of John, whom we are now considering. It is necessary to establish the identity of each of them at the outset.

The Town Records contain the birth entries:
Elizabeth, daughter of John, born April 15, 1664.
John, son of John, born Sept. 29, 1666.
Jonathan, son of John, born Nov. 4, 1668.
Sarah, daughter of John born Dec. 2, 1670.
Hannah, daughter of John, the glazier, born Nov. 13, 1676.

John Brown, the glazier, had wife Mary, in 1668. On April 22, 1668, John Brown, glazier, his wife, Mary, releasing right of dower, sold two divisional lots in Plum Island to Francis Wainwright (23:70). On March 20, 1674–5, he sold his house on High St., in Ipswich, to Thomas Lull and Robert Paine, his wife, Mary, signing release (Ips. Deeds, 3: 335).

John, the glazier, was a notorious drunkard. The Town authorities ordered him not to frequent any of the ordinaries "as he neglects his vocations and spends much time and expense " (1672) and the Ipswich Court ordered, "No person whatsoever shall sell or give unto John Brown the glazier, any strong drink etc." This notice was to be posted at the meeting house and ordinaries, 1679. (Court Papers, Vol. XXXI: 19.) The Grand Jury presentment calls him John Brown, the drummer (XXXI: 18.) At the same Court, John Brown, son of John, was released from paying extra money to his sisters and mother. The term, glazier, is used to distinguish the tippler from the farmer.

A neighborhood scandal on High Street arose in 1682. John Brown, aged 44, and Mary his wife, testified; also Elizabeth Brown and Mary Brown aged 19. (Court Papers, Vol. XXXVII: 89.) The Grand Jury made presentment against Mary Brown and Elizabeth, the glazier's daughters, for arranging their hair too showily and wearing silk scarfs, April 14, 1682. (Court Papers, Vol. XXXVII: 116.)

In 1690, he was before the Court again for his evil habits and on March 29, 1692, John Brown, the glazier, was presented for being a common drunkard, and for throwing a fire brand at his wife, which struck her on the thigh. (Court Papers, Vol. LII: 112.)

These citations establish the fact that Elizabeth born 1664, the first of the children named[1] was the daughter of John, the glazier and Mary, that Hannah, born in 1676, was the daughter of the glazier, that Mary was his wife in 1682 and that all the children named above were of this family. The deposition of Nathaniel Brown already quoted,[2] made on April 2, 1679, affirmed that his father made objection not long before his death to his brother John's marriage with the woman, "which is now my brother John's wife." The Town Record contains the entry:

"John Brown... was married ... 1677." (his father died Sept. 13, 1677); also the birth entry, "John Brown, son of John at farme, July 1678."

On Sept. 17, 1684, John Browne, farmer, wife Hannah, sold 9 acres in Chebacco to Francis Wainwright, "free from all incumbrance whatsoever, done suffered and committed by the aforesaid John Brown's heirs or assigns or by John Browne his father deceased." (9: 228). The word 'farmer,' as we have already observed distinguished the thoroughly respectable resident of Candlewood from the notorious toper. Mary, the daughter of John and Hannah, was born July 3d, 1685. (Town Record). He bought the Bishop farm Jan. 1, 1684.[3] On April 18, 1707, John Brown Sen, farmer, conveyed to his son William, two acres of this farm, "Elizabeth my wife freely consenting to sd gift and freely surrenders and yields up her right of thirds or dower." (28: 19).

John Brown Sen. now house carpenter, conveyed to his son William, one third of the Bishop farm, on which he dwelt with no mention of wife, May 26, 1714 (27: 28) and to his sons, John and Nathaniel, various lots, including the common right which belonged to the Bishop dwelling, May 26, 1714 (27: 29). Nathaniel Brown died intestate, July 18, 1719; and on June 2, 1721, John Brown Jr., James Brown, William Brown, Sarah Cogswell, widow, and Samuel Choate and Mary his wife, surviving heirs of Nathaniel, agree in a written instrument that the estate of their brother shall revert to their father (313: 308). John Brown conveyed to his son, James, two thirds of the Bishop farm, except what he had given William out of

[1] Page 92.
[2] Page 92.
[3] Page 26.

one of their thirds, no wife mentioned, July 9, 1721 (39: 54). The Town Record states that Mr. John Brown died on April 9, 1727 aged 84, and Hannah, relict of farmer John Brown, died Nov. 19, 1727. A weatherworn headstone of red sandstone marks the place of their burial in the old High Street burying ground. Recent investigators have declared it illegible or have disagreed as to the inscription. I rubbed it with soft chalk, dusted it off carefully and the inscription was perfectly clear.

Here lyeth ye Body of John Brown who Died April ye 9 in ye 88 year of his Age 1727	Also Hannah Brown his wife died ye 17th of Novem. in ye 76 year of her Age 1727

This agrees perfectly with the reading of Mr. Hammatt who copied all the epitaphs many years ago. There is a slight discrepancy between the age of Mr. Brown and the date of his wife's death as given by the Record and the inscription. Preference is naturally given to the inscription, as many inaccuracies are found in the public records. The inference must be that he had three wives, Hannah, Elizabeth and Hannah. Their children were:

6   JOHN,[3] born July, 1678. See No. 6.
7   WILLIAM.[3] See No. 7.
8   JAMES.[3] See No. 8.
9   MARY,[3] born July 3, 1685; died Oct. 25, 1686.
10 SARAH,[3] married John Cogswell of Chebacco (pub. Sept. 25, 1708) his widow in 1721.
11 MARY, married Samuel Choate, son of the nearest neighbor (pub. March 31, 1716).
12 NATHANIEL,[3] died July 18, 1719 in his 29th year. (Gravestone).
13 ELIZABETH,[3] died May 7, 1716, in her 22nd year. (Gravestone)

5. NATHANIEL BROWN,[2] born about 1652, was a soap boiler by trade and had his "sope-house" near the dam on South Main st.[1] He lived near by at the time, but subsequently seems to have occupied a house on what is now Washington St. He was a tithing man and a farmer in 1681. In Jan., 1706, he sold to his son, Nathaniel, a weaver, a house, barn and 16 acres in his homestead in the Hamlet (19: 192). He married Judith Perkins, Dec. 16, 1673 and died in 1717. His will was proved, June 17, 1717. His wife survived him and made her home in Wenham for many years. Their children were:

[1] Ipswich in Mass. Bay Colony, p. 460.

14   JOHN,[2] born about 1674. He lived in Wenham and removed to Preston, Conn.[1] (44: 218).
15   NATHANIEL,[3] born about 1676. In 1706, a weaver by trade, he bought his father's homestead in the Hamlet. He also removed to Wenham before 1717 (44: 218).
16   ELIZABETH,[3] married William Hasey of Rumbly Marsh (Chelsea), April 5, 1702.
17   MARY,[3] married John Hubbard (pub. 22-2, 1710).
18   HANNAH,[3] married Edward Cogswell of Chebacco (pub. Aug. 21, 1708). Edward Cogswell sold to Nathaniel Brown "my father's house etc in Chebacco," May 3, 1709 (21: 73).
19   JACOB.[3] See No. 19.
20   JAMES,[3] born June 1, 1685. See No. 20.
20a BENJAMIN.[3]

Judith Brown, the widow of Nathaniel, conveyed to her sons, Nathaniel and Benjamin, the right to the houses where they then dwelt, given her by her husband's will, Oct. 10, 1716, and to her son James, all the lands given him by his father, March 9, 1741 (91: 168).

6. JOHN BROWN,[3] born July 1678, was called John Jr., in 1742 and Sergeant. Both yeoman and cordwainer, he lived on the farm in Fellows's Lane but enlarged it by the purchase of the John Ross farm adjoining[2] in 1737. He married Mary Fellows, his near neighbor, before 1712. He died on May 6, 1759 and his will (proved May 28, 1759), provided for his widow and children and for the children of his son John[3], deceased. He had conveyed to his son, called John 3d, a house and 2 acres, Jan., 1745, near the house now owned by William J. Cameron, at the fork of the Essex road and Lakeman's Lane.[4] To his daughter, Mary (Lufkin) he gave his negro child, Luie, and his negro woman, Phillis, after his wife's decease. Their children were:

20b JOHN.[4] See No. 20b.
21   MARY,[4] married Moses Lufkin of Ipswich, April 10, 1733.
22   JOSEPH,[4] removed to Topsfield and Boxford.[5]
23   NATHAN.[4] See No. 23.
24   DANIEL.[4]
25   SARAH.[4]

7. WILLIAM BROWN,[3] was a weaver and had built his house on a part of his father's farm on the Candlewood road before April, 1707.[6] His land holdings have already been noted.[7] He married Dorothy Giddings, April

---

[1] See The Essex Antiquarian, Vol. XII, No. 4, p. 156.
[2] Page 37.
[3] Page 38.
[4] Page 18.
[5] See The Essex Antiquarian, Vol. XII, No. 4, p. 160.
[6] Page 28.
[7] Pages 26, 28.

17, 1703. His will dated Aug. 3, 1752 was proved April 2, 1753, and his estate was appraised at £701-11s. 6d.¹ Their children were:

26 WILLIAM,⁴ See No. 26.
27 THOMAS.⁴ See The Essex Antiquarian, Vol. XII, No. 4, p. 161.
28 ELISHA.⁴ See No. 28.
29 DOROTHY,⁴ baptized 8–2 mo. 1711; married Caleb Burnam, Feb. 10, 1731; died July 28, 1784.
30 BENJAMIN,⁴ baptized April 12, 1713. See No. 30.
31 NEHEMIAH,⁴ baptized 5–12 mo. 1715. See No. 31.
32 STEPHEN,⁴ baptized 1–7 mo. 1718. See No. 32.
33 NATHANIEL,⁴ baptized July 17, 1726; not mentioned in his father's will, probably died young.

8. JAMES BROWN,³ received from his father two thirds of his farm on the Candlewood road with the dwelling.² He was a shop keeper and his home was probably on North Main St., where his business interests were located.³ He married Sarah Cogswell (pub. July 13, 1723.) His will, dated April 3, 1740 was proved June 1, 1741 and his large estate was appraised at £6530-11s.⁴ Their children were:

34 JAMES,⁴ baptized March 21, 1724–5; not living in 1760.
35 JONATHAN,⁴ baptized June 5, 1726; died July 19, 1726.
36 JONATHAN,⁴ baptized June 18, 1727. See No. 36.
37 FRANCIS,⁴ baptized Aug. 4, 1728; died Aug. 16, 1728.
38 FRANCIS,⁴ living in 1740.
39 LUCY,⁴ baptized Sept. 7, 1729; not living in 1760, probably died March 13, 1745.
40 EUNICE,⁴ baptized July 18, 1731; married Timothy Thornton of Boston (pub. Mar. 28, 1761) who married, second, widow Lydia Lord, July 14, 1785.
41 ELIZABETH,⁴ born Feb. 2, 1732; married Robert Perkins, July 19, 1753.
42 SARAH,⁴ baptized Nov. 24, 1734.

19. JACOB BROWN,³ called Lieut., Yeoman and cordwainer, lived in the Hamlet parish. He married Sarah Burnham of Chebacco (pub. Jan. 10, 1707–8) who died April 9, 1729 aged 50. He married second, widow Mary Dane of the Hamlet (pub. Nov. 30, 1735), and third, Elizabeth Brown of Ipswich (pub. Nov. 14, 1761). He died Feb. 26, 1769, and his estate was appraised at £1387-17s. 7d. His wife, Elizabeth, survived him and died at the age of eighty-eight, June 1, 1774.⁵ Their children were:

43 JACOB,⁴ lived in the Hamlet Parish until about 1758, when he removed to Preston, Conn. No son survived him.⁶

¹ Page 28.
² Page 26.
³ Ipswich in Mass. Bay Colony, page 352.
⁴ Inventory, page 27.
⁵ The Essex Antiquarian, Vol. XII, No. 4, p. 157.
⁶ The Essex Antiquarian, Vol. XII, No. 4, p. 158.

OF JOHN BROWN

44 SIMON,[4] See No. 44.
45 JOHN,[4] baptized Aug. 14, 1715.
46 JOHN,[4] baptized Jan. 20, 1716-7. See No. 46.
47 NATHANIEL,[4] baptized June 7, 1719. See No. 47.
48 ADAM,[4] baptized April 16, 1721.[1]
49 JAMES,[4] baptized March 1, 1723-4. See No. 49.
50 STEPHEN,[4] baptized Jan. 30, 1725-6.
51 JOSEPH,[4] baptized March 17, 1727-8; probably died Nov., 1728.

20. JAMES BROWN,[3] born June 1, 1685, called a trumpeter in 1713 and 1718, yeoman in 1714, inherited his father's dwelling. He married Mehitable Pengry, June 7, 1707, who died Aug. 29,1719, in her thirty-third year. James Brown Jr. died at the Hamlet, May 23, 1735. Their child was:
52 JAMES,[4] baptized April 3, 1715.

20b JOHN BROWN,[4] called John 3d in the conveyance by his father,[2] lived in the house at the fork of Essex Road and Lakeman's Lane. A clump of lilac bushes marks the site. By trade, he was a carpenter. He married Mary Fitts? Jan. 2, 1724-5. His will and inventory were filed June 9, 1746 and the estate was divided by a committee, May 26, 1759 (Pro. Rec. 336: 246). Their children were:
53 RUTH,[5] baptized June 30, 1728; probably, not living in 1759.
54 SAMUEL,[5] inherited ⅔ of estate, which he conveyed to Thomas Boardman.[2]
55 ABEL,[5] baptized Mar. 5, 1737.
56 MARY,[5] baptized April 13,1740; married Ammi Andrews of Chelmsford before 1759.
57 HEPHZIBAH,[5] baptized Aug. 30, 1741; married Nathaniel Brown, Feb. 1, 1768. See No. 88.
58 JOHN,[5] baptized July 21, 1745; died early.

Guardianship of Abel Brown, a minor of 14 years and of Mary and Hephzibah, under 14 years, all children of John Brown 3d was granted to Mary Brown, widow, Dec. 18, 1752 (Pro. Rec. 331: 94.) Guardianship of Hephzibah was granted Ammi Andrews, April 27, 1761 (Pro. Rec. 338: 123.) Abel received no share in the estate and probably was not living in 1759.

23. NATHAN BROWN,[4] bapt. 30-1, 1712, cordwainer and farmer, acquired the farm of his father on Fellows's Lane and lived there all his days.[3] He married Elizabeth Knowlton of the Hamlet (pub. Aug. 19, 1737) and

[1] The Essex Antiquarian, Vol. XII, No. 4, p. 159.
He married first Ester Parkman of Wenham (pub. July 7, 1743) and second Anna Whipple of the Hamlet parish (pub. May 9, 1761.) They removed to Moultonborough, N. H. in 1774, where Mrs. Brown died June 30, 1775, and her husband, July 20, 1775, aged 54 years.
[2] Page 18.
[3] Page 38.

died April 7, 1794. His widow died Nov. 27, 1798. He distributed his estate by will (proved June 2, 1794). Their children were:

59 JAMES,⁵ baptized March, 1739; died before 1794.
60 ELIZABETH,⁵ baptized May 4, 1740; died before 1794.
61 NATHAN,⁵ died Feb. 16, 1747.
62 JEREMIAH,⁵ baptized Nov. 9, 1746. See No. 62.
63 HANNAH,⁵ baptized Jan. 1, 1748; married Thomas Boardman before 1774; widow in 1794.
64 SUSANNA,⁵ baptized Nov. 25, 1750; unmarried in 1794.
65 NATHAN,⁵ baptized Nov. 19, 1752. See No. 65.
66 JOHN,⁵ baptized March 28, 1756. See No. 66.
67 ABRAHAM,⁵ baptized Dec. 9, 1759. See No. 67.

26. WILLIAM BROWN JR.⁴ received from his father a small piece of land on which his blacksmith shop stood, 1753.¹ He married Elizabeth Kinsman (No. 25, p. 56, pub. Jan. 1, 1726) and built his home near the dwelling of the late Manasseh Brown Jr., on the corner of Fellows Lane about 1732.² He was styled, Gentleman, in his latter years as his father had been before him. Mrs. Brown died Feb. 16, 1795 and her husband on Dec. 31, 1799. Their children were:

68 ELIZABETH,⁵ baptized Nov. 5, 1727; pub. to Samuel Langdon of Portsmouth, N. H., Oct. 25, 1746.
69 LUCY,⁵ baptized July 6, 1729; married Samuel Potter Jr., Jan. 14, 1748. Their home was on the Hobson lot so called on the Essex road.³
70 WILLIAM,⁵ baptized Aug. 8, 1731. See No. 70.
71 SUSANNA,⁵ baptized March 3, 1733; married Nehemiah Choate, Mar. 27, 1755.
72 PELATIAH,⁵ baptized May 2, 1736; removed to Wenham, where he became a prominent citizen.⁴
73 PRISCILLA,⁵ baptized April 1, 1739; married Oliver Carter Jr., of Leominster, Nov. 25, 1762.
74 MEHITABLE,⁵ baptized Aug. 31, 1740: married Job Giddings, Dec. 15, 1757.
75 EBENEZER,⁵ baptized Oct. 14, 1744. See No. 75.
76 ——,⁵ baptized Nov. 11, 1745.
77 JAMES,⁵ baptized Nov. 30, 1746. See No. 77.

28. ELISHA BROWN,⁴ a weaver by trade, married Lydia Brown at the Hamlet (pub. Mar. 10, 1736). In 1743, he bought land in equal shares with his brother, Benjamin Brown,⁵ and joined with him in building a house on the Essex road, near Mr. William G. Horton's residence. He sold his

¹ Page 28.
² Page 33.
³ Page 4.
⁴ The Essex Antiquarian, Vol. XII. No. 4. p. 163.
⁵ Page 12.

OF JOHN BROWN 99

interest to Francis Brown in 1781. He had inherited land from his father on the Candlewood road in 1753 and probably built the house, which was occupied by his heirs, the site of which is marked by a cellar, near the large barn of E. Newton Brown on the west side of the road.[1] He died Dec. 1, 1798; his widow died Nov.1,1801 at the age of eighty-seven. Their children were:

78   ELISHA,[5] baptized Feb. 19, 1737. See No. 78.
79   MOSES,[5] baptized Mar. 25, 1739.
80   AARON,[5] baptized Nov. 8, 1741
81   LYDIA,[5] baptized Dec. 12, 1742.
82   NEHEMIAH,[5] baptized July 7, 1745. See No. 82.
83   ELIZABETH,[5] baptized May 14, 1748.
84   JOSEPH,[5] baptized Sept. 29, 1751. See No. 84.
85   FRANCIS,[5] baptized Sept. 30, 1753. See No. 85.

30. BENJAMIN BROWN,[4] baptized April 12, 1713, a blacksmith by trade, was joint owner with his brother Elisha of the house on the Essex Road and also owned other land on Lakeman's lane on the Essex road.[2] He married Sarah Brown (pub. Feb. 25, 1736). She died Dec. 31, 1778 of fever aged "above sixty." He died in Feb., 1797. Their children were:

86   SARAH,[5] baptized Jan. 29, 1737; died Nov. 5, 1759 unmarried.
87   BENJAMIN,[5] baptized Jan. 6, 1739. See No. 87.
88   NATHANIEL,[5] baptized Nov. 6, 1743. See No. 88.
89   JOHN,[5] baptized May 25, 1746; died Dec. 31, 1778 of fever, on the same day with his mother.
90   HANNAH,[5] baptized July 31, 1748.
91   HANNAH,[5] baptized Nov. 5, 1749; married Joseph Proctor Feb. 4, 1773.
92   DAVID,[5] twin, baptized Sept. 17, 1752. See No. 92.
93   JONATHAN[5] twin, baptized Sept. 17, 1752; died Aug. 11, 1773.
94   ABNER,[5] baptized Jan. 11, 1756; married Sally Archibald, Jan. 29, 1809, who died Jan. 11, 1818 aged 55 years. He died Dec. 31, 1818, aged 63 years. Their daughter Sarah married John M. Cook of Salem and Sarah's son, William, was named as legatee in his will[3] 1819 (Pro. Rec. 394: 242).
95   EUNICE,[5] baptized Feb. 25, 1759; married Joseph Proctor of Londonderry, Dec. 25, 1808.

31. NEHEMIAH, BROWN,[4] baptized 5,12, 1715: married Mary Tanor (pub. June 2, 1743); administration on his estate was granted Feb. 29, 1748. His wife was published to Abijah How, March 10, 1749. Their children were:

96   MARY,[5] baptized Nov. 6, 1743, pub. to Jonathan Dodge Jr., April 26, 1766.
97   DOROTHY,[5] baptized Feb. 17, 1744.

[1] Page 32.
[2] Page 18.
[3] Page 12.

32. STEPHEN BROWN,[4] baptized 1:7 mo., 1718, inherited the homestead with his brother Elisha and bought his brother's interest in 1754.[1] It was located back from the Candlewood road, not far from the engine house. He married Ann Fellows (m. n. Start), daughter of William Start of Ipswich, the widow of Nathan Fellows of Fellows Lane, who was drowned March 15, 1743, while crossing Mile Brook with a loaded team, a year after his marriage, leaving an infant child.[2] Mr. Brown and the widow Fellows were published Aug. 10, 1746. He died Feb. 5, 1797, his widow on March 12, 1802. Their children were:

98 STEPHEN,[5] baptized June 14, 1747. See No. 98.
99 ANNE,[5] baptized June 21, 1752.

36. JONATHAN BROWN,[4] baptized June 18, 1727, married Elizabeth Lakeman, April 14, 1748 and was drowned in Ipswich bay, Oct. 10, 1751. His widow married Samuel Sawyer,[3] (pub. March 11, 1753). Their child was:

100 JAMES,[5] baptized April 15, 1750; died April 16, 1759.

44. SIMON BROWN[4] lived in the Hamlet Parish. He married first, Susanna Bennett of Ipswich, Dec. 23, 1734, who died Feb., 1769 and second Lydia Hooker of Ipswich (pub. Sept. 17, 1774); administration on his estate was granted May 15, 1804.[4] Their children were:[5]

101 STEPHEN,[5] baptized May 2, 1736. See No. 101.
102 NATHANIEL,[5] baptized Sept., 1737, inventory filed Jan. 4, 1811 (Pro. Rec. 380:246); the homestead assigned to widow Elizabeth (384: 551).
103 MARAH,[5] baptized Dec., 1739.
104 SUSANNA,[5] baptized Dec., 1739.
105 JACOB.[5]

46. JOHN BROWN,[4] baptized Jan. 20, 1716–7, married Sarah Emmerton of the Hamlet parish Dec. 8, 1736 and died Dec., 1777, his wife surviving. Their home was in the Hamlet, where he seems to have been a very prosperous inn keeper. His wardrobe, as the inventory reveals it, was particularly ample and gorgeous, including a blue serge coat 80/, a broad cloth coat 24/, fustian coat 27/, claret coat 20/, blue serge waist coat 30/, black ditto 15/, white holland ditto 15/, velvet breeches 18/, deerskin breeches 6/, striped waistcoat 12/, red waistcoat 3/, blue surtout 25/, 3 striped shirts 12/, one white shirt 30/, handkerchief 8/, wigg 6/, 2 caps 4/, trumpet 10/, silver buckles 12/, also a tavern table 24/, seed plough 60/, cart and wheels and hay rigging £25, plough 24/, 2 scythes and hangings 24/, tedder 30/. Their children were:[6]

[1] Pages 28, 29, 32.
[2] Page 77.
[3] Page 27.
[4] The Essex Antiquarian, Vol. XII, No. 4, p. 159.
[5] See The Essex Antiquarian, Vol. XII, No. 4. p. 162.
[6] See The Essex Antiquarian, Vol. XII, No. 4, p. 159.

106   SARAH,[5] baptized May 22, 1737: married . . . . Lufkin.
107   ELIZABETH,[5] baptized Dec. 21, 1738; married Nathaniel Brown of Ipswich (pub. Oct. 28, 1758). (perhaps No. 47.)
108   HANNAH,[5] baptized Jan. 25, 1741; unmarried in 1793.
109   JOHN,[5] cordwainer of Bow, N. H., quitclaimed to brothers David and Stephen, his interest in his father's estate, Sept. 2, 1778 (160: 6).
110   DAVID,[5] carpenter; married Ruth Story of the Chebacco Parish, April 19, 1772.
111   STEPHEN,[5] cordwainer; married Margaret Safford, July 17, 1780.
112   LUCY,[5] married Reuben Bowles of Ipswich, joiner, Aug. 12, 1773. They lived in New Salem, N. H., in 1789 and 1793.
113   LYDIA,[5] born about 1764.

47.   NATHANIEL BROWN,[4] baptized June 7, 1719, married Elizabeth ———. Their children were:

114   RHODA,[5] baptized Jan. 24, 1741.
115   NATHAN,[5] baptized Feb. 12, 1743.

49.   JAMES BROWN,[4] baptized March 1, 1723–4; a tailor by trade, married first, Lydia Dane (pub. June 27, 1746); second Sarah Lampson, July 25, 1751. His will, dated July 27, 1764, was proved Oct. 15, 1764, his wife surviving. They lived in the Hamlet Parish. Their children were:[1]

116   SARAH,[5] unmarried 1764.
117   LYDIA,[5] unmarried 1764.
118   JAMES,[5] born about 1753; living in 1784.
119   MARY,[5] married Moses Lufkin Jr., Aug. 22, 1780; died March 2 1784, aged 24.

62.   JEREMIAH BROWN,[5] baptized Nov. 9, 1746, married Lucy Potter Aug. 16, 1770, removed to Lyndeborough, N. H., about 1790. Their children were:[2]

120   ELIZABETH,[6] baptized April 28, 1771.
121   JEREMIAH,[6] baptized Sept. 20, 1772.
122   JOSIAH,[6] baptized June 12, 1774.
123   LUCY,[6] baptized April 14, 1776.
124   ISRAEL,[6] baptized Nov. 9, 1777.
125   ALLEN,[6] baptized May 21, 1780.
126   NATHAN,[6] baptized April 6, 1783.
127   HANNAH,[6] baptized July 9, 1786.
128   ———,[6] died May 21, 1788.

65.   NATHAN BROWN,[5] baptized Nov. 19, 1752, married Abigail Boardman (pub. July 11, 1776): died Jan. 10, 1823. His widow died Sept. 27,

[1] The Essex Antiquarian, Vol. XII, No. 4, p. 159.
[2] The Essex Antiquarian. Vol. XII, No. 4. p. 163.

1831, aged seventy-six. He owned and occupied the Ross farm, part of the homestead.¹ Their children were:

129 RHODA,⁶ baptized June 15, 1777; probably married Daniel Brown. See No. 165.
130 SUSANNA,⁶ baptized Dec. 20, 1778.
131 ABIGAIL,⁶ baptized Dec. 2, 1781; died Jan. 27, 1808.
132 ELIZABETH,⁶ baptized Oct. 24, 1784; married   Hosmer, before 1823.
133 NATHAN,⁶ baptized Nov. 12, 1786. See No. 133.
134 LANGLEY,⁶ baptized May 1, 1791. See No. 134.
135 SARAH N.,⁶ baptized Dec. 15, 1793; died unmarried Dec. 13, 1824, aged thirty-one.
136 FRANCIS,⁶ born June 27, 1798; sold his interest in father's estate in 1823; died in Roxbury, Feb. 1, 1848.

66. JOHN BROWN,⁵ baptized March 28, 1756, cordwainer and farmer, married Hannah Proctor, Dec. 1, 1789, who died a widow, Dec. 21, 1843, aged seventy-four. He inherited half the house occupied by his father² and lived in it until his death on Jan. 13, 1817 at the age of sixty-one. He left his widow with ten minor children; guardianship was granted her Dec. 2, 1817 (Pro. Rec. 3: 106). He was called John Brown Jr. and John Brown 3d. Their children were:

137 SAMUEL PROCTOR,⁶ baptized May 1, 1791; died young.
138 HANNAH,⁶ baptized Dec. 15, 1793; died unmarried, July 3, 1841, aged 48 years.
139 LOIS,⁶ baptized June 7, 1795; died unmarried July 8, 1830.
140 CLARISSA,⁶ baptized Oct. 16, 1796; died unmarried Nov. 1, 1830.
141 FRANCES,⁶ twin, baptized May 27, 1798; married Stephen Staples of Tamworth, N. H. (pub. Nov. 16, 1824).
142 LUCY,⁶ twin, baptized May 27, 1798; married Theodore Gibbs of Essex.
143 RELIEF,⁶ baptized Aug. 15, 1802; married Solomon Sanborn of Tamworth, Nov. 12, 1820.
144 ELIZABETH,⁶ born 1804; married Capt. Joseph Gardiner.
145 SAMUEL,⁶ born 1805. See No. 145.
146 ABIGAIL GILBERT,⁶ born 1807; died Feb., 1832 aged 24 years.
147 SARAH,⁶ born 1809; married Nathan Burnham Jr., of Essex, July 20, 1834.
148 MARY JANE,⁶ born 1812.
149 JOHN,⁶ born Jan. 3, 1815. See No. 149.

67. ABRAHAM BROWN⁵ baptized Dec. 9, 1759, married Sarah Boardman, Jan. 18, 1780.³ Their children were:

¹ Page 38.
² Page 39.
³ Page 34.

149a ——,⁶ died Jan. 31, 1781.
149b PRISCILLA,⁶ baptized Aug. 18, 1782.
149c JUDITH,⁶ baptized Nov. 3, 1782.
149d ABRAHAM,⁶ baptized April 24, 1785.
149e JOHN,⁶ baptized Jan. 27, 1788 (son of Abraham and Sarah, from Gloucester).
149f SARAH,⁶ baptized Jan. 3, 1798.

70. WILLIAM BROWN,⁵ called Jr. and 3d, baptized Aug. 8, 1731, married Eunice Wells, April 22, 1755; died April 22, 1759. Their child was:
149g EUNICE,⁶ baptized Feb. 5, 1758.

75. EBENEZER BROWN,⁵ baptized Oct. 14, 1744, married Elizabeth Perkins, March 24, 1768. Their home was in the Chebacco parish, now Essex. Their children were:
150 EBENEZER,⁶ baptized Feb. 19, 1769.
151 ISAAC,⁶ baptized Nov. 18, 1770.
152 WILLIAM,⁶ baptized Nov. 15, 1772.
153 ELIZABETH,⁶ baptized April 16, 1775, died April 30, 1775.
154 ELIZABETH PERKINS,⁶ baptized April 21, 1776.

77. JAMES BROWN,⁵ baptized Nov. 30, 1746, married Jemima Kinsman, Jan. 1, 1782; who died Aug. 13, 1822, aged eighty-four. He died Nov. 8, 1825, aged seventy-nine. He inherited his father's farm and lived there probably his whole life.¹ Their children were:
155 FANNY,⁶ born Feb. 24, 1782; married Benjamin Patch 3d, of Hamilton, Jan. 18, 1816; died March 20, 1871.
156 EUNICE,⁶ married Joseph Kinsman, May 18, 1809; died July 18, 1855 aged 81 years (Gravestone).
157 EPHRAIM,⁶ twin, baptized Oct. 30, 1785. See No. 157.
158 MANASSEH,⁶ twin, baptized Oct. 30, 1785; died Oct. 31, 1802 aged 18 years.
159 JOSIAH.⁶ See No. 159.

78. ELISHA BROWN JR.,⁵ baptized Feb. 19, 1737, married Elizabeth Roberts (pub. Dec. 15, 1759). His will, dated April 1, 1799, was proved July 1, 1799. His widow died Dec. 7, 1820, aged eighty-four. He lived in the homestead of his father.² Their children were:
160 ELISHA,⁶ baptized March 1, 1761. See No. 160.
161 EPHRAIM,⁶ born Feb. 8, 1763. See No. 161.
162 LYDIA,⁶ baptized Oct. 20, 1765; died unmarried Aug. 30, 1823.
163 ELIZABETH,⁶ baptized July 24, 1768; married John Raymond of Beverly, Aug. 25, 1791.
164 ASA,⁶ baptized Sept. 1, 1771; died unmarried Nov. 20, 1796.

¹ Page 33
² Page 32

165   DANIEL,⁶ baptized May 8, 1775. See No. 165.
166   LUCY,⁶ baptized Feb. 7, 1778; married 1st Timothy Tibbets, Dec. 11, 1796; married 2d, Joseph Heard of Boston (pub. Aug. 17, 1810).

82. NEHEMIAH BROWN,⁵ called Lieut., baptized July 7, 1745, married Mary Choate, Nov. 28, 1771. He died June 16, 1812, aged sixty-seven his widow April 3, 1825, aged seventy-one. He purchased the house built by Elisha Brown in 1789, and occupied it until his death. It was afterwards removed by Mr. Joseph Marshall to its present location.[1] Their children were:

167   MARY,⁶ born Aug. 29, 1772; married John Patch Jr., June 30, 1811; died 1838.
168   NEHEMIAH,⁶ born Aug. 8, 1774; died 1793.
169   AMMI,⁶ born June 27, 1776. See No. 169.
170   MICHAEL,⁶ born April 8, 1778. See No. 170.
171   DAVID,⁶ born July 25, 1780.
172   WILLIAM,⁶ born Jan. 12, 1783. See No. 172.
173   SALLY,⁶ baptized June 19, 1785; married Daniel Witham of Gloucester, Oct. 24, 1805; died 1826.
174   ELIZABETH,⁶ baptized Jan. 11, 1788; married Silas Chamberlain of Beverly, Dec. 1, 1813; died 1814.
175   JOHN,⁶ born June 29, 1791; married Sophia Raymond; died 1823; had child mentioned in Ammi's will.
176   NEHEMIAH,⁶ Feb. 18, 1794. See No. 176.
177   MARTHA,⁶ baptized Sept. 4, 1796; died 1797.

84. JOSEPH BROWN,⁵ baptized Sept. 29, 1751, married first, Elizabeth Perkins, daughter of Robert and Elizabeth (Brown) Perkins, Jan. 1, 1778, who died Feb. 26, 1803; married second, Martha Perkins, sister of Elizabeth, Nov. 27, 1806. The early home was in the old house of Joseph Marshall, but in 1797, he bought the interest of the surviving heirs in the old home farm of John Brown and his descendants on the Candlewood road.[2] The widow, Martha Perkins, died Nov. 21, 1850, at the age of seventy-six. The children by the first marriage were:

178   ELIZABETH,⁶ born April 14, 1780.
179   JOSEPH,⁶ born March 14, 1783. See No. 179.
180   LUCY,⁶ born Oct. 24, 1785; died May 9, 1806.
181   JAMES,⁶ born Feb. 22, 1789. See No. 181.
182   WINTHROP,⁶ born Aug. 26, 1791; died June 4, 1811.
183   ISAAC,⁶ born July 9, 1794. See No. 183.

The children by the second marriage were:

184   ELIZABETH,⁶ born July 1, 1811; married Thomas Brown Jr., May 26, 1839. See No. 241.

[1] Page 13
[2] Page 27, 28

185   MARY PERKINS,⁶ born June 23, 1814; married William Foster Wade, Dec. 16, 1841.

85. FRANCIS BROWN,⁵ baptized Sept. 30, 1753, married Judith Burnham, Jan. 1, 1779 and died May 23, 1790, aged 37 years. His widow died Jan. 27, 1834, aged seventy-four. He bought the Bragg farm (now owned by Alonzo B. Fellows) of Thomas Burnham Jr., in 1781 and there they made their home.¹   Their children were:

186   JOHN BURNHAM,⁶ born Sept. 12, 1779. See No. 186.
187   FRANCIS,⁶ born Feb. 3, 1781; died in Guadaloupe Feb. 3, 1803.
188   JUDITH,⁶ born Oct. 25, 1782; married Richard Manning, Jan. 10, 1819; died June 21, 1856.
189   SAMUEL,⁶ born Jan. 12, 1785; died Oct. 25, 1802 at Alexandria.
190   MARY,⁶ born Jan. 10, 1787; died unmarried April 16, 1860; at Ipswich.
191   CHARLES,⁶ born Jan. 12, 1789. See No. 191.

87. BENJAMIN BROWN,⁵ called 4th, 3d and Jr., baptized Jan. 6, 1739, a blacksmith by trade as his father was, married Martha Roberts (pub. March 20, 1762), who died April 20, 1797. He died May 12, 1816, aged seventy-six. Their home was on the triangular lot on the Essex Road and Lakeman's lane. Their children were:

192   MARTHA⁶ (daughter Benj. Jr.), baptized Jan. 8, 1764; married Capt. Elisha Brown, Aug. 26, 1790. See No. 160.
193   BENJAMIN,⁶ baptized Oct. 5, 1766. See No. 193.
194   THOMAS⁶ (son of Benj. 3d), baptized Dec. 25, 1768; not living in 1817 when the heirs quitclaimed.¹
195   MARY,⁶ baptized April 28, 1771; not living in 1817.
196   PARKER,⁶ baptized April 25, 1773. See No. 196.
197   JONATHAN ⁶ (son Benj. Jr.), born March 19, 1776; not living in 1817.
198   SARAH⁶ (child of Benjamin, baptized May 28, 1780) living in 1817.

88. NATHANIEL BROWN,⁵ baptized Nov. 6, 1743, married Feb. 1, 1768, Hepzibah Brown, daughter of John Brown 3d (See No. 57). They made their home in her father's homestead, which he bequeathed to his children² (will proved June 1, 1830. Pro. Rec. 407: 415.) He died April 9, 1830. Their children were:

198a HEPZIBAH,⁶ baptized Feb. 25, 1770; died in early life.
199   NATHANIEL,⁶ baptized Nov. 6, 1772; married   ; had daughter
199a   Lucy⁷ or Lucia P. He was not living in 1830. (Pro. Rec. 407: 415. Essex Co. Deeds, 261: 21).

200   DAVID.⁶ See No. 200.
201   SUSANNA,⁶ married William Lakeman 3d, June 27, 1797.

¹ Page 11.
² Page 18.

201a ABEL,⁶ baptized April 13, 1777; probably died young.
202 JOSHUA,⁶ baptized Oct. 17, 1784; administration of Joshua Brown, mariner, late of Ipswich, granted to Nathaniel Brown, Aug. 5, 1811 (Pro. Rec. 381: 116).

92. DAVID BROWN,⁵ baptized Sept. 17, 1752, married Mary Potter, June 5, 1797, who died Dec. 22, 1845, aged 87 years.
He died May, 1822. He was the doner of the Brown fund.¹

98. STEPHEN BROWN,⁵ called 3d, baptized June 14, 1747, married Elizabeth Potter (pub. Dec. 15, 1770), daughter of Robert and Mary Potter of the Bay Road. He bought the interest of Moses Potter, and lived in the Potter homestead, the small house moved by Asa Wade from the roadside.² He died Sept. 4, 1828, aged eighty-three. Their children were:

203 BETSEY,⁶ baptized March 22, 1772; married Isaac Hacket of Salem, Nov. 26, 1801.
204 SALLY,⁶ baptized March 27, 1774.
205 ROBERT,⁶ baptized Jan. 7, 1776.
206 JOHN POTTER,⁶ baptized June 21, 1778; removed to New Hampshire.
207 STEPHEN,⁶ baptized Nov. 3, 1782; married Rachel Meady, May 2, 1805, died in West Indies, 1810.³
208 GEORGE,⁶ baptized Oct. 10, 1784. See No. 208.
209 WALTER,⁶ baptized Dec. 3, 1786. See No. 209.
210 PARKER,⁶ baptized Sept. 30, 1787.
211 CHARLOTTE,⁶ baptized Nov. 1, 1789; married Alexander Meady, Nov. 21, 1811.
211a ANNA,⁶ baptized May 27, 1798.
211b HARRIET,⁶ baptized May 27, 1798; living in 1822; beneficiary in the will of David Brown (Pro. Rec. 399: 502); married — Webb of Salem.
211c MARY,⁶ married Stephen Holt of Salem, March 20, 1803.

101. STEPHEN BROWN,⁵ baptized May 2, 1736; married Elizabeth (Betty) Dodge of Wenham, Nov. 22, 1761; died July 5, 1819, age 84 yrs. Their home was in Hamilton. He bequeathed his homestead and lands, including 16 acres on Redwood Hill, to his daughter Sarah, and William Kinsman Jr., his son-in-law, was named as executor (Pro. Rec. 394: 547, proved Sept. 7, 1819). Their children were:

211d STEPHEN.⁶
211e BETTY,⁶ married William Poland of Ipswich (pub. July 4, 1781).
211f HANNAH,⁶ married Nathan Fellows of Ipswich (pub. Aug. 20 1785).

¹ Page 14.
² The Old Bay Road. No. xv. p. 8.
³ Administration on the estate of Stephen Brown, Jr., mariner, was granted to Thomas Meady of Topsfield, Nov. 6, 1811. Pro. Rec. 380:43.

211g SUSA,[6] baptized Jan. 1, 1769; unmarried in 1818.
211h AMMI,[6] baptized May 1, 1774; married Sarah Fellows of Ipswich, July 15, 1798.
211i SARAH,[6] baptized Oct. 21, 1781; married William Kinsman, Sept. 4, 1802; died March 11, 1860.
211j ANNA,[6] baptized May 22, 1785; married Ebenezer Goodhue of Ipswich, Nov. 27, 1806.

133. NATHAN BROWN,[6] baptized Nov. 12, 1786, called Jr., house carpenter, married Lydia Hood of Topsfield, Sept. 20, 1814, who died Nov. 10, 1859, aged seventy-three. He died Nov. 10, 1873, aged eighty-seven. He bought the Timothy Bragg[1] house on the Essex road of Oliver Appleton in 1824 and removed it to the corner of County Road and Ward Street and occupied it until his death. It is now the residence of Mr. Everett K. Brown. Their chilrden were:

212 NATHAN,[7] born Dec. 3, 1814.
213 ABIGAIL,[7] born April 27, 1816; died Dec. 10, 1848 unmarried.
214 LYDIA H.,[7] born Feb. 2, 1818; died Oct. 17, 1818.
215 SAMUEL H.,[7] born Oct. 21, 1820; died May 5, 1843.
216 LYDIA H.,[7] born Nov. 28, 1822; married Josiah Lord Jr., May 21, 1845.
217 FRANCIS E.,[7] born June 17, 1827.

134. LANGLEY BROWN,[6] baptized May 1, 1791, married Hannah Smith, Oct. 31, 1811, who died, his widow, May 1, 1831 aged thirty-seven years. They lived in Lincoln in 1823. Their child was:

218 ELIZABETH,[7] born 1816; died Dec. 21, 1831 aged 15 years.

145. SAMUEL BROWN,[6] born in 1805; married Eliza Saville of Gloucester (pub. June 15, 1829), died Oct. 26, 1830. Their child was:

218a OLIVER,[7] born   ; died May 7, 1891.

149. JOHN BROWN,[6] born Jan. 3, 1815, married Eunice Kinsman, Sept. 17, 1840. He bought the interest of the other heirs in the old homestead and lived there all his life. Mrs. Brown died Dec. 2, 1881, aged sixty-three years, three months. He died Feb. 12, 1889, aged 74 years 1 month 9 days. Their children were:

219 JOHN HENRY,[7] born Dec. 11, 1841. He occupies the homestead.
220 JOSEPH ALBERT,[7] born Oct. 11, 1844; married S. Lizzie Burnham of Essex, Nov. 23, 1877; have one son, Jesse Eliot.
221 PROCTOR KINSMAN,[7] born Feb. 27, 1852; lives in East Milton, unmarried.
222 CLARENCE E.,[7] born Dec., 21 1857. See No. 222.

157. EPHRAIM BROWN,[6] baptized Oct. 30, 1785, married Hannah Kinsman, daughter of Moses. Oct. 6, 1811. They lived in Gloucester. Their children were:

[1] Page 11.

222a　HANNAH,⁷ unmarried.
222b　ABBY.⁷
222c　EPHRAIM,⁷ died in Somerville, March, 1862, aged 35 yrs.

159. CAPT. JOSIAH BROWN,⁶ married 1st, Chrisse Baker, daughter of John Baker Jr. and Joanna, July, 17, 1806, who was born April 1, 1780 and died Jan. 10, 1818; married 2nd, Nabby Baker, her sister, May 13, 1819, who died a widow, Nov. 21, 1871, aged 89 yrs. 1 month. He inherited his father's farm and lived there. The children by the first marriage were:

223　JEMIMA PATCH,⁷ born Aug. 31, 1807; married Daniel Brown Jr., May 19, 1825. See No. 243.
224　JOSIAH,⁷ born Sept. 29, 1809; died Nov. 19, 1829.
225　JAMES,⁷ born April 15, 1813; married Eliza　　　; died May 15, 1864 in Adams Co., Illinois.
226　LUCRETIA,⁷ baptized Aug. 3, 1817; married Joel B. Stowe of Plymouth, N. H., Nov. 7, 1838.

The only child by the second marriage was:
227　MANASSEH JR.⁷　See No. 227.

160. CAPT. ELISHA BROWN,⁶ baptized March 1, 1761, married Martha Brown, daughter of Benjamin and Martha (Roberts) (No. 192), Aug. 26, 1790, who died his widow on March 21, 1865, at the great age of 101 years 2 months, 24 days. Capt. Elisha died March 11, 1808, leaving her a widow, with six children under age, including a babe of ten months. Guardianship was granted her, July 5, 1808 (Pro. Rec. 376: 457). They lived in several places in Candlewood. Their children were:

228　MARTHA,⁷ born April 27, 1791; died Aug. 31, 1818.
229　ELIPHALET,⁷ born Oct. 14, 1793. See No. 229.
230　ELISHA,⁷ born Nov. 3, 1796 in Gloucester. See No. 230.
231　Town Record, a child of Elisha Brown Jr. died Feb. 9, 1799 (not mentioned in family record).
233　ASA,⁷ born Jan. 23, 1800; died April 2, 1805.
234　JONATHAN,⁷ born Dec. 27, 1802. See No. 234.
235　ELIZA,⁷ born Jan. 25, 1804; died April 10, 1871, unmarried.
236　SARAH,⁷ born July 20, 1807; died Sept. 5, 1813.

161. EPHRAIM BROWN,⁶ born Feb. 8, 1763, married Elizabeth Boardman of the same neighborhood, who was born July 27, 1768, on Nov. 13, 1791, who died Oct. 2, 1824, aged fifty-six. He died March 28, 1842, aged seventy-nine. Their home was on the corner, occupied by Mr. E. Newton Brown, where Mr. Elisha Brown, father of Ephraim had erected buildings probably for the young couple's use.[1] Their children were:

237　INCREASE HOW,⁷ born Jan. 16, 1793. See No. 237.

[1] Page 30.

238   EPHRAIM,[7] born Nov. 12, 1795. See No. 238.
239   ASA,[7] born Oct. 31, 1797; died April 7, 1868 unmarried.
240   ELIZABETH,[7] born Jan. 30, 1800; married William Giddings, Dec. 26, 1843; died April 6, 1878.
241   THOMAS,[7] born July 20, 1802. See No. 241.
242   RHODA,[7] born Oct. 1, 1805; married James Potter, Dec. 2, 1830; died March 4, 1892 aged 86 years 5 months 4 days.

165.   DANIEL BROWN,[6] baptized May 8, 1775, married Rhoda Brown (No. 129), Aug. 2, 1801, who died Sept. 2, 1805. He inherited a portion of the homestead and dwelt there.[1]   Their children were:

243   DANIEL,[7] born Nov. 10, 1801. See No. 243.
244   SAMUEL,[7] born   ; died Sept. 2, 1805.

169.   AMMI BROWN,[6] born June 27, 1776, married Hannah Baker, Oct. 27, 1814. They made their home in Salem, as early as 1820. He died in 1827; his widow died in Salem, July 31, 1876. Their only child was:

245   FRANCIS,[7] born Aug. 5, 1815. See No. 245.

170.   MICHAEL BROWN,[6] born April 8, 1778, married Mary Baker, daughter of Asa Baker, Oct. 2, 1802. He died March 1, 1839, aged 61 years; his widow Sept. 9, 1862, aged 79 years 3 months 13 days. Their children were:

245a   HANNAH NEWALL,[7] born   ; died Dec. 12, 1804.
246   HANNAH N.,[7] married John H. Harris Jr., July 20, 1826.
247   ANN B.,[7] married Warren Kimball, May 13, 1835.
248   STEPHEN CHOATE.[7]   See No. 248.
249   WINTHROP.[7]   See No. 249.
250   GEORGE,[7] in 1827, heir in Uncle Ammi's will; unmarried.
251.   MICHAEL.[7]
252   ELIZABETH C.,[7] born 1816; died unmarried at the age of 92 years.
253   THOMAS B.,[7] born 1818; died Nov. 8, 1825 aged 7 years.
254   JOHN,[7] married in Hawaiian Islands.

172.   CAPT. WILLIAM BROWN,[6] born Jan. 12, 1783, married 1st, Dorcas Baker, Dec. 27, 1810. She was born July 25, 1786 and died April 5, 1822. He married 2nd, Ann Baker, sister of Dorcas, who died in 1875. He was a resident in Salem in 1826, when he conveyed his interest in his father's estate.[2]   He was an intrepid sailor and many of his exploits are told in the "Choates in America." He was the hero of a remarkable fight against Malay pirates, who cut off the ship Putnam in the Malay Archipelago, the account of which has often been published. He was lost overboard in a storm at sea, Aug. 23, 1833. The children by the first marriage were:

255   WILLIAM HENRY,[7] born Nov. 13, 1812; died unmarried in 1844;
            either at sea or at St. Helena, where he was buried.

[1] Page 32.
[2] Page 13.

256 EDWARD,⁷ born Jan. 13, 1815. See No. 256.
257 DORCAS BAKER,⁷ born Feb. 27, 1818; married Judge James R. Newhall of Lynn, 1840; died March 31, 1841.
258 SAMUEL NEWHALL,⁷ born May 29, 1821; died Sept. 28, 1822.

176. NEHEMIAH BROWN,⁶ born Feb. 18, 1794; married Susannah Smith, July 20, 1819, who died Jan. 31, 1826. He died Nov. 30, 1859. Their home was in Salem, where he was Deputy Sheriff. Their children were:

259 AMMI,⁷ a dentist in Boston; married
260. NEHEMIAH,⁷ married Ellen, daughter of William and Rebecca Brown. Their home was in Boston.

179. JOSEPH BROWN JR.,⁶ born March 14, 1783, married Rebecca Appleton, daughter of Samuel and Mary Appleton, Jan. 15, 1808. She was born March 19, 1783 and died his widow, Aug. 28, 1865. Mr. Brown died Dec. 9, 1852. Their home was on the ancestral farm.¹ Their children were:

261 LUCY,⁷ born Feb. 11, 1809; died Sept. 19, 1810.
262 SAMUEL APPLETON,⁷ born Nov. 4, 1810. See No. 262.
263 LUCY,⁷ born March 28, 1812; died Jan. 20, 1817.
264 JOSEPH PERKINS,⁷ born April 24, 1814. See No. 264.
265 MARY ELIZABETH,⁷ born May 31, 1816; married Joseph Kinsman, Sept. 20, 1842; died Feb. 19, 1861.
266 WINTHROP,⁷ born June 10, 1818; died Feb. 9, 1819.
267 REBECCA Appleton,⁷ born Jan. 23, 1821; died Oct. 28, 1857.
268 GARDINER APPLETON,⁷ born May 5, 1823. See No. 268.

181. JAMES BROWN,⁶ born Feb. 22, 1789, married July 2, 1812, Lucy Fellows, daughter of Ephraim and Eunice, of Lakeman's Lane, who was born on May 2, 1790. Their home was in the house built for their use, where all the children but the eldest were born, now owned and occupied by their grandson, Geo. A. Whipple. Mr. Brown died Oct. 11, 1848, his widow, Feb. 1, 1852. Their children were:

269 AARON FELLOWS,⁷ born Jan. 15, 1813. See No. 269.
270 MARTHA PERKINS,⁷ born Jan. 22, 1816; married Hervey Whipple of Hamilton, Jan. 1, 1835; died Nov. 7, 1896.
271 SALLY PERKINS,⁷ born Oct. 24, 1816; married Azor Bray of Gloucester, Dec. 1, 1836.
272 LUCY MARY⁷, born July 5, 1818; married Asa Rust of Gloucester, Dec. 3, 1851.
273 WINTHROP,⁷ born March 5, 1820; went to California in 1849, and never returned.
274 ELIZABETH FELLOWS,⁷ born June 5, 1822; married Joshua Lamson, April 15, 1841; died Nov. 1, 1862.

¹ Page 28.
² Page 22.

OF JOHN BROWN 111

275 DAVID,[7] born June 5, 1824. See No. 275.
276 EUNICE APPLETON,[7] born Aug. 6, 1826; married Manasseh Brown Jr., March 6, 1845. See No. 227.
277 JAMES FRANCIS,[7] born Nov. 4 1828; went to California in 1849 and married there. He preferred the name Charles Francis.
278 GEORGE WILLIAM,[7] born Dec. 1, 1830; married Thankful Burnham of Essex, daughter of Ebenezer and Susan, March 8, 1856. They had no children.
279 ADDISON,[7] born Dec. 14, 1832; died May 12, 1863.
280 EDWARD,[7] twin, born July 14, 1835. See No. 280.
281 ELLEN,[7] twin, born July 14, 1835; married John C. Low of Essex (pub. Dec. 7, 1855).

183. ISAAC BROWN,[6] born July 9, 1794, married Lydia Smith, April 1, 1825. They removed to Litchfield, N. H., where they kept an inn. Brown's Tavern, their former home, was a well remembered landmark, within the recollection of the present Town Clerk. Mr. Brown died Dec. 10, 1843 and the widow probably returned to Ipswich soon after, where the remainder of her life was spent. She died Nov. 12, 1887. Their children, all born in Litchfield, were:

282 LUCY JANE SMITH,[7] born May 4, 1826; died Dec. 1, 1826.
283 LYDIA LUCRETIA SMITH,[7] born Oct. 16, 1827; died May 3, 1883, unmarried, at Ipswich.
284 MARTHA ELIZABETH PERKINS,[7] born Aug. 20, 1829; died Oct., 1904, unmarried, at Chesterfield Co., Maryland.
285 SARAH ANSTICE MANNING,[7] born Sept. 23, 1831; died April 16, 1835.
286 CAROLINE COBURN,[7] born Oct. 11, 1833; died June 21, 1852.
287 EDWARD RICHMOND,[7] born June 16, 1837. See No. 287.

186. JOHN BURNHAM BROWN,[6] born Sept. 12, 1779, married 1st, Elizabeth Potter of Hamilton (pub. Oct. 12, 1809), who died May 17, 1814, aged 26 years. Their children were:

288 FRANCIS,[7] born Jan. 19, 1811; died May 12, 1814.
289 ELIZABETH POTTER,[7] born Aug. 24, 1812; married 1st, Alonzo Butler of Essex, Oct. 16, 1834. They made their home in Lowell, where Mr. Butler died Dec. 28, 1836. She married 2d, William Poor of South Danvers, now Peabody, April 14, 1842; who died June 10, 1865. Mrs. Poor died Aug. 25, 1893, leaving no children by either marriage.
290 INFANT,[7] born May 7, 1814; died May 20, 1814.

Mrs. Brown died at the same time and there were three funerals within a week. Mr. Brown married 2d, Mary Kinsman,[1] April 5, 1818, who died June 11, 1867, aged 82 years 8 months. Their children were:

[1] See The Kinsman Genealogy, page 81.

291 MARY KINSMAN,⁷ born Jan. 11, 1819; married Manasseh Brown, Dec. 15, 1836; died July 15, 1851.
292 LUCY,⁷ born Dec. 10, 1820; married Wilder J. Mellen of Quincy, Illinois, May 9, 1854; died Dec. 30, 1892.
293 JOHN ALLEN,⁷ born Sept. 28, 1822; died unmarried, June 21, 1903.
294 EMELINE,⁷ born July 17, 1824; died Feb. 7, 1825.
295 EMELINE FRANCES,⁷ born May 30, 1827; resides in Ipswich.
296 HANNAH BURNHAM,⁷ born April 18, 1831; married Theodore F. Cogswell, Oct. 27, 1853; who died Sept. 17, 1907. Mrs. Cogswell died May 16, 1909.

Mr. John Burnham Brown built the house now owned and occupied by Mr. Alonzo B. Fellows soon after his marriage, and the ancient house on the hill slope behind the new house fell into ruin. He died June 17, 1868.

191. CHARLES BROWN,⁶ born Jan. 12, 1789, married Beulah C. Burns of Rockport, Sept. 4, 1814. He was a baker, by trade, and removed from Rockport to Quincy, Illinois, where he spent the rest of his life. Their children were:

297 JOHN BURNS,⁷ born May 22, 1815.
298 FRANCIS,⁷ born Oct. 29, 1817.
299 ABIGAIL C.,⁷ born Oct. 27, 1819.
300 CHARLES,⁷ born Sept. 22, 1822.
301 MARY JANE,⁷ born July 11, 1824.
302 BEULAH C.,⁷ born Nov. 2, 1826.
303 EMELINE F. M.,⁷ born Nov. 5, 1828.
304 LUCINDA,⁷ born June 2, 1831.
305 SAMUEL,⁷ born April 20, 1834.

193. BENJAMIN BROWN,⁶ called Jr. and 4th, baptized Oct. 5, 1766; a tailor by trade, married Hannah Woodbury, July 29, 1792 who died his widow, Dec. 19, 1839. He built a house near the Goose Pond, so called, on the Essex road, which has disappeared.¹ He died April 21, 1836. Their children were:

306 EDMUND,⁷ a blacksmith, living in Lynn in 1838.
307 LEVI.⁷ See No. 307.
308 PERLEY.⁷ See No. 308.
309 JOHN JR.⁷ See No. 309.
310 SARAH,⁷ married John R. Lakeman of Salem, April 2, 1820; not living in 1838.
311 FRANCIS.⁷ See No. 311.
312 ISAAC,⁷ probably died early in life.
313 BENJAMIN,⁷ probably died early in life.
314 HANNAH,⁷ probably died in early life.

¹ Page 19.

196. PARKER BROWN,[6] married Ruth ——, at Bridgetown, April, 1794. They lived in Bridgetown, Mass., now Bridgton, Maine. Their children, all born in Bridgeton, were:

315 SALLY,[7] born May 1, 1804; married Francis Brown. See No. 311.
316 MARTHA,[7] born Oct. 18, 1805
317 JONATHAN,[7] born June 27, 1807.
318 PARKER,[7] born Aug. 19, 1809; died Oct. 9, 1810.
319 ISRAEL G.,[7] born Aug. 15, 1811.
320 HANNAH,[7] born Nov. 20 1813.
321 JOHN,[7] born Dec. 17, 1816.
322 BETSEY G.,[7] born Dec. 20, 1823.

The Town Clerk of Bridgeton writes that the old Town Records were destroyed by fire some years ago. The few that remain give no further trace of this family

200. DAVID BROWN,[6] married, Nov. 21, 1807, Mrs. Thankful Bagley (m. n. Burnham), who was born Feb. 28, 1780 and died in 1842. Mr. Brown died Jan. 7, 1827, aged 45 years. Their home was in Portland, Me., where he was a baker. In May 1831, Thankful Brown, his widow, guardian of Caroline, Nathaniel, Mary Ann and Abigail B. Brown, minor children, with guardians of other grandchildren of Nathaniel Brown, petitioned for liberty to sell the interest of their wards in their grandfather's estate[1] (Pro. Rec. 408: 88). Their children, all born in Portland, were:

323 DAVID,[7] born Oct. 6, 1808. He went west and died unmarried.
324 CAROLINE,[7] born Nov. 10, 1810; married Nathan Chapman of Portland (pub. Sept. 21, 1833); died in 1857.
325 NATHANIEL,[7] born Sept. 22, 1813. See No. 325.
326 MARY ANN,[7] born Aug. 15, 1816; married Levi T. Lincoln of Yarmouth, Me. (pub. Dec. 16, 1852); died Aug. 25, 1899.
327 ABIGAIL BURNHAM,[7] born Feb. 7, 1818; married William Hammond of Portland, Me. (pub. Aug. 11, 1838); died March 4, 1874.

208. GEORGE BROWN,[6] baptized Oct. 10, 1784, married 1st, Lucy Meady, Sept. 8, 1807, who died Dec. 16, 1807, at the age of 17½ years. He married 2d, Esther Ann Saunders of Folly Cove, Aug. 5, 1813, who died May 12, 1833. He inherited from David Brown[2] the part of the house he owned, whose wife was his aunt (Pro. Rec. 399: 502). Their children were:

328 GEORGE,[7] born March 17, 1814. See No. 323.
329 JOHN POTTER,[7] born 1818; died unmarried, April 25, 1878, aged 60 years.
330 ELIZABETH MEADY,[7] married Samuel Lufkin Jr. of Gloucester.
331 SUSAN,[7] married Louis ——.
332 LUCY MEADY,[7] married John Sweet, July 3, 1834.

[1] Pages 18, 19.
[2] Page 14.

333   MARY POTTER,[7] married Samuel Lufkin Jr after her sister's death.
334   DAVID ALLEN.[7] See No. 334.
335   CHARLOTTE,[7] married James R. Grant of Maine.

209. WALTER BROWN,[6] baptized Dec. 3, 1786, married 1st, Annis ——, who died Sept. 7, 1833, aged forty one; 2d, Mrs. Lucy Post of Newburyport (pub. Dec. 15, 1838). Their child was:
336   ELIZA,[7] born   ; married John R. Norfolk of Salem, Dec. 26, 1847.

222. CLARENCE E. BROWN,[7] born Dec. 21, 1857, married Alice L. Low, daughter of Andrew and Louisa (Willcomb) Low, Sept. 6, 1881, who died Aug. 13, 1908. Their home is in Beverly. Their children are:
337   EARL KINSMAN,[8] born May 8, 1885; died Feb. 5, 1889, at West Medford.
338   ETHEL LOUISE,[8] born July 4, 1889.
339   BERTHA EDWARDS,[8] born Dec. 2, 1901.

227. MANASSEH BROWN,[7] called Jr., married Eunice A. Brown (No. 276), daughter of James and Lucy (Fellows) Brown, March 6, 1845. They lived in the homestead of his father, Capt. Josiah Brown, where he was born.[1] He died Jan. 15, 1900, "at the age of 76 years 5 months." Mrs. Brown died April 6, 1899, aged 73 years 8 months. Their children were:
340   LUCY ABBY,[8] baptized July 5, 1846; married Emery Lawrence of Hamilton, March 22, 1862.
341   SARAH APPLETON,[8] baptized June 18, 1848; died Sept. 5, 1849 aged 1 year 7 months.
342   JOHN BAKER,[8] born Aug. 12, 1850.
343   SARAH APPLETON,[8] born   ; married John Hooper Jr., of Rockport, May 23, 1880.

229. ELIPHALET BROWN,[7] born Oct. 14, 1793, married Martha Pratt Gay, widow of —— Gay. He was drowned in Ipswich river, Nov. 27, 1836, aged forty-three. The widow, a delicate woman, with a large and helpless family was obliged to separate the family. Mary was adopted by Mr. Charles Giddings and removed with them to Wisconsin. The baby, Thomas, was adopted by a family of the name of Whitney. Their children were:
344   MARTHA,[8] born July 10, 1823; married Willard Goldthwait of Salem.
345   ASA,[8] born Sept. 30, 1826. See No. 345.
346   CHARLES,[8] born Oct. 26, 1827 in Roxbury. See No. 346.
347   MARY,[8] born Aug. 13, 1831; married —— Cole of Sheboygan, Wis.
348   JONATHAN,[8] born Sept. 20, 1833. See No. 348.
349   ELIPHALET,[8] born June 11, 1835; died in Wenham, July 8, 1866 unmarried.
350   THOMAS,[8] born Oct. 19, 1836. He was a soldier in the War of the Rebellion in a Maine regiment. He left a family, which cannot be traced.

[1] Page 33.

230. ELISHA BROWN,[7] born in Gloucester, Nov. 3, 1796, married Charlotte Kinsman, daughter of Aaron and Hannah Kinsman, July 2, 1840, who died March 29, 1860, aged 59 years 2 days. Mr. Brown died Nov. 3, 1877, aged 81 years. Their children were:
351   EVERETT KINSMAN,[8] born April 24, 1841; married Margaretta Wilson, daughter of Henry and Lucy (Patch) Wilson, Nov. 24, 1870. They have no children. They live on County Road, Ipswich.
352   CHARLOTTE ANNA,[8] born Jan. 17, 1843; married Alvin Story, June 6, 1877; died Aug. 2, 1897.
353   ELISHA NEWTON,[8] born June 18, 1845. See No. 353.

234. JONATHAN BROWN,[7] born Dec. 27, 1803, married Lucy Smith Kimball, in Ipswich, May 8, 1836. They removed to Salem, where he died Jan. 20, 1878. Their children were:
354   ELIZA,[8] born Jan. 7, 1841; married Charles P. Dodge, Jan., 1869.
355   AUGUSTUS,[8] born Oct. 18, 1843. See No. 355.
356   JOHN THOMAS,[8] born 1845; died in Salem, Sept. 16, 1852, aged 7 years.

237. INCREASE HOW BROWN,[7] married 1st, on June 18, 1820, Eliza Harris of Marblehead, where he made his home. He died Nov., 1869, aged 76 years. Their children were:
357   WILLIAM BLANCHARD.[8] See No. 357.
358   INCREASE HOW JR.,[8] baptized July 4, 1824. See No. 358.
359   JOHN HARRIS.[8] See No. 359.

He married 2d, Mary Warner Gerry, the niece of his former wife, Oct. 28, 1830. Their children were:
360   ELIZA HARRIS,[8] born Sept., 1832; married Joseph H. Robinson, Jan. 14, 1857.
361   MARY GERRY,[8] born Feb. 7, 1834; married Chas. W. Seymour, April 13, 1857.
362   GERRY BROWN,[8] born May 25, 1838. See No. 362.
363   ELBRIDGE,[8] born April 28, 1840. See No. 363.

238. EPHRAIM BROWN,[7] born Nov. 12, 1795, married Mary Blanchard of Marblehead, Aug. 11, 1825, who died Aug. 21, 1858, aged 54 years 5 months. Mr. Brown died Feb. 28, 1860, aged 65 years, 4 months. Their home was in Marblehead. Their children were:
364   EPHRAIM BLANCHARD,[8] born Oct. 24, 1826; married Hetty ———.
365   ELIZABETH BOARDMAN,[8] born May 1, 1828; married Peregrine Maitland Burnham, Sept. 27, 1847; died Dec. 28, 1847.
366   WILLIAM HENRY,[8] born July 8, 1830; died Dec. 27, 1859.
367   MARY BLANCHARD,[8] born Oct. 20, 1834; married Francis H. Bridge, Nov. 2, 1854; died Oct. 17, 1880.

368 SARAH ELLEN,[8] born Oct. 18, 1837; married Horace C. Bartlett, Aug. 28, 1866. Both were lost in the City of Columbus, wrecked on Gay Head, Jan. 18, 1884.

241. THOMAS BROWN,[7] called Jr., born July 20, 1802, married Elizabeth Brown, daughter of Joseph and Martha Brown (No. 184), May 26, 1839. Their home was on the Argilla farm, which was purchased by his father Ephraim. Mr. Brown died March 24, 1889; his widow, April 2, 1904. Their children were:

369 WARREN,[8] born Dec. 22, 1839; died at Pernambuco, July 7, 1859.
370 AUGUSTINE,[8] born Aug. 20, 1842. See No. 370.
371 HORACE,[8] born Sept. 8, 1844, lives on the Argilla farm.
372 OTIS,[8] born Dec. 16, 1847. See No. 372.
373 MARY ELIZABETH,[8] born Oct. 6, 1852; married John J. Sullivan, Oct. 21, 1880. Their home is in Ipswich.

243 DANIEL BROWN JR.,[7] born Nov. 10, 1801, married Jemima P. Brown, daughter of Capt. Josiah and Chrisse (Baker) Brown,(223) May 19, 1825, who died Jan. 17, 1837. They lived in the Elisha Brown homestead[1] on the Candlewood road. Their children were:

374 SOPHIA,[8] born Oct. 27, 1825; married Albert Perry of Salem; died Nov. 4, 1853, aged 28 years.
375 RHODA ANN,[8] born Jan. 14, 1828; married Enoch Fuller of Salem, Sept. 29, 1854. She lives in Ipswich.
376 LUCRETIA BAKER,[8] born Aug. 29, 1830; married James Potter of Salem, Jan. 20, 1853. She lives in North Beverly.
377 DANIEL CHOATE,[8] twin, born Oct. 22, 1833. See No. 377.
378 LYDIA,[8] twin, born Oct. 22, 1833; married Chas. Berry Cogswell of Essex (pub. Sept. 7, 1857).

245. FRANCIS BROWN,[7] born in Salem, Aug. 5, 1815, married Ellen M. Appleton, March 5, 1839. They made their home in Salem, where Mr. Brown died, Nov. 15, 1880, his widow, June 7, 1887. Their children were:

379 ELLEN APPLETON,[8] born Jan. 17, 1841.
380 FRANCIS ALBERT,[8] born March 4, 1842; died Dec. 16, 1843.
381 SUSAN WOODBURY,[8] born June 7, 1845.
382 ANNIE BAKER,[8] born March 21, 1847.
383 SARAH HALE,[8] born June 25, 1849.
384 FRANK APPLETON,[8] born July 17, 1853. See No. 384.
385 ARTHUR HOWARD,[8] born Sept. 6, 1856.
386 HENRY SARGENT,[8] born Dec. 2, 1858; died July 28, 1871.

248. STEPHEN CHOATE BROWN,[7] married Mary Lynde S. Dodge, April 2, 1834, who died April 27, 1887, aged 72 years 9 months. Their children were:

387 LUCY HAMMATT,[8] died July 1905, aged 70 years.

[1] Page 32.

388 KATE S.,[8] married John W. Philbrook, Jan. 19, 1860 and removed to California.
389 FRANK,[8] went to California; died unmarried.
390 FREDERICK,[8] died Oct. 2, 1843, aged 9 months.

249. WINTHROP BROWN,[7] married Louisa Jane Allen, Nov. 12, 1835. Their children were:
391 ——,[8] twin, died Oct. 10, 1844.
392 ——,[8] twin, died Oct. 18, 1844.
393 SON,[8] born in Salem; died Sept. 19, 1851, aged 2 months.
394 CHILD,[8] died in Danvers, aged 3 months.
395 SON,[8] died Aug. 19, 1857, aged 7 months.

256. EDWARD BROWN,[7] born Jan. 13, 1815, was a student for two years at Amherst College, though he did not graduate. Henry Ward Beecher, John Codman and James Roosevelt Bayley, afterwards R. C. Archbishop of Baltimore were among his classmates. Leaving college, he followed the sea for a time. He married 1st, Eliza Osgood Dalton, July 21, 1842, who died in 1849. Their children, all born in Salem, Mass., were:
396 EDWARD OSGOOD,[8] born 1843; died 1844.
397 LUCY OSGOOD,[8] born May 6, 1845; died 1848.
398 EDWARD OSGOOD,[8] born Aug. 5, 1847. See No. 398.

He married 2d, Jennie E. Taylor, 1859, who died in Jan., 1906. Their child was:
399 JENNIE TAYLOR,[8] born Nov. 1, 1866; married James W. Greig of London, England in 1890.

262. SAMUEL APPLETON BROWN,[7] born Nov. 4, 1810, married Sarah Butler of Pelham, Nov. 20, 1852 and made his home in Lowell. Their children were:
400 SARAH REBECCA,[8] born July 13, 1854; died May 13, 1862.
401 HARRY APPLETON,[8] born Sept. 25, 1856. See No. 401.
402 MARY ELIZABETH,[8] born Oct. 26, 1862; died April 29, 1874.

264. JOSEPH PERKINS BROWN,[7] born April 24, 1814, married Susan W. Lord, daughter of Philip and Susan Lord, March 26, 1846; died April 29, 1857, on the ancestral farm, where he had always lived.[1] His widow married William Foster Wade Jr., Dec. 13, 1865 and died May 11, 1881. Their chidren were:
403 JULIA APPLETON,[8] born Aug. 6, 1846; married Andrew Craigie Spring, April 16, 1868.
404 SAMUEL APPLETON,[8] born Oct. 1, 1848; unmarried, lives in Somerville.
405 JOSEPH,[8] born Jan. 23, 1852; married   ; died April 10, 1907.
406 ELIZABETH POTTER,[8] born Oct. 26, 1854; unmarried, lives in Somerville.

[1] Page 28.

268. GARDINER APPLETON BROWN,[7] born May 5, 1823, married 1st, Judith Ann Perley, Oct. 20, 1851, who died Jan. 13, 1853, aged 31 years. Their child was:

    407 CHARLES GARDINER,[8] born Jan. 8, 1853. See No. 407.

He married 2d, Leonora Abby Story, daughter of David and Eunice Story, Jan. 3, 1855. Their children were:

    408 ALVIN STORY,[8] born Nov. 27, 1855. See No. 408.
    409 JESSE APPLETON,[8] born Feb. 17, 1858; died June 2, 1879.

Mr. Brown died June 19, 1907 on the farm of his ancestors and in the house in which he was born.[1]

269. AARON FELLOWS BROWN,[7] born Jan. 15, 1813, married Nabby B. Brown, daughter of Tristram and Joanna, Dec. 25, 1839. They made their home for many years on the Argilla road, where Mr. Brown died, June 12, 1879. His widow died   . Their children were:

    410 ABIGAIL PATCH,[8] born Dec. 30, 1843; lives in Ipswich; unmarried.
    411 RUFUS ALLEN,[8] born March 29, 1849; died May 26, 1850.
    412 CAROLINE,[8] born   ; married Joseph Farley Kinsman, Oct. 1, 1873, a soldier in the War of the Rebellion, who died Aug. 31, 1906. The widow lives in the Kinsman homestead.

275. DAVID BROWN,[7] born June 5, 1824, married Sarah Coffin Currier of Newburyport, Oct. 22, 1846. They lived in Newburyport, where he was the first City Marshall. He served with honor as the Captain of a company in the War of the Rebellion. He died Dec. 30, 1876.

    413 They had one daughter.[8]

280. EDWARD BROWN,[7] born July 14, 1835, married 1st, Sarah E. Poor, daughter of Melzeard and Mary Poor, Nov. 25, 1858, who died Oct. 30, 1870, aged 35 years 2 months 22 days. He married 2d, Isabelle Coffin of Boston, May, 1876. His home is in Salisbury. The children, all by the first marriage, were:

    414 SON,[8] unnamed, born Nov. 21, 1859; died Nov. 22, 1859.
    415 CHARLES AUSTIN,[8] born Oct. 24, 1860.
    416 ASA R.,[8] born 1863. See No. 416.
    417 LUCY FELLOWS,[8] born Aug. 19, 1865; married Charles Franklin Hatch, Dec. 22, 1881. They live in Amesbury.
    418 SUSAN ARNOLD,[8] born May 22, 1868; died Oct. 26, 1868.

287. EDWARD RICHMOND BROWN,[7] born June 16, 1837, married Annie Marion Hood, Oct. 31, 1866, died at Ipswich, Nov. 6, 1873. Their child was:

    419 RICHMOND HOOD,[8] born July 22, 1867.

307. LEVI BROWN,[7] married Susan Mears of Essex (pub. May 12, 1826). He died Oct. 7, 1840; his widow, March 28, 1857, aged 55 years.

[1] Page 28.

He built a dwelling which forms part of the house now occupied by Miss Emily Patch on the Essex road.[1] Their children were:

420　SUSAN.[8]
421　ABBY ANN,[8] born 1829; died July 17, 1855, aged 26 years.
422　LEVI WOODBURY,[8] baptized Sept. 11, 1836.

308. PERLEY BROWN,[7] a cabinet maker by trade, married Betsey Tappan of Manchester, Sept. 12, 1827. Their home was in Manchester, where all their children were born. Their children were:

423　ELIZA T.,[8] born May 8, 1829; married 1st, Ariel P. Lee, April 30, 1848, who died Dec. 28, 1858. She married 2d,——Spooner.
424　ANN MARIA,[8] born May 22, 1831; married Laban F. Cushing, Oct. 26 1854.
425　PERLEY,[8] born Feb. 23, 1833. He went to California in '49 and married there. His later history is not known.
426　CAROLINE,[8] born Aug. 11, 1836; married Chas. C. Parsons, Dec. 3, 1854.
427　MARTHA T.,[8] born Feb. 12, 1839; married William Atwood. She died, his widow, in Malden in Nov., 1907.

309. JOHN BROWN JR.,[7] born in 1811, a cordwainer by trade, married, Mary L. Caldwell, daughter of Nathaniel and Mary N. Caldwell, June 16, 1836. He died Oct., 1839, his widow May 27, 1881. Their son:

428　SYLVESTER,[8] born Feb. 6, 1838, still lives in Ipswich.

311. FRANCIS BROWN,[7] married Sally Brown (No. 315), Sept. 28, 1830, who died July 6, 1862, aged fifty-seven. Their house was the dwelling now owned by William J. Cameron at the fork of Lakeman's Lane and Essex road, which he built about 1850.[2] Mr. Brown died Aug. 23, 1873, aged 69 years. Their children were:

429　FRANCIS PARKER,[8] born Feb. 6, 1832; unmarried; lives in Ipswich.
430　CHARLES,[8] born Nov.,1834; went to California, his later history not known.
431　BENJAMIN,[8] born Nov., 1837. See No. 431.

325. NATHANIEL BROWN,[7] born in Portland Me., Sept. 22, 1813, married 1st, Juliet Davis, who lived only a year; 2d, Mrs. Julia Blanchard (Bryant) March 31, 1842, who died in Feb., 1881; 3d, Mrs. Sarah Jaquith, Feb., 1882, who died in Sept., 1893. Mr. Brown died in Boston, where he had lived many years, Sept. 3, 1891. The children were by the second marriage:

432　EDWIN,[8] born Oct. 12, 1844. See No. 432.
433　CHARLES E.,[8] born July 21, 1854; is unmarried.

[1] Page 9.
[2] Pages 18, 19.

328. GEORGE BROWN JR.,[7] born March 17, 1814, married Eunice A. Tucker, April 14, 1836. He died March 12, 1884. Their home was in Ipswich. Their children were:

434   GEORGE ALLEN,[8] born April 12, 1838. See No. 434.
435   JESSE FRANKLIN,[8] born Nov. 22, 1840. See No. 435.
436   WALTER,[8] born March 19, 1843. See No. 436.
437   ESTHER ANN,[8] born Feb. 11, 1847; married Moses S. Saunders of Rowley, Nov. 28, 1866.
438   MARY POTTER,[8] born Oct. 24, 1851; married Chas. W. Davis; died March 28, 1853.
439   FREDERIC HERBERT,[8] born   ; died 1852.
440   HENRY HOWARD,[8] born Nov. 7, 1859. See No. 440.
441   JOHN WISE,[8] born   ; married and lives in Middletown, N. Y. He has a family.

334. DAVID ALLEN BROWN,[7] married 1st, Mary L. Lakeman, Feb. 27, 1845.

441a   A DAUGHTER,[8] died Aug. 22, 1845 aged 3 mos.

He married 2d, Lucy Parsons of Gloucester.

345. ASA BROWN,[8] born Sept. 30, 1826, married Olive E. Rollins. Their home is in Wakefield, N. H. Their son is

441b   DANIEL R.[9] See No. 441b.

346. CHARLES BROWN,[8] born in Roxbury, Oct. 26, 1827, married, Mary Ann Woodbridge of Wenham. They made their home in Wenham, where their children were born, but they have lived in Georgetown many years. Their children are:

442   ELNATHAN DODGE,[9] born May 20, 1851; married Angeline Allexia, Feb. 5, 1874. They have no children. They live in Georgetown.
443   GEORGE WOODBRIDGE,[9] born Dec. 9, 1856; died June 8, 1904.
444   WILLARD EUGENE,[9] born Dec. 31, 1870. See No. 444.

348. JONATHAN BROWN,[8] born in Ipswich, Sept. 20, 1833, married Martha B. Hatch, in Lynn, Feb. 13, 1859, who was born in Falmouth, Mass., Sept. 8, 1838 and died in Berwick, Me., at the home of her son, Henry, Nov. 16, 1908. Mr. Brown served in the War of the Rebellion. Their children were:

445   FRANK W.,[9] twin, born in Lynn, Nov. 12, 1859. See No. 445.
446   HENRY N.,[9] twin, born in Lynn, Nov. 12, 1859. See No. 446.

353. ELISHA NEWTON BROWN,[8] born June 18, 1845, married Eliza A. Philbrook, daughter of John and Mary A. (Baker) Philbrook, Nov. 30, 1871. They own and occupy the farm on the Candlewood road, formerly owned by Manasseh Brown Jr., who built the present dwelling.[1] Their children are:

[1] Page 30.

447   EVA KINSMAN,[9] born April 26, 1875; died March 3, 1895.
448   BERTHA ASHLEY,[9] born Oct. 29, 1876; married John L. Russell, Sept. 16, 1896.
449   KATHERYN LORD,[9] born Sept. 14, 1883; married Curtis E. Lakeman, June 13, 1908. Their residence is in Albany, N. Y.

355.   AUGUSTUS BROWN,[8] born Oct. 18, 1843 in Salem, married Helen F. Smith, Sept 7, 1869. They lived in Salem, where he died Aug., 1879. Their children are:

450   JULIUS CLARKE,[9] born May 20, 1870.
451   PORTER DODGE,[9] born Feb. 11, 1872. See No. 451.
452   LUCY STEVENS,[9] born Feb. 13, 1874.
453   HORACE MANSFIELD,[9] born Sept. 3, 1876. See No. 453.
454   HELEN AUGUSTA,[9] born Dec. 18, 1878; died April 8, 1896.

357.   WILLIAM BLANCHARD BROWN,[8] born in Marblehead Aug. 12, 1821, married Caroline Dixey, daughter of Capt. John Dixey and Rebecca (Cowell), of Marblehead, Nov. 4, 1844; died Jan. 13, 1892. Their children were:

455   THEODORE PARKER,[9] born Sept. 3, 1845. See No. 455.
456   CAROLINE DIXEY,[9] born Dec. 17, 1847.
457   ELIZABETH BOARDMAN,[9] born Oct. 8, 1849.
458   REBECCA COWELL,[9] born Aug. 26, 1851; died Jan. 19, 1889.
459   MARY,[9] born Dec. 29, 1854.

358.   INCREASE HOW BROWN JR.,[8] born in Marblehead, married 1st, Catherine Twisden Green, daughter of Major Joseph W. Green of Marblehead, a Dartmoor prisoner in the war of 1812; married 2nd, Mary Knight Gregory, April 8, 1860. Their children were:

460   HENRY,[9] born Nov. 26, 1847. See No. 460.
461   FREDERICK WARNER,[9] born Dec. 9, 1853. See No. 461.

359.   JOHN HARRIS BROWN,[8] born in Marblehead, March 20, 1827; married Hannah E. Blanchfield, Dec. 8, 1852. He died Feb. 20, 1895, his widow, Dec. 19, 1907. Their children were:

462   FANNIE,[9] born April 1, 1854; died July 6, 1871.
463   FRANK HARRIS,[9] born April 17, 1856; married Ellen Tucker Gardner, Dec. 6, 1882. They have no children. Their home is in Melrose, Mass.
464   AUGUSTUS MAGOUN,[9] born Sept. 10, 1865. See No. 464.

362.   GERRY BROWN,[8] born May 25, 1838, in Marblehead, where he spent his life; married Anne Scobie Bowden, Dec. 24, 1863. He died April 6, 1893. Their children were:

464a   BESSIE,[9] born May 15, 1865, at Taunton, Mass.; married Dr. Carolus M. Cobb (born in Maine) July 15, 1897.

465   MARY GERRY,[9] born Feb. 12, 1867 at Taunton, married George S. Bliss (born in Troy, N. Y.) June 24, 1903.
465a   DAUGHTER,[9] still born Sept. 1, 1869 at Lynn.
466   ELIZABETH GOODWIN,[9] born Sept. 15, 1870 at Lynn, died Jan. 10, 1879.
466a   DAUGHTER,[9] died one day old, March 19, 1872 at Lynn.

363. ELBRIDGE BROWN,[8] born April 28, 1840 in Marblehead, where he lives. He married Caroline L. Mason, Nov. 23, 1865. Their children are:

467   GEORGE MASON,[9] born June 10, 1867; died March 25, 1868.
468   HARRY WINTHROP,[9] born Dec. 31, 1868; died Jan. 4, 1890.
469   ELBRIDGE GERRY,[9] born Nov. 18, 1871; married 1st, Marie Carrie Gardner of Lynn, Oct. 9, 1895; married 2d, Florence Elsie Woodworth of New Haven, April 28, 1903. They have no children.
470   PERCIVAL HOWE,[9] born Aug. 11, 1875; married Anna May Redfern of Philadelphia Nov. 23, 1908. They live in Philadelphia.
471   EDITH WARNER,[9] born Jan. 2, 1881; married Charles H. Brown, Jr., Sept. 18, 1907. They live in Buffalo, N. Y.

370. AUGUSTINE BROWN,[8] born Aug. 20, 1842; married Susan M. Russell, daughter of David and Susan (Lakeman) Russell, May 4, 1871. He died April 29, 1884. Their child is:

472   BLANCHE R.,[9] born Feb. 24, 1872; married John W. Goodhue of Ipswich, Sept. 16, 1897.

372. OTIS BROWN,[8] born in Ipswich Dec. 16, 1847, married Mary A. Leonard, daughter of Fred N. Leonard of Agawam, Nov. 20, 1873. Their home is in Peabody, Mass. Their children are:

473   ETHELYN WARREN,[9] born Oct. 17, 1874.
474   RENA MAY,[9] born March 2, 1883.

377. DANIEL CHOATE BROWN,[8] baptized Jan. 7, 1837, married Elizabeth S. Harris of Marblehead, Dec. 25, 1855, where he made his home. He died Feb. 3, 1907. Their children are:

475   DANIEL CHOATE JR.,[9] born Nov. 13, 1861; died Nov. 6, 1863.
476   DANIEL CHOATE JR.,[9] born Nov. 5, 1864. See No. 476.
477   FANNY,[9] born July 31, 1866; died Aug. 22, 1866.

384. FRANK APPLETON BROWN,[8] born July 17, 1853 in Salem, where he has always made his home. He married Caroline Lewis Pease, daughter of George W. Pease of Salem, Oct. 19, 1881. Their children are:

478   FRANCIS,[9] born Oct. 5, 1882, Harvard A. B. 1904, S. B. 1905.
479   EDITH DOANE,[9] born Dec. 15, 1887.
480   CAROLINE APPLETON,[9] born April 16, 1889.

398. EDWARD OSGOOD BROWN,[8] born in Salem, Aug. 5, 1847, was graduated at Brown University, class of 1867, studied in the Harvard Law School and in the offices of Ives and Lincoln at Salem and Francis Miner at Providence, was Assistant Clerk of the Supreme Court of Rhode Island for a year; practised law in the firm of Gorman and Brown in Providence for a year and a half; came to Chicago with his classmate at Brown, Orville Peckham, and engaged with him in the general practise of law for thirty-one years, under the firm name of Peckham and Brown; was elected Judge of the Circuit Court, June 1, 1903 and appointed a Justice of the Appellate Court of Illinois for the First District in November, 1904, which position he still holds. He married Helen Gertrude Eagle June 25, 1884. Their children are:

481 EDWARD EAGLE,[9] born June 4, 1885. Harvard A. B. 1905, practices law in Chicago.
482 HELEN DALTON,[9] born Jan. 13, 1887; student in Bryn Mawr College, Class of 1909.
483 WALTER ELLIOTT,[9] born Aug. 11, 1888; student in U. S. Naval Academy, Class of 1910.
484 ROBERT OSGOOD,[9] born Feb. 13, 1890; student in University of Chicago, Class of 1910.
485 MARY WILMARTH,[9] born Sept. 15, 1891; student in Bryn Mawr College, Class of 1912.

401. HARRY APPLETON BROWN,[8] born in Lowell, Sept. 25, 1856 was educated in the public schools of Lowell, and spent two years at the Mass. Institute of Technology, studied law one year in the office of D. S. and G. F. Richardson in Lowell, and one year in the Boston University School of Law, taking the lectures of two years; was admitted to the bar in 1881, and still continues the practice of his profession. He married Mary Eugenia Sawyer, Oct. 6, 1887. Their child is:
486 BARBARA,[9] born Sept. 2, 1895.

407. CHARLES GARDINER BROWN,[8] born Jan. 8, 1853, married Susan M. Peatfield, daughter of Joseph and Caroline (Heard) Peatfield, May 10, 1877. Mr. Brown inherited and occupies the Moses Kinsman farm[1] on the Essex Road. Their children are:
487 MARION GARDINER,[9] born Aug. 14, 1881, married Chester L. Harvey of Essex, Oct. 16, 1901. They live in Essex.
488 JESSE APPLETON,[9] born Nov. 14, 1883.

408. ALVIN STORY BROWN,[8] born Nov. 27, 1855, married Ella Thurston, daughter of Timothy and Rebecca (Morley) Thurston, May 10, 1879. Mr. Brown inherited and occupies the ancestral farm on the Candlewood road.[2] Their children are:

[1] Pages 14, 15.
[2] Page 28.

489   EMMA APPLETON,⁹ born Jan. 27, 1880; married Chester A. Bolles, Nov. 25, 1908.
490   ELSIE FRANCIS,⁹ born Dec. 15, 1882; married Charles F. Scotton, June 8, 1904.
491   RUTH STORY,⁹ born Sept. 23, 1887.

416.   ASA R. BROWN,⁸ born 1853, married Lottie A. Joyce, June 2, 1895. He died in Ipswich, Nov. 28, 1906, aged 43 years 5 months. Their children are:
492   GRACIE M.,⁹ born Aug. 27, 1895; died Aug. 21, 1896.
493   FREDERICK,⁹ born Aug. 21, 1897.
494   ELMER,⁹ born June 11, 1899.
495   ETHEL EUNICE,⁹ born Sept. 27, 1900.
496   WARREN,⁹ born Sept. 8, 1902.
497   WALTER,⁹ born Sept. 5, 1903.

431.   BENJAMIN BROWN,⁸ born Nov., 1837, married Rebecca W. Baker, Dec. 12, 1858. He died Aug. 10, 1888, aged 50 years 9 months; his widow, Feb. 15, 1896, aged 65 years. Their children were:
498   NELLY COGSWELL,⁹ born Jan. 26, 1859.
499   ANNIE GERTRUDE,⁹ born July 8, 1861.

They both make their home in Ipswich, unmarried.

432.   EDWIN BROWN,⁸ born Oct. 12, 1844, married Emma F. Green of Brooklyn, N. Y. on June 4, 1868. They live in Boston. Their child is:
500   GRACE C.,⁹ born Oct. 31, 1878.

434.   GEORGE ALLEN BROWN,⁸ born in Ipswich, April 12, 1838, married Catherine Houlden of Nottingham, England, June 24, 1874. Their children are:
501   AGNES H.,⁹ born Dec. 3, 1877; married Charles W. Woodbury, May 8, 1898.
502   MAUD A.,⁹ born Mar. 30, 1885; died April 22, 1885.
503   WALTER HARLAND,⁹ born Sept. 18, 1888.

435.   JESSE FRANKLIN BROWN,⁸ born in Ipswich, Nov. 22, 1840, married 1st, Rebecca P. Kenney of Salem, Oct. 5, 1865. She was born Sept. 6, 1847 and died Nov. 10, 1881. Their children are:
504   GEORGE FRANKLIN,⁹ born in Ipswich, Aug. 15, 1866. See No. 504.
505   CHARLES DAVIS,⁹ born in Ipswich, July 28, 1868; married Sarah Steeves of Moncton, N. B.; died June 19, 1903.
506   MINNIE APPLETON,⁹ born in Lawrence, Mar. 6, 1872.
507   JESSIE REBECCA,⁹ born in Lawrence, Mar. 16, 1878.

He married 2d, on April 6, 1883, Emma J. Wing, who was born in Salem, Jan. 4, 1844 and died in Lawrence, Feb. 25, 1884. His third marriage on Aug. 14, 1884, was with Sarah H. Sproul, born in Wilmot, N. S. Jan. 15, 1851. Mr. Brown is an official in the County Jail in Lawrence.

436. WALTER BROWN,[8] born in Ipswich, March 19, 1843, married 1st Evelyn A. Kimball, Dec. 24, 1866, who died March 6, 1881. Their home is in Georgetown, Mass. Their children are:

508   EUNICE ANNA,[9] born Nov. 21, 1867.
509   GRACE E.,[9] born June 17, 1870.
510   CHARLES HENRY,[9] born Feb. 19, 1874. See No. 510.

He married 2d, Sarah B. Lord, daughter of Jeremiah and Sarah (Baker, Lord, Oct. 15, 1885.

440. HENRY HOWARD BROWN,[8] born in Ipswich, Nov. 7, 1859, married Philena Margaret Mooney, Sept. 24, 1891. Their home is in Rowley Mass. Their children are:

511   ELMER HOWARD,[9] born Aug. 18, 1893.
512   FRED DAVIS,[9] born Oct. 15, 1895.
513   ESTHER ELIZABETH,[9] born Oct. 30, 1897.

441b. DR. DANIEL R. BROWN,[9] born Oct. 28, 1856, a physician in Salem, Mass., married Mary Paul, June 25, 1890. Their children are:

514   ROLLINS,[10] born April 16, 1891.
515   PAUL HARRINGTON,[10] born Nov. 17, 1892.
516   OLIVE,[10] born May 9, 1895.

444. WILLARD EUGENE BROWN,[9] born in Wenham, Mass., Dec. 31, 1870, married Edith May Garrette, June 23, 1897. Their home is in George town. Their child is:

517   ALICE GARRETTE,[10] born July 16, 1898.

445. FRANK W. BROWN,[9] born in Lynn, Nov. 12, 1859, married Nellie M. Thissell, Nov. 24, 1883, in Lynn, where they reside. Their children are:

518   WALLACE,[10] born Dec. 6, 1884.
519   ETHEL MAY,[10] born Dec. 5, 1886.
520   HERBERT LEO,[10] born Feb. 21, 1890.

446. HENRY N. BROWN,[9] born in Lynn, Nov. 12, 1859, married Alice A. Hartford, July 4, 1893. Their home is in Berwick, Maine. Their child is:

521   LURA M.,[10] born Aug. 23, 1894.

451. PORTER DODGE BROWN,[9] born in Salem, Feb. 11, 1872, married Fannie Maynard Davis, Sept. 19, 1899. They live in Danvers, Mass. Their children are:

522   MARGARET,[10] born June 3, 1901; died Dec. 24, 1901.
523   FRANCES,[10] born Feb. 7, 1903.
524   MAYNARD AUGUSTUS,[10] born Dec. 30, 1904.

453. HORACE MANSFIELD BROWN,[9] born in Salem, Sept. 3, 1876, married Vinnie Baker Hartshorn, Oct. 4, 1905. Their home is in Salem. Their children are:

   525 AUGUSTA BAKER,[10] born Feb. 23, 1808; died Feb. 24, 1908.
   526 EUGENE CLARK,[10] born April 1, 1909.

455. THEODORE PARKER BROWN,[9] born in Marblehead, Sept. 3, 1845 married Hannah Hammond Flynn, July 8, 1869; died Feb. 8, 1898, in Marblehead, where he always made his home. Their children were:

   526a EDWARD GLOVER,[10] born July 23, 1869; married Jennie Glover Swasey, Sept. 28, 1896. They live in Marblehead; have no children.
   526b MABEL CROWNINSHIELD,[10] born Sept. 27, 1871; married Herbert A. Harris, Nov. 12, 1891.
   526c FANNIE DIXEY,[10] born 1874; died April 11, 1876, aged 2 years 4 months 20 days.
   526d BESSIE PARKER,[10] born April 2, 1876; married Frank Randolph Washburn, May, 1904. They live in New Rochelle, N. Y.
   526e THEODORE PARKER,[10] born July 31, 1878; lives in New York unmarried.
   526f WILLIAM BLANCHARD,[10] born Dec. 6, 1881; lives in New Rochelle, N. Y., unmarried.
   526g JENNIE STACEY,[10] born April 29, 1883; married Joseph Matthias March 30, 1904. They live in Melrose.
   526h ROBERT INGERSOLL,[10] born May 3, 1884; died Nov. 16, 1894.
   526i CHARLES SEWALL,[10] born Oct. 31, 1887; died Feb. 21, 1889.

460. HENRY BROWN,[9] born in Lynn, Nov. 26, 1847, married at Providence, Ellen M. Hawkins, daughter of Albert L. and Fannie M. Hawkins, Aug. 22, 1871. He was engaged in business in Providence, 1865–1870, when he entered the employ of H. C. Cook in Boston and became foreign buyer in 1872. In 1880, he became proprietor of the business. Their home was in Melrose but later in Ipswich. Their children, all born in Melrose, are:

   527 HENRY HOWARD.[10] born August 4, 1872; married at Melrose, Emma Louise Linnell of Melrose, Dec. 17, 1894. They have no children.
   528 FRANK WARNER,[10] born Nov. 29, 1873. See No. 528.
   529 MAUD ETHEL,[10] born Aug. 7, 1875.
   530 ROBERT,[10] born Jan. 19, 1877. See No. 530.
   531 KARL,[10] born Sept. 22, 1879. See No. 531.
   532 WILLIAM OSCAR,[10] born Feb. 23, 1881; died Dec. 10, 1883.
   533 SON unnamed,[10] born May 1, 1885; died Sept. 10, 1885.
   534 HOPE CATHERINE,[10] born April 17, 1887.
   535 KENNETH POTTER,[10] born June 5, 1889.

461. FREDERICK WARNER BROWN,[9] born in Marblehead, December 9, 1853, married Caroline Maria Gould, daughter of James Lewis and Helen Maria (Gregory) Gould of Bridgeport, Conn., at Bridgeport, Nov. 1, 1877. Their home is in Melrose, Mass. Their children are:

536   HELEN GOULD,[10] born in Melrose, Aug. 6, 1882; married Oswyn T. Bourdon at Melrose, April 5, 1905.
537   CATHERINE WARNER,[10] born Feb. 22, 1887; married at Melrose, Jonathan Thatcher Sears, Aug. 3, 1907.
538   DORIS GERRY,[10] born April 4, 1889.

464. AUGUSTUS MAGOUN BROWN,[9] born in Marblehead, Sept 10, 1865, married Laura Belle Snelling, April 26, 1900. They live in Melrose, Mass. Their children are:

538a   OLIVER BLANCHFIELD,[10] born March 27, 1901.
538b   REGINALD,[10] born Nov. 10, 1902.
538c   FANNIE,[10] born July 21, 1904.

476. DANIEL CHOATE BROWN JR.,[9] born in Marblehead, Nov. 5, 1864, married Elizabeth M. Chamberlain, Dec. 4, 1890. Their child is:

539   HARRY C.,[10] born May 19, 1891.

504. GEORGE FRANKLIN BROWN,[9] born in Ipswich, Aug. 15, 1866, married Helen Kunert of Lawrence, June 28, 1894. Their home is in Lawrence. Their child is:

540   HAROLD KUNERT,[10] born May 20, 1896.

510. CHARLES HENRY BROWN,[9] born Feb. 19, 1874, married Emma J. Bergereon, Oct. 2, 1899. Their children are:

541   RUTH A.,[10] born Sept. 5, 1900.
542   BERNARD C.,[10] born Aug. 29, 1902.

528. FRANK WARNER BROWN,[10] born in Melrose, Nov. 29, 1873 married Violet Hamlin Kinnear at Sussex, N. B., Sept. 16, 1901. They removed to Trinidad, Colorado, where they still reside. Their children are:

543   CARL HAMLIN,[11] born Nov. 19, 1902.
544   MARGERY WARNER,[11] born July 18, 1905.

530. ROREBT BROWN,[10] born in Melrose, Jan. 19, 1877, married at Ipswich, Susan Lord Kimball, Aug. 12, 1902. They live in Ipswich. Their child is:

545   MARGARET,[11] born June 11, 1909.

531. KARL BROWN,[10] born in Melrose, Sept. 22, 1879, married at Ipswich, Marion Willard Olive, June 3, 1907. Their child is:

546   THEODORE CLINTON,[11] born in Chelsea, April 21, 1908.

INDEX

Abbe, Joseph, original lot, 16.
Adams, Ephraim, married Lydia Kinsman[5] (43), 1749, 58.
Adams, Joseph, married Dorothy Kinsman[6] (91), 1774, 61.
Adams, Margaret, married George Fellows[6] (134), 85.
Alford, William, married Lydia Fellows[5] (73), 1765, 76.
Allen, Louisa J., married Winthrop Brown[7] (249), 1835, 117.
Allexia, Angeline, married Elnathan D. Brown[9] (442), 1874, 120.
Amory, Jonathan, Jr., married Lydia Fellows[6] (105), 1794, 78.
Andrews, Ammi, married Mary Brown[6] (56), 97.
Andrews, Asa, bought farm, 1809, 3, 6, 9; 1815, 17.
Andrews, John, original grant, 33.
Andrews, Capt. John, married Sarah Kinsman[6] (90), 1766, 61.
Andrews, John Dudley, bought lot, 1815, 17.
Andrews, Martha, married Jeremiah Kinsman[6] (92), 1769, 65.
Andrews, Theodore, sold farm, 1835, 3; bought lots, 1842, 25, 28, 31.
Annable, John, original grant, 20.
Annable, John, Sen., bought Jacobs farm, 1701-2, 42.
Appleton, Daniel bought the Fellows farm, 46, 48, 49.
Appleton, Daniel W., inheritance, 49; bought Low's Island, 50.
Appleton, Ellen M., married Francis Brown[7] (245), 1839, 116.
Appleton, Eunice, married Ephraim Fellows[5] (77), 1778, 80.
Appleton, Joseph, bought Philemon Dane lot, 1742, 15.
Appleton, Margaret, married John Kinsman[5] (45), 1773, 61.
Appleton, Oliver, Jr., bought Jas. Burnham lot, 1823, 11; Ross farm, 1823, 39.
Appleton, Rebecca, married Joseph Brown, Jr.[6] (179), 1808, 110.
Appleton, Tristram, bought Ross farm, 1835, 39.
Appleton, William, married Sarah Kinsman[5] (49), 1764, 59.
Archibald, Sally, married Abner Brown[5] (94), 1809, 99.
Atwood, William, married Martha T. Brown[8] (427), 119.
Ayres, Aiden, married Elizabeth Fellows[6] (84), 77.
Ayres, Samuel, Sen., original lot, 16; bought Samuel Fellows farm, 1701, 40.

Bagley, Mrs. Thankful, married David Brown[6] (200), 1807, 113.
Bailey, Enoch, bought lot, 1892, 3.

Baker, Ann, married Capt. William Brown[6] (172), 109.
Baker, Chrisse, married Capt. Josiah Browne[6] (159), 1780, 109.
Baker, Dorcas, married Capt. William Brown[6] (172), 1810, 109.
Baker, Hannah, married Ammi Brown[6] (169), 1814, 109.
Baker, Mary, married Michael Brown[6] (170), 1802, 109.
Baker, Nabby, married Capt. Josiah Brown[5] (159), 1819, 108.
Baker, Rebecca W., married Benjamin Brown[8] (431), 1858, 124.
Baker, Samuel, interest in Argilla farm, 1749, 13.
Bancroft, Joseph, married Hannah P. Fellows[6] (90), 77.
Bartlett, Horace C., married Sarah E. Brown[8] (368), 1866, 116.
Bartlett, John P., married Hannah Kinsman[6] (111), 63.
Bemont, Susanna, married Jonathan Kinsman[5] (51), 1796, 62.
Bennett, John, Jr., married Sarah Fellows[4] (26). 1754, 73.
Bennett, Susanna, married Simon Brown[4] (44), 1734, 100.
Bergereon, Emma J., married Charles H. Brown[9] (510), 1899, 127.
Bird, Oliver W., married Clara R. Fellows[8] (228), 1860, 86.
Bishop, John, widow Sarah, son and heir of Thomas, 1670, 25.
Bishop, Sarah, wife of John, conveys title to Anthony Checkley, 1683, 25.
Bishop, Thomas, Sen., owned Howlett farm, 25.
Bishop, Thomas, Jr., inherited farm, 1670, 25.
Blake, widow Abigail, married Isaac Fellows[4] (34), 75.
Blanchard, Mrs. Julia, married Nathaniel Brown[7] (325), 1842, 119.
Blanchard, Mary, married Ephraim Brown[7] (238), 1825, 115.
Blanchfield, Hannah E., married John H. Brown[8] (359), 1852, 121.
Blaney, Aaron, Jr., married Betsey Kinsman[6] (103), 63.
Blatchford, Stephen, married Nancy Kinsman[8] (161), 1834, 67.
Bliss, George S., married Mary G. Brown[9] (465), 1903, 122.
Blois, H. Maud, married Frederick W. Fellows[8] (251), 1902, 87.
Boardman, Boareman, Boreman, Borm, Abigail, married Nathan Brown[5] (65), 1776, 101.
Boardman, Elizabeth, married Ephraim Brown[6] (161), 1791, 108.
Boardman, Hannah, inheritance, 1794, 38.

(129)

INDEX

Boardman, Jacob, married widow Martha Rogers, conveyance, 1714, 7.
Boardman, Joanna, married Isaac Fellows² (2), 1672, 72.
Boardman, Capt. John, bought Fellows farm, 1747, 34.
Boardman, John, son and heir of Capt. John, 1760, 34.
Boardman, John How, bought lots, 1796, 30; 1811, 19; family, 34, 35.
Boardman, Joseph, bought Thornton lot, 1796, 30; family, 34, 35.
Boardman, Mary, married Robert Kinsman² (2), 22, 55.
Boardman, Mary, daughter of Capt. John, 1760, 34; married James Kinsman⁵ (46), 1760, 62.
Boardman, Sarah, daughter of Capt. John, 1760, 34; married Abraham Brown⁵ (67), 1780, 102.
Boardman, Stephen, married Martha Kinsman⁶ (98), 1791, 62.
Boardman, Thomas, married Hannah Brown⁵ (63), 98; lands, 18, 29, 34; wife Elizabeth, 35.
Boardman, Capt. Winthrop, married¹ Abigail E. Kinsman⁶ (126), 1821; married² Elizabeth Kinsman⁶ (123), 1824, 64; lands, 30, 35.
Bolles, Chester A., married Emma A. Brown⁹ (489), 1908, 124.
Bolles, Robert W., bought lot, 1888, 9.
Bowdon, Oswyn T., married Helen G. Brown¹⁰ (536), 1905, 127.
Bowden, Anne S., married Gerry Brown⁸ (362), 1863, 121.
Bowles, Reuben, married Lucy Brown⁵ (112), 1773, 101.
Bradley, David W., married Elizabeth Fellows⁶ (93), 1788, 78.
Bragg, Abiel, son and heir of Timothy, 1709, 10.
Bragg, Ebenezer, quitclaim, 1723–4, 11.
Bragg, Edward, bought lot of Thomas Firman, 1647, 40; other lots, his will, 10.
Bragg, Edward, of Andover, quitclaim, 1723–4, 11.
Bragg, John, son and heir of Edward, 1709, 10.
Bragg, Nathaniel, quitclaim, 1723–4, 11.
Bragg, Samuel, bought farm, 1773, 6.
Bragg, Timothy, son and heir of Edward, house, 1693; sons, 10.
Bragg, Timothy, Jr., 10, 11; married Elizabeth Low, 8.
Bragg's Hill, 1743, 16.
Bray, Azor, married Sally P. Brown⁷ (271), 1836, 110.
Bridge over Mile River, 1658, 41.
Bridge, Francis H., married Mary B. Brown⁸ (367), 1854, 115.
Brooks, Noah, married Caroline A. Fellows⁷ (206), 1856, 85.
Brown, Aaron⁵ (80), 1741, 99.
Brown, Aaron F.⁷ (269), married Nabby B. Brown, 1839, 118.
Brown, Abby⁷ (222b), 108.
Brown, Abby A.⁸ (421), 1829, 119.
Brown, Abel⁵ (55), 1737, 97; heir of estate, 1759, 38.
Brown, Abel⁶ (201a), 1777, 106.
Brown, Abigail⁶ (131), 1781, 102.
Brown, Abigail⁷ (213), 1816, 107.
Brown, Abigail B.⁷ (327), married William Hammond, 1838, 113.
Brown, Abigail C.⁷ (299), 1819, 112.
Brown, Abigail G.⁶ (146), 1807, 102; 1834, 39.

Brown, Abigail P.⁸ (410), 1843, 118.
Brown, Abner⁵ (94), 12; married Sally Archibald, 1809, 99.
Brown, Abraham⁵ (67); married Sarah Boardman, 1780, 102; land, 16, 17, 38.
Brown, Abraham⁸ (149d), 1785, 103.
Brown, Adam⁴ (48), 1721, 97.
Brown, Addison⁷ (279), 1832, 111.
Brown, Agnes H.⁹ (501), married Charles W. Woodbury, 1898, 124.
Brown, Alice G.¹⁰ (517), 1898, 125.
Brown, Allen⁶ (125), 1780, 101.
Brown, A. Story⁸ (408), married Ella Thurston, 1879, 123; farm, 14, 24, 25, 28, 32.
Brown, Ammi⁶ (169), married Hannah Baker, 1814, 109; bought lot, 1818, 12, 13.
Brown, Ammi⁶ (211h), married Sarah Fellows⁶ (119), 1798, 79, 107.
Brown, Ammi⁷ (259), 110.
Brown, Ann B.⁷ (247), married Warren Kimball, 1835, 109.
Brown, Ann M.⁸ (424), married Laban F. Cushing, 1854, 119.
Brown, Anna, married William Kinsman⁶ (93), 1773, 65.
Brown, Anna⁶ (211a), 1798, 106.
Brown, Anna⁶ (211j), married Ebenezer Goodhue, 1806, 107.
Brown, Anne⁵ (99), 1752, 100.
Brown, Annie B.⁸ (382), 1847, 116.
Brown, Annie G.⁹ (499), 1861, 124.
Brown, Arthur H.⁸ (385), 1856, 116.
Brown, Asa⁶ (164), 1771, 103.
Brown, Asa⁷ (233), 1800, 108.
Brown, Asa⁷ (239), 1797, 109; bought lots, 3, 12, 18, 30.
Brown, Asa⁸ (345), married Olive E. Rollins, 120.
Brown, Asa B.⁸ (416), married Lottie A. Joyce, 1895, 124.
Brown, Augusta B.¹⁰ (525), 1808, 126.
Brown, Augustine⁸ (370), married Susan M. Russell, 1871, 122.
Brown, Augustus⁸ (355), married Helen F. Smith, 1869, 121.
Brown, Augustus M.⁹ (464), married Laura B. Snelling, 1900, 127.
Brown, Barbara⁹ (486), 1895, 123.
Brown, Benjamin³ (20a), 95.
Brown, Benjamin⁴ (30), married Sarah Brown, 1736 99; blacksmith, owned lands, 12, 13, 14, 18, 24, 28.
Brown, Benjamin⁵ (87), married Martha Roberts, 1762, 105; called 3d, owned lands, 17, 18, 24.
Brown, Benjamin, Jr.⁶ (193), married Hannah Woodbury, 1792, 112; Tailor, bought lot, 1797, 10.
Brown, Benjamin⁷ (313), 112.
Brown, Benjamin⁸ (431), married Rebecca W. Baker, 1858, 124.
Brown, Bernard C.¹⁰ (542), 1902 127.
Brown, Bertha A.⁹ (448), married John L. Russell, 1896, 121.
Brown, Bertha E.⁸ (339), 1901, 114.
Brown, Bessie⁹ (464a), married Dr. Carolus M. Cobb, 1897, 121.
Brown, Bessie P.¹⁰ (526d), married Frank R. Washburn, 1904, 126.
Brown, Betsey (Elizabeth)⁶ (203), married Isaac Hacket, 1801, 106.
Brown, Betsey G.⁷ (322), 1823, 113.
Brown, Betty⁶ (211e), married William Poland, 1781, 106.
Brown, Beulah C.⁷ (302), 1826, 112.

Brown, Blanche R.⁹ (472), married John W. Goodhue, 1897, 122.
Brown, Carl H.¹¹ (543), 1902, 127.
Brown, Caroline⁷ (324), married Nathan Chapman, 1833, 113; sold lot, 19.
Brown, Caroline⁸ (412), married J. Farley Kinsman⁸ (175), 1873, 68, 118.
Brown, Caroline⁹ (456), 1847, 121.
Brown, Caroline A.⁹ (480), 1889, 122.
Brown, Caroline C.⁷ (286), 1833, 111.
Brown, Catherine W.¹⁰ (537), married Jonathan T. Sears, 1907, 127.
Brown, Charles⁵ (191), married Beulah C. Burns, 1814, 112.
Brown, Charles⁷ (300), 1822, 112.
Brown, Charles⁸ (346), married Mary A. Woodbridge, 120.
Brown, Charles⁸ (430), 1834, 119.
Brown, Charles A.⁸ (415), 1860, 118.
Brown, Charles D.⁹ (505), married Sarah Steeves, 124.
Brown, Charles E.⁸ (433), 1854, 119.
Brown, Charles F.⁷ (277), 1828, 111.
Brown, Charles G.⁸ (407), married Susan M. Peatfield, 1877, 123.
Brown, Charles H.⁹ (510), married Emma J, Bergereon, 1899, 127.
Brown, Charles H., Jr., married Edith W. Brown⁹ (471), 1907, 122.
Brown, Charles S.¹⁰ (526i), 1887, 126.
Brown, Charlotte⁶ (211), married Alexander Meady, 1811, 106.
Brown, Charlotte⁷ (335), married James R. Grant, 114.
Brown, Charlotte, wife of Elisha, conveyance from Winthrop Low, 1851, 33.
Brown, Charlotte A.⁸ (352), married Alvin Story, 1877, 115.
Brown, Clarence E.⁷ (222), married Alice L. Low, 1881, 114.
Brown, Clarissa⁶ (140), 1796, 39, 102.
Brown, Daniel⁴ (24), 95.
Brown, Daniel⁶ (165), married Rhoda Brown (129), 1801, 109; owned lands, 24, 28, 31, 32.
Brown, Daniel, Jr.⁷ (243), married Jemima (223), 1825, 116.
Brown, Daniel C.⁸ (377), married Elizabeth S. Harris, 1855, 122.
Brown, Daniel C., Jr.⁹ (475), 1861, 122.
Brown, Daniel C., Jr.⁹ (476), married Elizabeth M. Chamberlain, 1890, 127.
Brown, Dr. Daniel R.⁹ (441b), married Mary Paul, 1890, 125.
Brown, David⁵ (92), married Mary Potter, 1797, 106; inheritance, 1809, 24; bequest for school fund, 1822, 12, 14, 24.
Brown, David⁵ (110), married Ruth Story, 1772, 101.
Brown, David⁶ (200), married Mrs. Thankful Bagley, 1807, 113; inheritance, 18.
Brown, David⁷ (275), married Sarah C. Currier, 1846, 118, 22.
Brown, David⁷ (323), 1808, 113.
Brown, David A.⁷ (334), married¹ Mary L. Lakeman, 1845; married² Lucy Parsons, 120.
Brown, Dorcas B.⁷ (251), married James R. Newhall, 1840, 110.
Brown, Doris G.¹⁰ (538), 1889, 127.
Brown, Dorothy⁴ (29), married Caleb Burnam, 1731, 96.
Brown, Dorothy⁵ (97), 1744, 99.
Brown, Earl K. (337), 1885, 114.
Brown, Ebenezer⁵ (75), married Elizabeth Perkins, 1768, 103.
Brown, Ebenezer⁵ (150), 1769, 103.

Brown, Edith D.⁹ (479). 1887, 122.
Brown, Edith W.⁹ (471), married Charles H. Brown, Jr., 1907, 122.
Brown, Edward⁷ (256), married¹ Eliza O. Dalton, 1842; married² Jennie E. Taylor, 1859, 117.
Brown, Edward⁷ (280), married¹ Sarah E. Poor, 1858; married² Isabelle Coffin, 1876, 118.
Brown, Edward E.⁹ (481), 1885, 123.
Brown, Edward O.¹⁰ (526a), married Jennie G. Swasey, 1896, 126.
Brown, Edward O.⁸ (396), 1843, 117.
Brown, Edward O.⁸ (398), married Helen G. Eagle, 1884, 123.
Brown, Edward R.⁷ (287), married Annie M. Hood, 1866, 118.
Brown, Edwin⁸ (432), married Emma F. Green, 1868, 124.
Brown, Edmund⁷ (306), 112; quitclaim, 1838, 19.
Brown, Elbridge⁸ (363), married Caroline L. Mason, 1865, 122.
Brown, Elbridge G.⁹ (469), married¹ Marie C. Gardner, 1895; married² Florence E. Woodworth, 1903, 122.
Brown, Eliphalet⁷ (229), married Mrs. Martha P. Gay, 114.
Brown, Eliphalet⁸ (349), 1835, 114.
Brown, Elisha⁴ (28), married Lydia Brown, 1736, 99; widow Lydia, weaver, owned lands, 12, 13, 14, 24, 28, 31, 32.
Brown, Elisha, Jr.⁵ (78), married Elizabeth Roberts, 1759, 103; owned lands, 24, 28, 30, 31, 32.
Brown, Capt. Elisha⁶ (160), married Martha Brown⁶ (192), 1790, 108; owned lands, 22, 24, 33.
Brown, Elisha⁷ (230), married Charlotte Kinsman⁶ (131), 1840, 64, 65, 115; owned lands, 17, 19, 24, 31.
Brown, Elisha Newton⁸ (353), married Eliza A. Philbrook, 1871, 120; lands, 24, 30.
Brown, Eliza⁷ (235), 1804, 108.
Brown, Eliza⁷ (336), married John R. Norfolk, 1847, 114.
Brown, Eliza⁸ (354), married Charles P. Dodge, 1869, 115.
Brown, Eliza, widow of James, conveyance, 1871, 33.
Brown, Eliza H.⁸ (360), married Joseph H. Robinson, 1857, 115.
Brown, Eliza T.⁸ (423), married¹ Ariel P. Lee, 1848; married² —— Spooner, 119.
Brown, Elizabeth, daughter of John, the glazier, 1664, 92, 93.
Brown, Elizabeth,³ (13), 1694, 94.
Brown, Elizabeth³ (16), married William Hasey, 1702, 95.
Brown, Elizabeth⁴ (41), married Robert Perkins, 1753, 96, 27.
Brown, Elizabeth, married Jacob Brown⁸ (19), 1761, 96.
Brown, Elizabeth⁵ (60), 1740, 98.
Brown, Elizabeth⁵ (68), married Samuel Langdon, 1746, 98.
Brown, Elizabeth⁵ (83), 1748, 99.
Brown, Elizabeth⁵ (107), married Nathaniel Brown, 1758, 101.
Brown, Elizabeth⁶ (120), 1771, 101.
Brown, Elizabeth⁶ (132), married —— Hosmer, 102.
Brown, Elizabeth⁶ (144), married Capt. Joseph Gardiner, 102.
Brown, Elizabeth⁶ (153), 1775, 103.
Brown, Elizabeth⁶ (163), married John Raymond, 1791, 103.

Brown, Elizabeth[6] (174), married Silas Chamberlain, 1813, 104; conveyance, 1820 13.
Brown, Elizabeth[6] (178), 1780, 104.
Brown, Elizabeth[6] (184), married Thomas Brown, Jr., (241) 1839, 104.
Brown, Elizabeth[7] (218), 1831, 107.
Brown, Elizabeth[7] (240), married William Giddings, 1843, 109.
Brown, Elizabeth B.[8] (365), married Peregrine M. Burnham, 1847, 115.
Brown, Elizabeth B.[9] (457), 1849, 121.
Brown, Elizabeth C.[7] (252), 1816, 109.
Brown, Elizabeth F.[7] (274), married Joshua Lamson, 1841, 110.
Brown, Elizabeth G.[9] (466), 1870. 122.
Brown, Elizabeth M.[7] (330), married Samuel Lufkin, Jr., 113.
Brown, Elizabeth P.[6] (154), 1776, 103.
Brown, Elizabeth P.[7] (289), married[1] Alonzo Butler, 1834; married[2] William Poor, 1842, 111.
Brown, Elizabeth P.[8] (406), 1854, 117.
Brown, Ellen, married Nehemiah Brown[7] (260), 110.
Brown, Ellen[7] (281), married John C. Low, 1855, 111.
Brown, Ellen A.[8] (379), 1841, 116.
Brown, Elnathan D.[9] (442), married Angeline Allexia, 1874, 120.
Brown, Elsie F.[9] (490), married Charles F. Scotton, 1904, 124.
Brown, Elmer[9] (494), 1899, 124.
Brown, Elmer H.[9] (511), 1893, 125.
Brown, Emeline[7] (294), 1824, 112.
Brown, Emeline F.[7] (295), 1827, 112.
Brown, Emeline F.[7] (303), 1828, 112.
Brown, Emma A.[9] (489) married Chester A. Bolles, 1908, 124.
Brown, Ephraim, Jr.[6] (157), married Hannah Kinsman[5] (122), 1811, 64 107.
Brown, Ephraim[6] (161), married Elizabeth Boardman, 1791, 108; owned lands, 29, 30, 31, 32.
Brown, Ephraim[7] (222c), 108.
Brown, Ephraim[7] (238), married Mary Blanchard, 1825, 115.
Brown, Ephraim B.[8] (364), 1826, 115.
Brown, Esther A.[8] (437), married Moses S. Saunders, 1866, 120.
Brown, Esther E.[9] (513), 1897, 125.
Brown, Ethel E.[9] (495), 1900, 124.
Brown, Ethel L.[8] (338), 1889, 114.
Brown, Ethel M.[10] (519), 1886, 125.
Brown, Ethelyn W.[9] (473), 1874, 122.
Brown, Eugene C.[10] (526), 1909, 126.
Brown, Eunice[4] (40), married Timothy Thornton, 1761, 27, 96.
Brown, Eunice[5] (95), married Joseph Proctor, 1808, 99.
Brown, Eunice[6] (149g), 1758, 103.
Brown, Eunice[6] (156), married Joseph Kinsman[6] (119), 1809, 66, 103.
Brown, Eunice, wife of John Brown, inheritance, 31.
Brown, Eunice A.[7] (276), married Manasseh Brown, Jr. (227), 1845, 111.
Brown, Eunice A.[9] (508), 1867, 125.
Brown, Eva K.[9] (447), 1875, 121.
Brown, Everett K.[8] (351), married Margaretta Wilson, 1870, 115.
Brown, Fanny[6] (155), married Benjamin Patch, 3d, 1816, 103.
Brown, Fanny[9] (462), 1854, 121.
Brown, Fanny[9] (477), 1866, 122.
Brown, Fanny[10] (538c), 1904, 127.
Brown, Fanny D.[10] (526c), 1874, 126.

Brown, Frances[6] (141), married Stephen Staples, 1824, 102.
Brown, Frances[10] (523), 1903, 125.
Brown, Francis[4] (37), 1728, 96.
Brown, Francis[4] (38), 1741, 96, 27.
Brown, Francis[5] (85), married Judith Burnham, 1779, 105; land purchases, 11, 12, 14, 21.
Brown, Francis[5] (136), 1798, 102; conveyances, 39.
Brown, Francis[6] (187), 1781, 105.
Brown, Francis[7] (288), 1811, 111.
Brown, Francis[7] (298), 1817, 112.
Brown, Francis[7] (245), married Ellen M. Appleton, 1839, 116.
Brown, Francis[7] (311), married Sally Brown (315), 1830, 119; land purchases, 9, 18, 19.
Brown, Francis[9] (478), 1882, 122.
Brown, Francis A.[8] (380), 1842, 116.
Brown, Francis E.[7] (217), 1827, 107.
Brown, Francis P.[8] (429), 1832, 119.
Brown, Frank[8] (389), 117.
Brown, Frank A.[8] (384), married Caroline L. Pease, 1881, 122.
Brown, Frank H[9] (463), married Ellen T. Gardner, 1882, 121.
Brown, Frank W.[9] (445), married Nellie M. Thissell, 1883, 125.
Brown, Frank W.[10] (528), married Violet H. Kinnear, 1901, 127.
Brown, Frederick[8] (390), 117.
Brown, Frederick[9] (493), 1897, 124.
Brown, Frederick[9] (512), 1895, 125.
Brown, Frederick H.[8] (294), 120.
Brown, Frederick W.[9] (461), married Caroline M. Guild, 1877, 127.
Brown, Gardner A.[7] (268), married[1] Judith A. Perley, 1851; married[2] Leonora Abby Story, 1855, 118; land ownerships, 14, 15, 24, 25, 28, 32.
Brown, George[6] (208), married[1] Lucy Meady, 1807; married[2] Esther A. Saunders, 1813, 208.
Brown, George[7] (250), 109.
Brown, George, Jr.[7] (328), married Eunice A. Tucker, 1836, 120.
Brown, George A.[8] (434), married Catherine Houlden, 1874, 124.
Brown, George F.[9] (504), married Helen Kunert, 1894, 127.
Brown, George M.[9] (467), 1867, 122.
Brown, George W.[7] (278), married Thankful Burnham, 1856, 111; land, 15.
Brown, George W.[9] (443), 1856, 120.
Brown, Gerry[8] (362), married Anne S. Burden, 1863, 121.
Brown, Grace C.[9] (500), 1878, 124.
Brown, Grace E.[9] (509), 1870, 125.
Brown, Grace M.[9] (492), 1895, 124.
Brown, Hannah[3] (18), married Edward Cogswell, 1708, 95.
Brown, Hannah[5] (63), married Thomas Boardman, 98.
Brown, Hannah[5] (90), 1748, 99.
Brown, Hannah[5] (91), married Joseph Proctor, 1773, 99.
Brown, Hannah[5] (108), 1741, 101.
Brown, Hannah[6] (127), 1786, 101.
Brown, Hannah[6] (138), 1793, 102.
Brown, Hannah[6] (211f), married Nathan Fellows[6] (79), 1785. 81, 106.
Brown, Hannah[7] (222a), 108.
Brown, Hannah[7] (314), 112.
Brown, Hannah[7] (320), 1813, 113.
Brown, Hannah B.[7] (296), married Theodore F. Cogswell, 1853. 112.
Brown, Hannah N.[7] (245a), 109.

INDEX 133

Brown, Hannah N.[7] (246), married John H. Harris, Jr., 1828, 109.
Brown, Harold K.[10] (540), 1896, 127.
Brown, Harriet[6] (211b), 1798; married —— Webb, 106.
Brown, Harry A.[8] (401), married Mary E. Sawyer, 1887, 123.
Brown, Harry C.[10] (539), 1891, 127.
Brown, Harry W.[9] (468), 1868, 122.
Brown, Helen A.[9] (454), 1878, 121.
Brown, Helen D.[9] (482), 1887, 123.
Brown, Helen G.[10] (536), married Oswyn T. Bourdon, 1905, 127.
Brown, Henry[9] (460), married Ellen M. Hawkins, 1871, 126.
Brown, Henry H.[8] (440), married Philena M. Mooney, 1891, 125.
Brown, Henry H.[10] (527), married Emma L. Linnell, 1894, 126.
Brown, Henry N.[9] (446), married Alice A. Hartford, 1893, 125.
Brown, Henry S.[8] (386), 1858, 116.
Brown, Hepzibah[8] (57), married Nathaniel Brown, 1768, 97.; inheritance, 38.
Brown, Hepzibah[6] (198a), 1770, 105.
Brown, Herbert L.[10] (520), 1890, 125.
Brown, Hope C.[10] (534), 1887, 126.
Brown, Horace[8] (371), 1844, 116.
Brown, Horace M.[9] (453), married Vinnie B. Hartshorn, 1905, 126.
Brown, Increase H.[7] (237), married[1] Eliza Harris, 1820; married[2] Mary W. Gerry, 1830, 115; land, 3, 6, 18.
Brown, Increase H., Jr.[8] (358), married[1] Catherine T. Green; married[2] Mary K. Gregory, 1860, 121.
Brown, Isaac[6] (151), 1770, 103.
Brown, Isaac[6] (183), married Lydia Smith, 1825, 111.
Brown, Isaac[7] (312), 112.
Brown, Israel[6] (124), 1777, 101.
Brown, Israel G.[7] (319), 1811, 113.
Brown, Jacob[3] (19), married[1] Sarah Burnham, 1707; married[2] Mary Dane, 1735; married[3] Elizabeth Brown, 1761, 96.
Brown, Jacob[4] (43), 96.
Brown, Jacob[5] (105), 100.
Brown, James[3] (8), married Sarah Cogswell, 1723, 96; land, 26, 30, 31, 93, 94.
Brown, James[3] (20), married Mehitable Pengry, 1707, 97.
Brown, James[4] (34), 1724, 96.
Brown, James[4] (49), married[1] Lydia Dane, 1746; married[2] Sarah Lampson, 1751, 101.
Brown, James[4] (52), 1715, 97.
Brown, James[5] (59), 1739, 98.
Brown, James[5] (77), married Jemima Kinsman, 1782, 103; land, 29, 33.
Brown, James[5] (100), 1750, 100.
Brown, James[5] (118), 1753, 101.
Brown, James, Jr.[6] (181), married Lucy Fellows[6] (132), 1812, 80, 110; land, 15, 22, 24.
Brown, James[7] (225), married Eliza ——, 108; land, 29, 33.
Brown, James F.[7] (277), 1828, 111.
Brown, Jeannie M., married Joseph E. Fellows[8] (246), 1908, 87.
Brown, Jemima P.[7] (223), married Daniel Brown, Jr. (243), 1825, 108.
Brown, Jennie S.[10] (526g), married Joseph Matthias, 1904, 126.
Brown, Jennie T.[8] (399), married James W. Greig, 1890, 117.
Brown, Jeremiah[5] (62), married Lucy Potter, 1770, 101; inheritance 38.

Brown, Jeremiah[6] (121), 1772, 101.
Brown, Jesse A.[8] (409), 1858, 118.
Brown, Jesse A.[9] (488), 1883, 123.
Brown, Jesse E.[8], 107.
Brown, Jesse F.[8] (435), married[1] Rebecca P. Kenney, 1865, 124; married[2] Emma I. Wing, 1883; married[3] Sarah H. Sproul, 1884, 125.
Brown, Jessie R.[9] (507), 1878, 124.
Brown, Joanna, married Nathaniel Kinsman[6] (128), 1828, 66.
Brown, John, farm; original grant, 36; Sen., owned lot in Heartbreak Road, 1660, 4; genealogy of, inventory, 89.
Brown, John, the glazier, widow Mary, 92, 93.
Brown, John, son of John, glazier, 92.
Brown, John[2] (2), wife[1] Hannah, 1684; wife[2] Elizabeth, 1707; wife[3] Hannah 92, 93, 94; land, 26, 37, 40
Brown, John[3] (14), 1674, 95.
Brown, John, Jr.[3] (6), 1678, married Mary Fellows[3] (20), 1712, 73, 94, 95, 96; land, 17, 18, 19, 37, 38, 44.
Brown, John, 3d[4] (20b), married Mary Fitts, 1724, 97; carpenter, lands, will, 17, 18.
Brown, John[4] (45), 1715, 97.
Brown, John[5] (58), 1745, 97.
Brown, John[5] (66), married Hannah Proctor, 1789, 102; lands, 38, 39.
Brown, John[5] (89) 1746, 99.
Brown, John[5] (109), of Bow, N. H., 101.
Brown, John[6] (149), married Eunice Kinsman[7] (155), 1840, 66, 107, 31; homestead, 39.
Brown, John[6] (149e), 1788, 103.
Brown, John[6] (175), 1791, married Sophia Raymond, 104.
Brown, John[7] (254), 109.
Brown, John[7] (321), 1816, 113.
Brown, John, Jr.[7] (309), married Mary L. Caldwell, 1836, 119; quitclaim, 19
Brown, John A.[7] (293), 112; land, 11, 12.
Brown, John B.[6] (186), married[1] Elizabeth Potter, 1809; married[2] Mary Kinsman,[6] (62) 111; land, 11, 12.
Brown, John B.[7] (297), 1815, 112.
Brown, John B.[8] (342), 1850, 114.
Brown, John H.[7] (219), 1841, 107.
Brown, John H.[8] (359), married Hannah E. Blanchfield, 1852, 121.
Brown, John P.[6] (206), 1778, 106.
Brown, John P.[7] (319), 1818, 113.
Brown, John T.[8] (356), 1845, 115.
Brown, John W.[8] (441), 120.
Brown, Jonathan, son of glazier, 1668, 92.
Brown, Jonathan[4] (35), 1726, 96.
Brown, Jonathan[4] (36), married Elizabeth Lakeman, 1748, 100, 27.
Brown, Jonathan[5] (93), 1752, 99.
Brown, Jonathan[5] (197), 1776, 105.
Brown, Jonathan[7] (234), married Lucy S. Kimball, 1836, 115.
Brown, Jonathan[7] (317), 1807, 113.
Brown, Jonathan[8] (348), married Martha B. Hatch, 1859, 120.
Brown, Joseph[4] (22), 95; land, 17, 38.
Brown, Joseph[4] (51), 1727, 97.
Brown, Joseph[5] (84), married[1] Elizabeth Perkins, 1778; married[2] Martha Perkins, 1806, 104; land, 13, 14, 24, 27, 28, 32.
Brown, Joseph, Jr.[6] (179), married Rebecca Appleton, 1808, 110; land, 14, 22, 24, 25, 28.
Brown, Joseph[8] (405), 1852, 117.

Brown, Joseph A.[7] (220), married S. Lizzie Burnham, 1877, 107; land, 39.
Brown, Joseph P.[7] (264), married Susan W. Lord, 1846, 117; land, 14, 28.
Brown, Joshua[6] (202), 1784, 106.
Brown, Josiah[6] (122), 1774, 101.
Brown, Capt. Josiah[6] (159), married[1] Chrisse Baker, 1780; married[2] Nabby Baker, 1819, 108; land, 28, 29, 30, 33.
Brown, Josiah[7] (224), 1809, 108.
Brown, Judith, widow of Francis, 12.
Brown, Judith[6] (149c), 1782, 103.
Brown, Judith[6] (188), married Richard Manning, 1819, 105.
Brown, Julia A.[8] (403), married Andrew C. Spring, 1868, 117.
Brown, Julius C.[9] (450), 1870, 121.
Brown, Karl[10] (531), married Marion W. Olive, 1907, 127.
Brown, Kate S.[8] (388), married John W. Philbrook, 1860, 117.
Brown, Katheryn L.[9] (449), married Curtis E. Lakeman, 1908, 121.
Brown, Kenneth P.[10] (535), 1889, 126.
Brown, Langley[6] (134), married Hannah Smith, 1811, 107; land, 22, 38, 39.
Brown, Levi[7] (307), married Susan Mears, 1826, 118; land, 9, 19.
Brown, Levi W.[8] (422), 1836, 119.
Brown, Lois[6] (139), 1795, 102, 39.
Brown, Lucinda[7] (304), 1831, 112.
Brown, Lucretia[7] (226), married Joel B. Stowe, 1838, 108.
Brown, Lucretia B.[8] (376), married James Potter, 1853, 116.
Brown, Lucy[4] (39), 1729, 96, 27.
Brown, Lucy[5] (69), married Samuel Potter, Jr., 1748, 98.
Brown, Lucy[5] (112), married Reuben Bowles, 1773, 101.
Brown, Lucy[6] (123), 1776, 101.
Brown, Lucy[6] (142) 1798, married Theodore Gibbs, 102.
Brown, Lucy[6] (166), married[1] Timothy Tibbets, 1796; married[2] Joseph Heard, 1810, 104.
Brown, Lucy[6] (180), 1785, 104.
Brown, Lucy[7] (199a), also called Lucia P., 18, 19, 105.
Brown, Lucy[7] (261), 1809, 110.
Brown, Lucy[7] (263), 1812, 110.
Brown, Lucy[7] (292), married Wilder J. Mellen, 1854, 112.
Brown, Lucy A.[8] (340), married Emery Lawrence, 1862, 114.
Brown, Lucy F.[8] (417), married Chas. F. Hatch, 1881, 118.
Brown, Lucy H.[8] (387), 1835, 116.
Brown, Lucy M.[7] (272), married Asa Rust, 1851, 110.
Brown, Lucy M.[7] (332), married John Sweet, 1834, 113.
Brown, Lucy O.[8] (397), 1845, 117.
Brown, Lucy S.[9] (452), 1874, 121.
Brown, Lura M.[13] (521), 1894, 125.
Brown, Lydia, married Elisha Brown,[4] (28), 1736, 98.
Brown, Lydia[5] (81), 1742, 99.
Brown, Lydia[5] (113), 1764, 101.
Brown, Lydia[5] (117), 1764, 101.
Brown, Lydia[6] (162), 1765, 103.
Brown, Lydia[8] (378), married Chas. B. Cogswell, 1857, 116.
Brown, Lydia H.[7] (214), 1818, 107.
Brown, Lydia H.[7] (216), married Josiah Lord, Jr., 1845, 107.
Brown, Lydia L. S.[7] (283) 1827, 111.

Brown, Mabel C.[10] (526b), married Herbert A. Harris, 1891, 126.
Brown, Manasseh[6] (158), 1785, 103.
Brown, Manasseh, Jr.[7] (227), married Eunice A. Brown (276), 1845, 114; land, 29, 30, 33.
Brown, Manasseh, married Mary K. Brown,[7] (291) 1836, 112.
Brown, Marah[5] (103), 1739, 100.
Brown, Margaret[10] (522), 1901, 125.
Brown, Margaret[11] (545) 1909, 127.
Brown, Margery W.[11] (544), 1905, 127.
Brown, Marion G.[9] (487), married Chester L. Harvey, 1901, 123.
Brown, Martha[2] (3), married Barnard Thorne, 92.
Brown, Martha[6] (192), married Capt. Elisha Brown (160), 1790, 105; quitclaim, 18.
Brown, Martha[7] (228), 1791, 108.
Brown, Martha[7] (316), 1805, 113.
Brown, Martha[8] (344), married Willard Goldthwait, 114.
Brown, Martha E. P.[7] (284), 1829, 111.
Brown, Martha P.[7] (270), married Hervey Whipple, 1835, 110.
Brown, Martha T.[8] (427), married William Atwood, 119.
Brown, Mary, daughter of the glazier, 1682, 93.
Brown, Mary[3] (9), 1685, 94.
Brown, Mary[3] (11), married Samuel Choate, 1716, 93, 94.
Brown, Mary[3] (17), married John Hubbard, 1710, 95.
Brown, Mary[4] (21), married Moses Lufkin, 1733, 95.
Brown, Mary[5] (56), married Ammi Andrews, 97; inheritance, 38.
Brown, Mary[5] (96), married Jonathan Dodge, Jr., 1766, 99.
Brown, Mary[5] (119), married Moses Lufkin, Jr., 1780, 101.
Brown, Mary[6] (167), married John Patch, Jr., 1811, 104.
Brown, Mary[6] (190), 1787, 105; land, 11, 12.
Brown, Mary[6] (195), 1771, 105.
Brown, Mary[6] (211c), married Stephen Holt, 1803, 106.
Brown, Mary[8] (347), married —— Cole, 114.
Brown, Mary[9] (459), 1854, 121.
Brown, Mary A.[7] (326), married Levi T. Lincoln, 1852, 113.
Brown, Mary B.[8] (367), married Francis H. Bridge, 1854, 115.
Brown, Mary E.[7] (265), married Joseph Kinsman[7] (153), 1842, 68, 110.
Brown, Mary E.[8] (373), married John J. Sullivan, 1880, 116.
Brown, Mary E.[8] (402), 1862, 117.
Brown, Mary G.[8] (361), married Chas. W. Seymour, 1857, 115.
Brown, Mary G.[9] (465), married Geo. S. Bliss, 1903, 122.
Brown, Mary J.[6] (148), 1812, 102.
Brown, Mary J.[7] (301), 1824, 112.
Brown, Mary K.[7] (291), married Manasseh Brown, 1836, 112.
Brown, Mary P.[6] (185), married William F. Wade, 1841, 105.
Brown, Mary P.[7] (333), married Samue Lufkin, Jr., 114.
Brown, Mary P.[8] (438), married Chas. W. Davis, 120.
Brown, Mary W.[9] (485), 1891, 123.
Brown, Maud A.[9] (502), 1885, 124.

INDEX 135

Brown, Maud E.[10] (529), 1875, 126.
Brown, Maynard A.[10] (524), 1904, 125.
Brown, Mehitable[6] (74), married Job Giddings, 1757, 98.
Brown, Michael[6] (170), married Mary Baker, 1802, 109; inheritance, 13.
Brown, Michael[7] (251), 109.
Brown, Minnie A.[9] (506), 1872, 124.
Brown, Nabby G., married Aaron P. Brown,[7] (269) 1839, 118.
Brown, Nathan[4] (23), married Elizabeth Knowlton, 1737, 97; land, will, 38.
Brown, Nathan[5] (61), 98.
Brown, Nathan[5] (65), married Abigail Boardman, 1776, 101; land, will, 38, 39.
Brown, Nathan[5] (115), 1743, 101.
Brown, Nathan[5] (126), 1783, 101.
Brown, Nathan[6] (133), married Lydia Hood, 1814, 107; land, 3, 11, 38, 39.
Brown, Nathan[7] (212), 1814, 107.
Brown, Nathaniel[2] (5), married Judith Perkins, 1673, 92, 93, 94; land, 37.
Brown, Nathaniel[3] (12), 1690, 93, 94.
Brown, Nathaniel[3] (15), 1676, 95.
Brown, Nathaniel[4] (33), 1726, 96.
Brown, Nathaniel[4] (47), married Elizabeth Brown,[5] (107) 1758, 101.
Brown, Nathaniel[5] (88), married Hepzibah Brown (57), 1768, 105; land, 17, 18; will and division, 24.
Brown, Nathaniel[5] (102), 1737, 100.
Brown, Nathaniel[6] (199), 1772, 105.
Brown, Nathaniel[7] (325), married[1] Juliet Davis; married[2] Mrs. Julia Blanchard 1842; married[3] Sarah Jaquith, 1882, 119.
Brown, Nehemiah[4] (31), married Mary Tanor, 1743, 99.
Brown, Nehemiah[5] (82), married Mary Choate, 1771, 104; land, 13, 14, 22, 24.
Brown, Nehemiah[6] (168), 1774, 104.
Brown, Nehemiah[6] (176), married Susanna Smith, 1819, 110; land, 11, 13.
Brown, Nehemiah[7] (260), married Ellen Brown, 110.
Brown, Nelly C.[9] (498), 1859, 124.
Brown, Olive[10] (516), 1895, 125.
Brown, Oliver[7] (218a), 107.
Brown, Oliver B.[10] (538a), 190, 127.
Brown, Otis[8] (372), married Mary A. Leonard, 1873, 122.
Brown, Parker[6] (210), 1787, 106.
Brown, Parker[6] (196), married Ruth —— 1794, 113; land, 17, 18.
Brown, Parker[7] (318), 1809, 113.
Brown, Paul H.[10] (515), 1892, 125.
Brown, Pelatiah[5] (72), 1736, 98.
Brown, Percival H.[9] (470), married Anna M. Redfern, 1908, 122.
Brown, Perley[7] (308), married Betsey Tappan, 1827, 119; quitclaim, 1838, 19.
Brown, Perley[8] (425), 1833, 119.
Brown, Porter D.[9] (451), married Fannie M. Davis, 1899, 125.
Brown, Priscilla[5] (73), married Oliver Carter, Jr., 1762, 98.
Brown, Priscilla[6] (149b), 1782, 103.
Brown, Proctor K.[7] (221), 1852, 107.
Brown, Rebecca A.[7] (267), 1821, 110.
Brown, Rebecca C.[9] (458), 1851, 121.
Brown, Reginald[10] (538b), 1902, 127.
Brown, Relief[6] (143), married Solomon Sanborn, 1820, 102.
Brown, Rena M.[9] (474), 1883, 122.
Brown, Rhoda[5] (114), 1741, 101.
Brown, Rhoda[6] (129), married Daniel Brown, 102.
Brown, Rhoda[7] (242), married James Potter, 1830, 109.
Brown, Rhoda A.[8] (375), married Enoch Fuller, 1854, 116.
Brown, Richmond H.[8] (419), 1867, 118.
Brown, Robert[6] (205), 1776, 106.
Brown, Robert[10] (530), married Susan L. Kimball, 1902, 127.
Brown, Robert I.[10] (526h), 1884, 126.
Brown, Robert O.[9] (484), 1890, 123.
Brown, Rollins[10] (514), 1891, 125.
Brown, Rufus A.[8] (411), 1849, 118.
Brown, Ruth[5] (53), 1728, 97.
Brown, Ruth A.[10] (541), 1900, 127.
Brown, Ruth S.[9] (491), 1887, 124.
Brown, Sally[6] (173), married Daniel Witham, 1805, 104.
Brown, Sally[6] (204), 1774, 106.
Brown, Sally[7] (315), married Francis Brown (311), 1830, 113.
Brown, Sally P.[7] (271), married Azor Bray, 1836, 110.
Brown, Samuel[5] (54), 97; land, 18, 38.
Brown, Samuel[6] (145), married Eliza Saville, 1829, 107.
Brown, Samuel[6] (189), 1785, 105.
Brown, Samuel[7] (244), 109.
Brown, Samuel[7] (305), 1834, 112.
Brown, Samuel A.[7] (262), married Sarah Butler, 1852, 117.
Brown, Samuel A.[8] (404), 1848, 117.
Brown, Samuel H.[7] (215), 1820, 107.
Brown, Samuel N.[7] (258), 1821, 110.
Brown, Samuel P.[6] (137), 1791, 102.
Brown, Sarah, daughter of John the glazier, 1670, 92.
Brown, Sarah, married Benjamin Brown[4] (30), 1736, 99.
Brown, Sarah[2] (4), married Thomas Jacobs, 1671, 92.
Brown, Sarah[3] (10), married John Cogswell, 1708, 93, 94.
Brown, Sarah[4] (25), 95; inheritance, 1759, 38.
Brown, Sarah[4] (42), 96; inheritance, 1741, 27.
Brown, Sarah,[5] (86) 1737, 99.
Brown, Sarah[5] (106), married —— Lufkin, 101.
Brown, Sarah[5] (116), 1764, 101.
Brown, Sarah[6] (147), married Nathan Burnham, Jr., 1834, 102.
Brown, Sarah[6] (149f), 1798, 103.
Brown, Sarah[6] (198), 1780, 105; land, 18.
Brown, Sarah[6] (211i), married William Kinsman[7] (144), 1802, 66, 107.
Brown, Sarah[6] married John M. Cook, 99.
Brown, Sarah[7] (280), 1807, 108.
Brown, Sarah[7] (310), married John R. Lakeman, 1820, 112.
Brown, Sarah A. M.[7] (285), 1831.
Brown, Sarah A.[8] (341), 1848, 114.
Brown, Sarah A.[8] (343), married John Hooper, Jr., 1880, 114.
Brown, Sarah E.[8] (368), married Horace C. Bartlett, 1866, 116.
Brown, Sarah H.[8] (383), 1849, 116.
Brown, Sarah N.[8] (135), 1793, 102.
Brown, Sarah N.[8] (400), 1854, 117.
Brown, Simon[4] (44), married[1] Susanna Bennett, 1734; married[2] Lydia Hooker, 1774, 100.
Brown, Simon, bought Fellows farm, 1845, 47.
Brown, Sophia[8] (374), married Albert Perry, 1853, 116.
Brown, Stephen[4] (32), married Ann Fellows, 1746, 100; land, 28, 31, 32.

Brown, Stephen[4] (50), 1725, 97.
Brown, Stephen[5] (98), married Elizabeth Potter, 1770, 106.
Brown, Stephen[5] (101), married Elizabeth Dodge, 1761, 106.
Brown, Stephen[5] (111), married Margaret Safford, 1780, 101.
Brown, Stephen[6] (207), married Rachel Meady, 1805, 106.
Brown, Stephen[6] (211d), 106.
Brown, Stephen C.[7] (248), married Mary L. S. Dodge, 1834, 116.
Brown, Susa[6] (211g), 1769, 107.
Brown, Susan[7] (331), 113.
Brown, Susan[8] (420), 119.
Brown, Susan A.[8] (418), 1868, 118.
Brown, Susan W.[8] (381), 1845, 116.
Brown, Susanna[5] (64), 1750, 98; inheritance, 1794, 38.
Brown, Susanna[5] (71), married Nehemiah Choate, 1775, 98.
Brown, Susanna[5] (104), 1739, 100.
Brown, Susanna[6] (130), 1778, 102.
Brown, Susanna[6] (201), married William Lakeman, 3d, 1797, 105.
Brown, Sylvester[8] (428), 1838, 119.
Brown, Theodore C.[11] (546), 1908, 127.
Brown, Theodore P.[9] (455), married Hannah H. Flynn, 1869, 126.
Brown, Theodore P.[10] (526e), 1878, 126.
Brown, Thomas[4] (27), 96; inheritance, 1753, 28.
Brown, Thomas[6] (194), 1768, 105; land 24.
Brown, Thomas, Jr.[7] (241), married Elizabeth Brown[6] (184), 1839, 116.
Brown, Thomas[8] (350), 1836, 114.
Brown, Thomas B.[7] (253), 1818, 109.
Brown, Wallace[10] (518), 1884, 125.
Brown, Walter[6] (209), married[1] Annis ———, married[2] Mrs. Lucy Post, 1808, 114.
Brown, Walter[8] (436), married[2] Evelyn A. Kimball, 1836; married[2] Sarah B. Lord, 1885, 125.
Brown, Walter[9] (497), 1903, 124.
Brown, Walter E.[9] (483), 1888, 123.
Brown, Walter H.[9] (503), 1888, 124.
Brown, Warren[8] (369), 1839, 116.
Brown, Warren[9] (496), 1902, 124.
Brown, Willard E.[9] (444), married Edith M. Garrette, 1897, 125.
Brown, William[3] (7), called Sergeant, married Dorothy Giddings, 1703, 95, 96; land, 21, 26, 28, 29, 31, 32, 33, 37, 93, 94.
Brown, William, Jr.[4] (26), married Elizabeth Kinsman[4] (25), 1726, 56, 98; land, 28, 29, 30, 33.
Brown, William[5] (70), married Eunice Wells, 1755, 103.
Brown, William[6] (152), 1772, 103.
Brown, Capt. William[6] (172), married[1] Dorcas Baker, 1810; married[2] Ann Baker, 109; land, 12, 13.
Brown, William B.[8] (357), married Caroline Dixey, 1844, 121.
Brown, William B.[10] (526f), 1881, 126.
Brown, William H.[7] (255), 1812, 109.
Brown, William H.[8] (366), 1830, 115.
Brown, William O.[10] (532), 1881, 126.
Brown, Winthrop[6] (182), 1791, 104.
Brown, Winthrop[7] (249), married Louisa J. Allen, 1835, 117.
Brown, Winthrop[7] (266), 1818, 110.
Brown, Winthrop[7] (273), 1820, 110.
Buckley, William, original lot, 20, 21.
Burley, Rebecca, married Robert Kinsman[3] (15), 1705, 57.

Burney, Elizabeth P., married Jonathan Fellows[6] (95), 1801, 81.
Burnham, Aaron, bought farm of Josiah, 1812, 9.
Burnham, Abigail, 8.
Burnham, Andrew, 2nd, married Charlotte A. Kinsman[8] (168), 1844, 67.
Burnham, Betsey, widow of James, inheritance, 21.
Burnham, Betsey, daughter of James and Betsey, married Jabez Richards; conveyances, 11, 21.
Burnham, Caleb, married Dorothy Brown[4] (29), 1731, 96.
Burnham, Dorothy, daughter of William; inheritance, 1753, 28.
Burnham, Elizabeth, married Thomas Kinsman[3] (10), 1687, 56.
Burnham, Eunice, inheritance, 1712, 23.
Burnham, Hannah, married Capt. John Kinsman[4] (26), 1733, 58.
Burnham, Hannah, married Jonathan Kinsman[5] (51), 62.
Burnham, Isaac, bought Capt. John Kinsman homestead, 1790, 9.
Burnham, James, son of Thomas, wife Mary, lands, 3, 4, 5, 6, 14, 16.
Burnham, James, Jr., wife Hannah, 6, 7, 8, 10, 11, 19, 20.
Burnham, James, wife Elizabeth, son of Thomas, Jr.; land, 11, 21.
Burnham, Jane, married Isaac Fellows[6] (61), 79.
Burnham, John, married Mehitable Kinsman[6] (94), 1780, 61.
Burnham, Josiah, land, 9, 19.
Burnham, Judeth, married Francis Brown[5] (85), 1779, 105.
Burnham, Nathan, Jr., married Sarah Brown[6] (147), 1834, 102.
Burnham, Nathaniel, married Eunice Kinsman[3] (130), 56.
Burnham, Peregrine M., married Elizabeth B. Brown[8] (365), 1847, 115.
Burnham, Rose, married Aaron Kinsman[6] (77), 1765, 60.
Burnham, Sarah, married Jacob Brown[8] (19), 1707, 96.
Burnham, S. Lizzie, married Joseph A. Brown[7] (220), 1877, 107.
Burnham, Thankful, married George W. Brown[7] (278), 1856, 111.
Burnham, Thomas, land, 3, 5, 6, 10, 11, 21; deposition, 1723, 37.
Burns, Beulah C., married Charles Brown[8] (191), 1814, 112.
Butler, Alonzo, married Elizabeth P. Brown[7] (289), 1834, 111.
Butler, Sarah, married Samuel A. Brown[7] (262), 1852, 117.
Butman, Betsey, married Isaac Fellows, Jr.[6] (117), 1801, 83.
Butman, Joanna, married Isaac Fellows, Jr.[6] (117), 1795, 83.

Caldwell, Mary L., married John Brown, Jr.[7] (309), 1836, 119.
Calef, John, land, 1748, 17.
Calef, Robert, original lot, 17.
Cameron, William J., land, 19, 49.
Campbell, Lydia, married Jeremiah Kinsman[6] (92), 1812, 65.
Candlewood, origin of name, 1; Island, 1; Street, 22.
Carlisle, Ira B., land, 3, 11, 12, 21.
Carlisle, John C., land, 11, 19.
Carter, Jacob, married daughter of Thorndike Low, 9.

INDEX

Carter, Oliver, Jr., married Priscilla Brown⁵ (73), 1762, 98.
Caryl, Elizabeth, married Stephen Kinsman⁶ (75), 1762, 60.
Cassell, William C., married Frances D. Fellows⁷ (215), 1861, 85.
Caverly, Carl, farm, 3, 6.
Chambellau, Gratau de, married Nathaniel Fellows, Jr.⁶ (101), 1803, 82.
Chamberlain, Elizabeth M., married Daniel C. Brown, Jr.⁹ (476), 1890, 127.
Chamberlain, Silas, married Elizabeth Brown⁶ (1788), 104.
Chapman, Edward, island, 1677, 4.
Chapman, George, married Elizabeth A. Fellows⁷ (189), 1846, 84.
Chapman, Joseph, married Hannah Fellows⁶ (139), 1805, 81.
Chapman, Nathan, married Caroline Brown⁷ (324), 1833, 113.
Chapman, Samuel, farm, 1701, 41.
Chase, Joseph W., married Sarah Fellows⁶ (85), 77.
Chebacco, ancient name, 1.
Checkley, Anthony, farm, 1683, 25.
Choate, Abraham, land, 3, 13.
Choate, David, widow Elizabeth, land, 2.
Choate, Elizabeth, married Nathaniel Kinsman⁵ (54), 1786, 63.
Choate, Sergeant John, farm, 1665, 1684. 26, 29.
Choate, John, Jr., land, 1692, 29.
Choate, John, son of Abraham, land, 3, 13.
Choate, Mary, married Nehemiah Brown⁵ (82), 1771, 104.
Choate, Nehemiah, married Susanna Brown⁵ (71), 1755, 98.
Choate Road or Street, 26, 29.
Choate, Samuel, son of John, married Mary Brown³ (11), 1716, 93, 94; land, 26, 29.
Choate, Samuel, son of Abraham, land, 3.
Clark, Phillip, married Sophia Fellows⁶ (88), 77.
Clarke, Philip E., married Mary E. Fellows⁷ (220), 1860, 86.
Cobb, Dr. Carolus M., married Bessie Brown⁹ (464a), 121.
Coffin, Isabelle, married Edward Brown⁷ (280), 1876, 118.
Cogswell, Aaron, married Lucy Kinsman⁶ (108), 1802, 64, 31.
Cogswell, Charles B., married Lydia Brown⁸ (378), 1857, 116.
Cogswell, Daniel, land, 22.
Cogswell, Ebenezer, land, 39.
Cogswell, Edward, married Hannah Brown³ (18), 1708, 95.
Cogswell, Elizabeth, daughter of Capt. Thos. Wade, 1737, 2.
Cogswell, John, married Sarah Brown³ (10), 94.
Cogswell, Lucy, married Moses Kinsman⁵ (58), 1780, 63.
Cogswell, Dr. Nathaniel, land, 2, 3, 15.
Cogswell, Susanna, married Moses Kinsman⁵ (58), 1809, 63, 64.
Cogswell, Theodore F., married Hannah B. Brown⁷ (296), 1853, 112; land, 3.
Cogswell, William, heir of Jonathan Wade, 1727, 2.
Cole, ——, married Mary Brown⁸ (347), 114.
Combey, Sarah, married Pelatiah Kinsman³ (16), 1708, 58.
Cook, John M., married Sarah Brown⁶ (94), 99.
Cook, William, son of John M., 12.

Crafts, Israel, married Susan C. Kinsman, (149), 1834, 66.
Crafts, Mary, married William Fellows⁸ (65), 1760, 76.
Crocker, William B., married Alice Fellows⁸ (234), 1866, 86.
Cross, Frederick G., land, 31, 36.
Cross, William T., land, 31.
Cunningham, Peter, married Elizabeth Fellows⁵ (54), 75.
Cunningham, William, married Abigail Fellow⁵ (58), 1766, 75.
Currier, Sarah C., married David Brown⁷ (275), 1846, 118.
Cushing, Laban F., married Ann M. Brown⁸ (424), 1854, 119.

Dalton, Eliza O., married Edward Brown⁷ (256), 1842, 117.
Dane, George, land, 39.
Dane, John, married Jemima Fellows, 1773, 76.
Dane, Lydia, married James Brown⁴ (49), 1746, 101.
Dane, Mary, married Jacob Brown³ (19), 1735, 96.
Dane, Philemon, original lot, 15.
Danford, William, married Hannah Kinsman² (5), 1670, 55.
Davis, Caroline, married William Fellows⁷ (152), 1829, 86.
Davis, Charles, married Harriet Fellows⁶ (103), 1799, 78.
Davis, Charles W., married Mary P. Brown⁸ (438), 120.
Davis, Fanny M., married Porter D. Brown⁹ (451), 1899, 125.
Davis, Isaac, married Elizabeth Fellows⁶ (84), 77.
Davis, Joseph, married Elsy D. Fellows⁶ (102), 78.
Davis, Juliet, married Nathaniel Brown⁷ (325), 119.
Day, Benjamin B., married Betsey Fellows⁵ (138), 1811, 81.
Day, Jonathan, married Jonathan Fellows⁸ (13), 1712, 73.
De Les Dernier, L. F., married Sophia (Fellows) Clark⁶ (88), 77.
De Les Dernier, Emily, 77.
Denison, Col. John, 20.
Dennis, David, married¹ Susanna Kinsman⁵ (56), 1779, 59; married² widow Mary Kinsman, 1809, 63.
Dennis, David, Jr., married Sarah Kinsman⁶ (107), 63.
Dennis, Capt. Joseph, married Susanna Fellows⁸ (126), 1809, 80.
Dennis, Martha, inheritance, 1741, 23.
Dennis, Thomas, married Martha Kinsman⁴ (28), 56.
Dennison, Elizabeth A., married Joseph B. Fellows⁶ (144), 1821, 85.
Dennison, Jonathan, married Susanna Fellows⁶ (143), 1821, 81.
Dick, slave of Jonathan Wade, 1727, 2.
Dike, George W., married Lavinia Fellows⁷ (202), 1848, 84.
Dingley, Eliza, 1712, 23.
Dixey, Caroline, married William B. Brown⁸ (357), 1844, 121.
Dodge, Barnabas, married Martha Burnham, 8.
Dodge, Betty, married Nathan Fellows⁶ (79), 80.
Dodge, Mrs. Betsey, married Nathan Fellows⁶ (124), 1840, 84.

INDEX

Dodge, Charles P., married Eliza Brown⁶ (354), 1869, 115.
Dodge, Elizabeth, married Stephen Brown⁵ (101), 1761, 106.
Dodge, Jonathan, Jr., married Mary Brown⁶ (96), 1766, 99.
Dodge, Mary L. S., married Stephen C. Brown⁷ (248), 1834, 116.
Dodge, Moses, married Sarah Fellows⁴ (43), 1761, 74
Dudley, Sarah, married Jonathan W. Fellows⁶ (97), 1795, 78.
Durgey, William, 1705, 34.
Dutch, Elizabeth, 1704, 73.
Dutch, Hannah, married Jonathan Fellows⁸ (13), 1705, 73.
Dutch, Susanna, married Joseph Kinsman³ (14), 56.

Eagle, Helen G., married Edward O. Brown⁸ (398), 1884, 123.
Elwell, widow Sarah, married Benjamin Fellows⁴ (40), 1749, 76.
Emerson, Elijah, married Mary A. Fellows⁷ (217), 1854, 85.
Emerson, Lewis, married Maria D. Kinsman⁸ (166), 1844, 67.
Eustace, Nannie C., married William Fellows⁸ (229), 1874, 88.

Fall, Ebenezer, land, 15.
Families, of great size, 51, 52.
Farley, Jane, married Pelatiah Kinsman⁴ (30), 59.
Farley, John, land, 1801, 15.
Farley, Thomas, land, 15.
Fawn, John, original lot, 22.
Fellows, Aaron⁶ (129), 1795, 80.
Fellows, Abby M.⁷ (224), 1846, 86.
Fellows, Abigail² (7), 1677, 72.
Fellows, Abigail³ (25), married Thomas Low, Jr., 1721, 73.
Fellows, Abigail⁵ (58), married William Cunningham, 1766, 75.
Fellows, Abigail⁵ (59), 1759, 75.
Fellows, Abigail⁵ (71), married Josiah Haskell, 1772, 76.
Fellows, Abigail C.⁶ (83), married Perrin May, 1789, 77.
Fellows, Abner⁴ (35), 1720, 74.
Fellows, Adelia A.⁸ (251), 1876, 87.
Fellows, Alfred⁷ (203), married Nancy Putnam, 1845, 87.
Fellows, Alice⁸ (234), married William B. Crocker, 1866, 86.
Fellows, Alice⁹ (260), 1886, 88.
Fellows, Alice J.⁸ (233), 86.
Fellows, Alonzo B.⁷ (216), married Henrietta Wheeler, 1876, 87; land, 4, 11, 39, 47.
Fellows, Alva⁶ (114), 1817, 79.
Fellows, Anna³ (17), 1693, 72.
Fellows, Anna⁶ (140), married Robert Tuck, 1810, 81.
Fellows, Anne L.⁸ (244), 1859, 87.
Fellows, Annie⁸ (239), 1855, 87.
Fellows, Anstice⁶ (146), 1800, 81.
Fellows, Anstice, 80.
Fellows, Asa W.⁷ (177), 1836, 83.
Fellows, Benjamin⁴ (40), married¹ Eunice Dodge, 1736; married² widow Sarah Elwell, 1749; married³ widow Rebecca Souther, 1778, 76; land, 18, 43, 44, 45.
Fellows, Benjamin⁵ (1750), 74.
Fellows, Benjamin, Jr.⁵ (78), married Anna Webber, 1784, 80.

Fellows, Bertha A.⁸ (252), 1872, 87.
Fellows, Betsey⁶ (137), 1789, 80.
Fellows, Betsey⁶ (138), married Benjamin B. Day, 1811, 81.
Fellows, Birney⁸ (235), married Henrietta Lonsdale, 1883, 88.
Fellows, Birney⁹ (261), 1890, 88.
Fellows, Caleb⁵ (56), 1744, ⁵ (57), 1746, 75.
Fellows, Caleb⁶ (96), married Mrs. Sarah Currier, sketch of life, founder of Fellows Athenæum, 82.
Fellows, Caroline⁷ (167), 1832, 82.
Fellows, Caroline⁸ (227), married D. P. Morgan, 1858, 86.
Fellows, Caroline A.⁷ (206), married Noah Brooks, 1856, 85.
Fellows, Caroline W.⁹ (258), 1882, 88.
Fellows, Carrie E.⁸ (240), 1856, 87.
Fellows, Catherine E.⁸ (236), married Benjamin T. Tilton, 1867, 87.
Fellows, Charlotte⁷ (162), 82.
Fellows, Charlotte⁷ (199), 1809, 84.
Fellows, Clara Rafaela⁷ (156), 82.
Fellows, Clara Rafaela⁸ (228), married Oliver W. Bird, 1860, 86.
Fellows, Cornelius⁵ (53), married¹ Sarah Williams, 1763; married² Hannah Parker, 1794, 77, 78.
Fellows, Cornelius⁵ (98), 1774, ⁶(100), 1778, 78.
Fellows, Cornelius⁷ (153), 81.
Fellows, Cornelius⁸ (231), married Caroline S Whitney, 1874, 88.
Fellows, Cornelius⁹ (257), 1879, 88.
Fellows, Daniel⁴ (41), 1713, 76; land, 43, 46.
Fellows, Daniel⁵ (150), 1808, 81.
Fellows, Daniel F.⁷ (192), 1816, 84.
Fellows, Daniel H.⁷ (225), married J. Augusta Archer, 1866, 87.
Fellows, David³ (14), 1687, 72.
Fellows, David B.⁷ (187), 1835, 83.
Fellows, Deborah⁵ (67), married Jonathan Goodhue, 1758, 76; inheritance, 46.
Fellows, Dolly P.⁷ (190), married Joseph Moody, 1838, 84.
Fellows, Elijah⁶ (111), 1809, 79.
Fellows, Eliza A.⁷ (186), 1830, 82.
Fellows, Eliza B.⁷ (154), 1808, 81.
Fellows, Eliza B.⁸ (226), married¹ Thomas R. Ingraham, 1856; married² I. M. Wardwell, 1863, 86.
Fellows, Elizabeth² (9), 72.
Fellows, Elizabeth³ (16), 1835, 72.
Fellows, Elizabeth⁴ (30), married¹ Joseph Perkins, 1728; married² Capt. John Kinsman, 1753, 73.
Fellows, Elizabeth⁴ (47), 1700, 74.
Fellows, Elizabeth⁵ (54), married Peter Cunningham, 75.
Fellows, Elizabeth⁵ (60), 1762, 75.
Fellows, Elizabeth⁶ (84), married¹ Isaac Davis; married² Aiden Ayres, 77.
Fellows, Elizabeth⁶ (93), married David W. Bradley, 1788, 78.
Fellows, Elizabeth⁶ (130), married John P. Lakeman, 1830, 80; inheritance, 49.
Fellows, Elizabeth A.⁷ (189), married George Chapman, 1846, 84.
Fellows, Elizabeth D.⁷ (213), 1822, 85.
Fellows, Elizabeth D.⁸ (249), 1888, 87.
Fellows, Ellen⁷ (207), 1835, 85.
Fellows, Ellen M.⁷ (171), 1844, 83.
Fellows, Elsy⁷ (155), married Joseph Saul, 82.
Fellows, Elsy D.⁶ (102), married Joseph Davis, 78.
Fellows, Elva A.⁸ (245), married Clarence I. Sherwood, 1905, 87.

INDEX 139

Fellows, Emily P.[8] (241), married Edwin Reed, 1871, 87.
Fellows, Ephraim[2] (3), family, 72; inheritance, 34.
Fellows, Ephraim[3] (12), married Hannah Warner, 1703, 73.
Fellows, Ephraim[5] (75), 1740, 76.
Fellows, Ephraim[5] (77), married Eunice Appleton, 1778, 80; farm, 45, 49.
Fellows, Ephraim[6] (125), married Charlotte Lakeman, 1806, 84; inheritance, 49, 50.
Fellows, Ephraim[7] (200), 1811, 86.
Fellows, Eunice[5] (72), married John Wood, 1758, 76.
Fellows, Eunice[6] (121), married Daniel Potter, Jr., 1796, 79.
Fellows, Eunice[6] (128), 1789, 80; inheritance, 49.
Fellows, Eunice[6] (147), 1802, 81.
Fellows, Eunice[7] (209), 1852, 85.
Fellows, Evelyn A.[8] (243), married Charles H. Masury, 1877, 87.
Fellows, Fanny[6] (112), 1812, 79.
Fellows, Frances[5] (89), married Jeremiah Plummer, 77.
Fellows, Frances D.[7] (215), married[1] William C. Cassell, 1861; married[2] Henry H. Wall, 1880, 85.
Fellows, Frederick W.[8] (251), married H. Maud Blois, 1902, 87.
Fellows, George[6] (131), 1800, 80.
Fellows, George[6] (134), married[1] Margaret Adams, married[2] Sarah E. Stanwood, 1847, 85; inheritance, 49.
Fellows, Gustavus[6] (86), married Abigail Kelly, 77.
Fellows, Hannah[4] (27), married Samuel Ingalls, 1723, 73.
Fellows, Hannah[4] (28), 1706, 73.
Fellows, Hannah[5] (82), 77.
Fellows, Hannah[6] (120), married John Lane, 1798, 79.
Fellows, Hannah[6] (139), married Joseph Chapman, 1805, 81.
Fellows, Hannah P.[5] (90), married Joseph Bancroft, 77.
Fellows, Hannah P.[6] (94), 1768, 78.
Fellows, Harriet[6] (103), married Charles Davis, 1799, 78.
Fellows, Harriet D.[8] (230), 1838, 86.
Fellows, Harriet D.[8] (256), 1877, 88.
Fellows, Harriet E.[7] (173), 1829, 83.
Fellows, Ira[6] (108), married Abigail Wright, 1827, 83.
Fellows, Ira P.[7] (179), 1840, 83.
Fellows, Irene F.[8] (247), 1884, 87.
Fellows, Isaac[2] (2), married Joanna Boardman, 1672, 72; inheritance, 34.
Fellows, Isaac[3] (10), 1673, 72.
Fellows, Isaac[4] (31), 1714, 73.
Fellows, Isaac[4] (34), married widow Abigail Blake, 75.
Fellows, Isaac[5] (61), married[1] Jane Burnham; married[2] widow Rebecca Hurlbut, 1804, 79.
Fellows, Isaac[5] (69), married Mary Roberts, 1764 79; farm, 46.
Fellows, Isaac[5] (74), 1740, 76.
Fellows, Isaac[6] (107), married[1] Annie T. Perley, 1823, 82; married[2] Urvilla Loomer, 1852, 83.
Fellows, Isaac, Jr.[6] (117), married[1] Joanna Butman, 1795; married[2] Betsey Butman, 1801, 83.
Fellows, Isaac[7] (168), 1835, 82.
Fellows, Isaac[7] (184), 1833, 83.

Fellows, Israel[7] (201), married Catherine H. Goldsmith, 1838, 86.
Fellows, Jacob[4] (39), married Sarah Frail, 1739, 74.
Fellows, James H.[7] (185), 1833, 83.
Fellows, James P.[6] (87), 77.
Fellows, Jane[6] (106), 1795, 79.
Fellows, Jemima, married John Dane, 1773, 76.
Fellows, Jeremiah[4] (37), 1724, 74.
Fellows, Jeremiah[5] (1749), 74.
Fellows, Jesse[5] (62), 1767, 75.
Fellows, Jesse[7] (188), 1809, 84.
Fellows, Joanna[3] (15), 1689, 72.
Fellows, Joanna[7] (181), 1799, 83.
Fellows, John[3] (19), married Rachel Young, 1692, 72.
Fellows, John[4] (32), 1716, 73.
Fellows, John[4] (48), 1702, 74.
Fellows, John[5] (76), married Martha Shatswell, 1772, 79; farm, 45, 47.
Fellows, John[6] (123), married Molly Willett, 1804, 79.
Fellows, John F.[7] (205), married Mary L. Sprague, 1843, 85.
Fellows, Jonathan[3] (13), married[1] Hannah Dutele, 1705; married[2] Sarah Day, 1712, 73; married[3] widow Sarah Rust, 1716; married[4] widow Deborah Tilton, 1733, 74; farm, 34.
Fellows, Jonathan, Jr.[4] (29), married[1] Abigail Gaines, 1729; married[2] widow Elizabeth Saunders, 1735, 75.
Fellows, Jonathan[5] (50), 1730, 75; 1757, 74.
Fellows, Jonathan[6] (91), 77.
Fellows, Jonathan[6] (92), 1765, 78.
Fellows, Jonathan[6] (95), married[1] Eunice F. Oliver, 1792; married[2] Elizabeth P. Burney, 1801, 81.
Fellows, Jonathan W.[6] (97), married Sarah Dudley, 1795, 78.
Fellows, Joseph[2] (5), married Ruth Fraile, 1675, 73; land, 34, 40, 42.
Fellows, Joseph[3] (21), married[1] Sarah Kimball, 1701; married[2] widow Mary Story, 1739, 74; farm, 16, 37, 42, 43.
Fellows, Joseph, Jr.[4] (38), married Susanna Giddings, 1731, 75, 76; farm, 43, 44, 45, 46.
Fellows, Joseph[5] (68), 1740, 76.
Fellows, Joseph[6] (116), 1770, 79.
Fellows, Joseph B.[6] (144), married Elizabeth A. Dennison, 1821, 85; farm, 47, 48.
Fellows, Joseph D.[7] (210), 1854; [7](211), 1856, 85.
Fellows, Joseph E.[7] (218), 1835, 85.
Fellows, Joseph E.[8] (246), married Jeannie M. Brown, 1908, 87.
Fellows, Judith[5] (64), 1773, 75.
Fellows, Julia M.[7] (219), 1840, 85.
Fellows, Julia P.[7] (174), 1831, 83.
Fellows, Laura[7] (212), 1856, 85.
Fellows, Lavinia[7] (202), married George W. Dike, 1848, 84.
Fellows, Lonsdale[9] (259), 1884, 88.
Fellows, Louis[7] (160), 82.
Fellows, Louisa J.[8] (242), 1848, 87.
Fellows, Louise[7] (161), 82.
Fellows, Lucinda M.[7] (176), 1835, 83.
Fellows, Lucy[6] (132), married James Brown, Jr.[6] (181), 1812, 80, 110.
Fellows, Lucy E.[7] (170), 1841, 83.
Fellows, Lydia[5] (73), married William Alford, 1765, 76.
Fellows, Lydia[6] (105), married Jonathan Amory, Jr., 1794, 78.

Fellows Lyman⁵ (109), 1805, 79.
Fellows, Martha⁵ (122), married Moses Willett, 1804, 79.
Fellows, Martha S.⁷ (195), married Isaac G. Johnson, 1842, 84.
Fellows, Mary² (8), 72.
Fellows, Mary³ (20), married John Brown, Jr.³ (6), 95.
Fellows, Mary⁴ (36), married Richard Tucker, 1768, 74.
Fellows, Mary⁴ (49), 75.
Fellows, Mary⁵ (113), 1814, 79.
Fellows, Mary⁵ (115), 1766, 79.
Fellows, Mary⁶ (145), married Moses Lane, 1828, 81.
Fellows, Mary A.⁷ (217), married Elijah Emerson, 1854, 85.
Fellows, Mary E.⁷ (220), married Philip E. Clarke, 1860, 86.
Fellows, Mary J.⁷ (164), 1825;⁷ (165), 1828, 82.
Fellows, Mary W.⁷ (191), 1815, 84.
Fellows, Mathilda⁷ (159), married M. Gaillardet, 82.
Fellows, Mehitable P.⁷ (193), married¹, Joseph Moody, 1843; married², Ebenezer Rolfe, 1853, 84.
Fellows, Melicent F.⁷ (194), married Benjamin Trefethan, 84.
Fellows, Morinda J.⁷ (221), married Tyler Parrott, Jr., 1859, 86.
Fellows, Morinda M.⁷ (178), 1837, 83.
Fellows, Moses A.⁷ (223), 1843, 86.
Fellows, Nancy⁵ (104), married¹ Charles Hunt; married² John S. Williams, 78.
Fellows, Nancy W.⁶ (135), 1785, 80.
Fellows, Nancy W.⁸ (232), 86.
Fellows, Nathan⁴ (42), married Anne Start, 1742, 77.
Fellows, Nathan⁵ (79), married¹ Betty Dodge; married² Hannah Brown⁶ (211f), 1785, 81, 106; farm, 31, 43, 47.
Fellows, Nathan⁶ (124), married¹ Dorothy Foster, 1807; married² Mrs. Betsey Dodge, 1840, 84.
Fellows, Nathan⁷ (137a), 1768, 80.
Fellows, Nathan⁷ (196), 1832, 84.
Fellows, Nathan W.⁶ (148), 81; farm, 47.
Fellows, Nathan W.⁸ (248), 1887, 87.
Fellows, Nathaniel⁴ (45), 1696, 74.
Fellows, Nathaniel⁵ (55), married Lydia Stanton, 1774, 78.
Fellows, Nathaniel, Jr.⁶ (101), married¹ Julia Hixon, 1803; married² A. L. A. H. Graton de Chambellan; married³ Lucy Lambert, 82.
Fellows, Nathaniel⁷ (157), 82.
Fellows, Nathaniel T.⁶ (80), 1764, 77.
Fellows, Olive⁶ (142), married Moses Lane, 1819, 81.
Fellows, Oliver⁶ (127), married Sally Foster, 1813, 84; land, 49.
Fellows, Pauline⁷ (158), 82.
Fellows, Rebecca⁶ (110) ,1806, 79.
Fellows, Reginald A.⁸ (250), 1891, 87.
Fellows, Ruth, wife of Joseph²; land, her will, 42, 43.
Fellows, Ruth³ (24), married Samuel Waite, 1717, 73.
Fellows, Ruth⁵ (1754), 74.
Fellows, Sally⁶ (136), 1787, 80.
Fellows, Sally W.⁶ (133), 80.
Fellows, Samuel² (4), family, 72; land, 34, 39, 40.
Fellows, Samuel³ (11), married Sarah Fuller, 1731, 73.

Fellows, Samuel, Jr.³ (18), 72.
Fellows, Samuel⁵ (51), married Mercy Treadwell, 1763, 77.
Fellows, Samuel⁶ (81), 1765, 77.
Fellows, Sarah² (6), married John Rust, 71.
Fellows, Sarah³ (23), married Peter Haraden, 1709, 73.
Fellows, Sarah⁴ (26), married John Bennett, Jr., 1754, 73.
Fellows, Sarah⁴ (33), married Samuel Knowlton, 1736, 74.
Fellows, Sarah⁴ (43), married Moses Dodge, 1761, 74.
Fellows, Sarah⁴ (44), 1741, 74.
Fellows, Sarah⁵ (63), 1770, 75.
Fellows, Sarah⁵ (66), married Moses Potter, 1757, 76.
Fellows, Sarah⁶ (85), married Joseph W. Chase, 77.
Fellows, Sarah⁶ (99), married Capt. Nathaniel Ruggles, 1786, 78.
Fellows, Sarah⁶ (119), married Ammi Brown⁶ (211h), 1798, 79, 107.
Fellows, Sarah⁶ (141), married Olphert Tuttle, 1820, 81.
Fellows, Sarah⁷ (208), married Charles R. Lord, 1873, 85.
Fellows, Sarah E.⁸ (238), married Charles W. Perkins, 1875, 87.
Fellows, Sarah G.⁷ (222), married Daniel L. Hodgkins, 1870, 86.
Fellows, Sarah J.⁷ (214), 1824, 85.
Fellows, Sarah S.⁸ (253), married Frank H. Spencer, 1900, 87.
Fellows, Simon⁶ (149), married Rebecca S. Graves, 1833, 85.
Fellows, Sophia⁵ (88), married¹ Phillip Clark; married² L. F. De Les Dernier, 77.
Fellows, Susan⁷ (163), married Geo. F. Williams, 82.
Fellows, Susan A.⁸ (255), 1879, 87.
Fellows, Susan C.⁷ (175), 1832, 83.
Fellows, Susanna⁵ (70), married Nehemiah Knowlton, 1771, 76.
Fellows, Susanna⁶ (126), married Capt. Joseph Dennis, 1809, 80.
Fellows, Susannna⁶ (143), married Jonathan Dennison, 1821, 81.
Fellows, Susanna⁷ (182), 1802, 83.
Fellows, Thomas B.⁷ (204), 1820, 84.
Fellows, Thomas B.⁸ (237), 1846, 87.
Fellows, Varney⁴ (19a), 1694, 72.
Fellows, William,¹ Genealogy, sketch of life, 71; farm, 33, 34.
Fellows, William³ (22), married¹ Elizabeth Rust, 1693; married² Deborah Frail, 1730, 75; farm, 43, 44.
Fellows, William⁴ (46), 1697, 74.
Fellows, William⁵ (65), married Mary Crafts, 1760, 76; land, 46.
Fellows, William⁶ (118), married Sally P. Haskell, 1823, 83; homestead, 46.
Fellows, William⁷ (152), married Caroline Davis, 1829, 86.
Fellows, William⁷ (180), 1797, 83.
Fellows, William⁸ (229), married Nannie C. Eustace, 1874, 88.
Fellows, William H.⁷ (169), 83.
Fellows, Winthrop⁷ (186), 1833, 83.
Firman, Thomas, farm of, 45.
Fitts, Abraham, land, 1730, 35.
Fitts, Mary, married John Brown⁴ (20b), 1724, 97.
Fitz, Rev. Daniel, land, 48, 50.

INDEX 141

Flynn, Hannah H., married Theodore P. Brown⁹ (455), 1869, 126.
Foster, Dorothy, married Nathan Fellows⁶ (124), 1807, 83.
Foster, Jacob, married Martha Kinsman² (6), 1658, 55.
Foster, Nathaniel, Jr., married Mary Low, 8.
Foster, Sally, married Oliver Fellows⁶ (127), 1813, 84.
Frail, Deborah, married William Fellows² (22), 1730, 75.
Frail, Ruth, married Joseph Fellows² (5), 1675, 73.
Frail, Sarah, married Jacob Fellows⁴ (39), 1739, 74.
Fuller, Ebenezer, owner in Fuller's Pasture, 1733, 32.
Fuller, Enoch, married Rhoda A. Brown⁸ (375), 1854, 116.
Fuller, Jacob, owner in Fuller's Pasture, 1733, 32.
Fuller, John, farm, 1659, 32, 35.
Fuller, Nathaniel, land, 16, 17.
Fuller, Pasture, 32.
Fuller, Sarah, married Samuel Fellows³ (11), 1731, 73.
Fuller, William, owner in Fuller's Pasture, 32.

Gaillardet, M., married Mathilda Fellows⁷ (159), 82.
Gaines, Abigail, married Jonathan Fellows, Jr.⁴ (29), 1729, 75.
Gardiner, Capt. Joseph, married Elizabeth Brown⁶ (144), 1804, 102; land, 39, 46.
Gardner, Ellen T., married Frank H. Brown⁹ (463), 1882, 121.
Gardner, Marie C., married Elbridge G. Brown⁹ (469), 1895, 122.
Garland, Albert S., land, 19.
Garrette, Edith M., married Willard E. Brown⁹ (444), 1897, 125.
Gay, Mrs. Martha P., married Eliphalet Brown⁷ (229), 1793, 114.
Gerry, Mary W., married Increase H. Brown, 1830, 115.
Gibbs, Theodore, married Lucy Brown⁶ (142), 1798, 102; land, 38.
Giddings, Charles, land, 1835, 2.
Giddings, Dorothy, married William Brown³ (7), 1703, 95.
Giddings, Job, married Mehitable Brown⁵ (74), 1757, 98.
Giddings, Susanna, married Joseph Fellows⁴ (38), 1731, 76..
Giddings, William, married Elizabeth Brown⁷ (240), 1843, 109.
Gilman, Capt. Samuel, married Martha Kinsman⁵ (52), 1779, 59.
Goldsmith, Catherine H., married Israel Fellows⁷ (201), 1838, 86.
Goldthwait, Willard, married Martha Brown⁸ 344, 114.
Goodhue, Ebenezer, married Anna Brown⁶ (211j) 1806, 107.
Goodhue, John W., married Blanche R. Brown⁹ (472), 1897, 122.
Goodhue, Jonathan, married Deborah Fellows⁵ (67), 1758, 76.
Goodwin, Silas Henry, land, 49.
Gordon, Samuel, land, 2.
Gordon, Samuel C., land, 2.
Gould, Caroline M., married Frederick W. Brown⁹ (461), 1877, 127.

Gould's Pasture, occupied by Henry Gould, 1728, 29.
Grant, James R., married Charlotte Brown⁷ (335), 114.
Graton de Chambellan, A. L. A. H., married Nathaniel Fellows, Jr.⁶ (101), 82.
Gravel Pit, Fellows's Lane, 48.
Graves, Rebecca S., married Simon Fellows⁶ (149), 1833, 85.
Green, Emma F., married Edwin Brown⁸ (432), 1868, 124.
Green, Catherine T., married Increase H. Brown, Jr.⁸ (358), 121.
Green, Nancy D., married William Kinsman⁸ (174), 69.
Gregory, Mary K., married Increase H. Brown, Jr.⁸ (358), 1860, 121.
Greig, James W., married Jennie T. Brown⁸ (399), 1890, 117.
Griffin, Humphrey, lot, 3.

Hacket, Isaac, married Betsey Brown⁶ (203), 1801, 106.
Hall, Mary, married Aaron Kinsman⁶ (77), 1775, 60.
Hamlet Road, 1740, 44.
Hammond, William, married Abigail B. Brown⁷ (327), 1838, 113.
Harden, Peter, married Sarah Fellows³ (23), 1709, 73; land, 44.
Harris, Eliza, married Increase H. Brown⁷ (237), 1820, 115.
Harris, Elizabeth S., married Daniel C. Brown⁸ (377), 1855, 122.
Harris, Herbert A., married Mabel C. Brown¹⁰ (526b), 1891, 126.
Harris, John H., Jr., married Hannah N. Brown⁷ (246), 1826, 109.
Harris, Sarah, married Jeremiah Kinsman⁵ (42), 1743, 61.
Hartford, Alice A., married Henry N. Brown⁹ (446), 1893, 125.
Hartshorne, Vinnie B., married Horace M. Brown⁹ (453), 1905, 126.
Harvey, Chester L., married Marion G. Brown⁷ (487), 1901, 123.
Hasey, William, married Elizabeth Brown³ (16), 1702, 95.
Haskell, original right, 16.
Haskell, Elias, married Martha (Kinsman) Boardman⁶ (98), 1812, 62.
Haskell, George, land, 1831, 2.
Haskell, Josiah, married Abigail Fellows⁵ (71), 1772, 76.
Haskell, Lieut. Mark, married Jane Kinsman⁵ (55), 1798, 59.
Haskell, Perley, land, 1837, 3.
Haskell, Sally P., married William Fellows⁶ (118), 1823, 83.
Haskell, Samuel M., land, 39, 46.
Hatch, Charles F., married Lucy F. Brown⁸ (417), 1881, 118.
Hawes, Edwin W., married Mary E. Kinsman⁹ (199), 1908, 69.
Hawkes, Benjamin, land, 3.
Hawkins, Ellen M., married Henry Brown⁹ (460), 1871, 126.
Heard, Elizabeth, 2.
Heard, George W., land, 9, 19.
Heard, John, land, 9, 19.
Heard, Joseph, married Lucy (Brown) Tibbets⁶ (166), 1810, 104.
Henchman, Mrs. Dorothy, land, 13.
Highway, original layout, 20.
Hill, Red-root or Red-wood, 29.
Hixon, Julia, married Nathaniel Fellows, Jr.⁶ (101), 1803, 82.

INDEX

Hobson, Daniel C., lot, 4, 10.
Hodgkins, Daniel L., married Sarah G. Fellows[7] (222), 1870, 86.
Hodgkins, Thomas, married Priscilla Kinsman[6] (109), 1795, 63.
Holmes, Capt. Henry S., married Louisa Kinsman[5] (159), 1825, 67; land, 9.
Holt, Stephen, married Mary Brown[6] (211c), 1803, 106.
Homans, Charles A., married Lydia A. Kinsman[9] (180), 1856, 68.
Hood, Annie M., married Edward R. Brown[7] (287), 1866, 118.
Hood, Lydia, married Nathan Brown[5] (133), 1814, 107.
Hooker, Lydia, married Simon Brown[4] (44), 1774, 100.
Hooper, John, Jr., married Sarah A. Brown[5] (343), 1880, 114.
Horton, Benjamin R., farm, 35.
Horton, Joseph, farm, 35.
Horton, William G., farm, 12, 13, 21, 31.
Hosmer, ———, married Elizabeth Brown[5] (132), 102.
Houlden, Catherine, married George A. Brown[8] (434), 1874, 124.
How, Hannah, married Aaron Kinsman[5] (59), 1795, 64.
How, Increase, married Susanna Kinsman[4] (21), 56, 57, 23.
How, Mark, death of children, 1736, 52.
Howard, Samuel, original lot, 17.
Howlett, Thomas, original lot, 25.
Hubbard, John, married Mary Brown[3] (17), 1710, 95.
Huckins, Joseph, land, 11, 12, 13, 21, 31.
Hunt, Charles, married Nancy Fellows[6] (104), 78.
Hurlburt, widow Rebecca, married Isaac Fellows,[5] (61) 1804, 79.

Ingalls, Samuel, married Hannah Fellows[4] (27), 1723, 73.
Ingraham, Thomas R., married Eliza B. Fellows[8] (226), 1856, 86.

Jacobs, Joseph, farm, 1701, 41.
Jacobs, Nathaniel, land, 40, 41.
Jacobs, Richard, grant, 1638; bridge over Mile River, 41; land, 34.
Jacobs, Thomas, married Sarah Brown[2] (4), 1671, 92, 41.
Jaquith, Mrs. Sarah, married Nathaniel Brown[7] (325), 1882, 119.
Jewett, Richard D., married Lucy Kinsman[5] (61), 1791, 59.
Johnson, Isaac G., married Martha S. Fellows[7] (195), 1842, 84.
Jones, Amos, land, 15.
Joyce, Lottie A., married Asa R. Brown[8] (416), 1895, 124.

Kelly, Abigail, married Gustavus Fellows[6] (86), 77.
Kenney, Rebecca P., married Jesse F. Brown[8] (435), 1865, 124.
Killum, Nathaniel, pub. widow, Sarah Fellows, 1738, 73.
Kimball, Alfred, land, 3.
Kimball, Evelyn A., married Walter Brown[8] (436), 1836, 125.
Kimball, Lucy, married Stephen Kinsman[4] (17), 1711, 58.
Kimball, Lucy S., married Jonathan Brown[7] (234), 1836, 115.
Kimball, Lydia, married Stephen Kinsman[4] (17), 1716, 58.
Kimball, Sarah, married Joseph Fellows[3] (21), 1701, 74.
Kimball, Susan L., married Robert Brown[10] (530), 1902, 127.
Kimball, Susan M., married Gustavus Kinsman[8] (177), 1875, 69.
Kimball, Warren, married Anne B. Brown[7] (247), 1835, 109.
Kinnear, Violet H., married Frank W. Brown[10] (528), 1901, 127.
Kinsman, Aaron[5] (59), married Hannah Howe, 1795, 64.
Kinsman, Aaron[5] (77), married[1] Rose Burnham, 1765; married[2] Mary Hall, 1775, 60.
Kinsman, Aaron[6] (133), 1804, 64.
Kinsman, Aaron[7] (77a), 1766, 60.
Kinsman, Abigail[6] (86), 1763, 60.
Kinsman, Abigail[7] (157), married Joseph Marshall, 1860, 66.
Kinsman, Abigail E.[6] (126), married Capt. Winthrop Boardman, 1821, 64.
Kinsman, Alice A.[9] (188), 1864, 68.
Kinsman, Alice F.[9] (184), 1858; (186), 1861, 68.
Kinsman, Anna[7] (143), married Benjamin Potter, 1794, 65.
Kinsman, Annie M.[9] (191), 1846, 69.
Kinsman, Arthur D.[9] (189), married Mary A. G. Smith, 1899, 69.
Kinsman, Asa[7] (142), 1793, 65.
Kinsman, Asa[7] (154), married Caroline A. Parsons, 1858, 66; land, 31.
Kinsman, Benjamin[4] (31), married Elizabeth Perkins, 1740, 59; land, 23, 33, 34.
Kinsman, Benjamin[5] (67), 1743, 60.
Kinsman, Bethiah D.[9] (198), 1841, 69.
Kinsman, Betsey[6] (99), married John Wells, Jr., 1796, 62.
Kinsman, Betsey[6] (103), married Aaron Blaney, Jr., 63.
Kinsman, Betsey B.[8] (158), 1803, 67.
Kinsman, Charles H.[9] (185), 1860, 68.
Kinsman, Charlotte[6] (131), married Elisha Brown[7] (230), 1840, 64, 65, 115.
Kinsman, Charlotte[7] (171), 1803, 67.
Kinsman, Charlotte A.[8] (168), married Andrew Burnham 2nd, 1844, 67.
Kinsman, Clarissa[7] (132), 1821, 64.
Kinsman, Daniel[5] (41), married Mary Perkins, 1794, 60, 61.
Kinsman, Daniel[7] (137), 1778, 65.
Kinsman, Daniel C.[6] (87), 1741; (88), married Abigail Morse, 1768, 61.
Kinsman, Daniel F.[8] (170), married Mattie A. Wood, 1855, 67.
Kinsman, Dorothy[6] (91), married Joseph Adams, 1774, 61.
Kinsman, Dorothy Q.[11] (203), 1904, 70.
Kinsman, Ebenezer[5] (70), 1750; (71), 1751, 60.
Kinsman, Ebenezer[6] (81), 1752; (83), 1758, 60, 61.
Kinsman, Edward[8] (176), 1845, 68.
Kinsman, Elizabeth[4] (18), married Jacob Perkins, 1713, 56; inheritance, 35.
Kinsman, Elizabeth[4] (25), married William Brown, Jr.[4] (26), 1726, 56, 98.
Kinsman, Elizabeth[5] (66), 1741, 60.
Kinsman, Elizabeth[6] (79), 1748, 60.
Kinsman, Elizabeth[6] (115), 1791, 63.
Kinsman, Elizabeth[6] (123), married Capt. Winthrop Boardman, 1824, 64.
Kinsman, Elizabeth[7] (147), married James L. Wells, 1832, 65.
Kinsman, Elizabeth[9] (182), 1846, 68.

INDEX 143

Kinsman, Elizabeth G.[10] (202), married Charles E. MacGlashan, 1909, 70.
Kinsman, Ephraim[6] (84), married Mary Hall, 60.
Kinsman, Eunice[3] (13), married Nath. Burnham, 56.
Kinsman, Eunice[4] (23), married Moses Wells, 1724, 23, 56, 57.
Kinsman, Eunice[5] (57), 1752, 59.
Kinsman, Eunice[6] (82), 1754, 60.
Kinsman, Eunice[7] (155), married John Brown[6] (149), 1840, 66, 107.
Kinsman, Farley[6] (124), married Jerusha Norwood, 64.
Kinsman, George[8] (169), married Elzina A. Tilton, 1865, 67.
Kinsman, Grace L.[9] (200), 1883, 69.
Kinsman, Gustavus[8] (177), married Susan M. Kimball, 1875, 69; land, 19.
Kinsman, Hannah[2] (5), married William Danford, 1670, 55.
Kinsman, Hannah[4] (27), married Robert Wallis, Jr., 1735, 56.
Kinsman, Hannah[5] (44), 1735, 58.
Kinsman, Hannah[5] (47), married James Perkins, 1762, 59.
Kinsman, Hannah[5] (63), 1760, 59.
Kinsman, Hannah[6] (111), married John P. Bartlett, 63.
Kinsman, Hannah[6] (122), married Ephraim Brown, Jr.[6] (151), 1811, 64, 107.
Kinsman, Hannah[6] (129), 1796, 64.
Kinsman, Hannah B.[6] (101), 1774, 62.
Kinsman, Harriet M.[9] (192), married Edward B. Wildes, 1870, 69.
Kinsman, Isaac[6] (78), 1745, 60.
Kinsman, Israel[5] (60), 1756, 59.
Kinsman, Israel[6] (106), 1789, 63.
Kinsman, Jacob[8] (162), married Abbie Staniford, 1837, 67.
Kinsman, Jacob[8] (173), 1808, 68.
Kinsman, Jacob B.[7] (145), married Bethiah Dodge, 1802, 67.
Kinsman, James[6] (46), married Mary Boardman, 1760, 62; land, 9.
Kinsman, James[6] (96), 1764, 61.
Kinsman, Jane[5] (55), married Mark Haskell, 1798, 59.
Kinsman, Jane[6] (130), married Moses Kinsman[6] (127), 1834, 64.
Kinsman, Jemima, married James Brown[5] (77), 1782, 103.
Kinsman, Jeremiah[5] (42), married Sarah Harris, 1743, 61; land, 36.
Kinsman, Jeremiah[6] (92), married[1] Martha Andrews, 1769; married[2] Lydia Campbell, 1812, 65; farm, 36.
Kinsman, Jeremiah[7] (134), 1770; (136), 1775, 65.
Kinsman, Jeremy[4] (37), 1719, 58.
Kinsman, Joanna[3] (11), married Nath. Rust, Jr., 1684, 55; inheritance, 23.
Kinsman, Joanna[4] (34), 1710, 58.
Kinsman, Joanna[7] (156), 1829, 66; land, 13.
Kinsman, Captain John[4] (26), married[1] Hannah Burnham, 1733; married[2] widow Elizabeth (Fellows) Perkins[4] (30), 1753, 58, 73; land, 8, 9, 14, 17, 18, 19, 23, 24.
Kinsman, John, Jr.[5] (45), married[1] Abigail Wells, 1758; married[2] Margaret Appleton, 1773, 61; land, 14.
Kinsman, John[6] (95), 1762, 61.
Kinsman, John[7] (140), 1786, 65.
Kinsman, John[7] (146), 1810, 66.
Kinsman, John C.[8] (114), married Anna Lord, 1810, 65.

Kinsman, John E.[11] (205), 1908, 70.
Kinsman, Jonathan[5] (51), married[1] Hannah Burnham; married[2] Susanna Bemont, 1796, 62.
Kinsman, Joseph[3] (14), married[1] Susanna Dutch; married[2] Sarah Peabody, 1736, 56; land, 23, 26; Lieutenant, 32, 34.
Kinsman, Joseph[4] (22), 1701, 56.
Kinsman, Joseph[5] (48), 1743, 59.
Kinsman, Joseph[5] (73), 1760, 60.
Kinsman, Joseph[6] (119), married Eunice Brown[6] (156), 1809, 66, 103; land, 30, 31.
Kinsman, Joseph[7] (153), married[1] Mary E. Brown[7] (265), 1842; married[2] Hannah S. Pert, 1863, 68, 110; land, 31.
Kinsman, J. Farley[8] (175), married Caroline Brown[8] (412), 1873, 68, 118; farm, 6.
Kinsman, Louisa[8] (159), married Capt. Henry S. Holmes, 1825, 67.
Kinsman, Louise E.[9] (196), 1861, 69.
Kinsman, Lucy[5] (61), married Richard D. Jewett, 1791, 59.
Kinsman, Lucy[6] (89), married Ebenezer Trask, 1768, 61.
Kinsman, Lucy[6] (118), married Aaron Cogswell, 1802, 64.
Kinsman, Lucy[7] (139), 1783, 65.
Kinsman, Lucy A.[7] (148), 1814, 66.
Kinsman, Lydia[5] (43), married Ephraim Adams, 1749, 58.
Kinsman, Lydia[6] (80), married Francis Knight, 1768, 60.
Kinsman, Lydia[7] (135), 1772, 65.
Kinsman, Lydia A.[9] (180), married Charles A. Homans, 1856, 68.
Kinsman, Maria D.[8] (166), married Lewis Emerson, 1844, 67.
Kinsman, Margaret[3] (12), 56; inheritance, 23.
Kinsman, Margaret[4] (36), 1718, 58.
Kinsman, Martha[2] (6), married Jacob Foster, 1658, 55.
Kinsman, Martha[4] (28), married Thomas Dennis, 1732, 56.
Kinsman, Martha[5] (52), married Samuel Gilman, Jr., 1779, 59.
Kinsman, Martha[6] (98), married[1] Stephen Boardman, 1791; married[2] Elias Haskell, 1812, 62.
Kinsman, Martha[6] (117), 1798, 63.
Kinsman, Martha[7] (152), 1829, 66.
Kinsman, Martha F.[9] (181), 1839, 68.
Kinsman, Mary[2] (3), married[1] Daniel Ringe; married[2] Uzall Wardell, 55.
Kinsman, Mary[3] (8), 23, 55.
Kinsman, Mary[4] (20), married Thomas Waite, Jr., 1717, 59; inheritance, 35.
Kinsman, Mary[4] (33), 1707, 58.
Kinsman, Mary[5] (74), 1763, 60.
Kinsman, Mary[6] (97), married James Remmick, 1782, 62.
Kinsman, Mary[6] (105), married Henry Little, Jr., 63.
Kinsman, Mary[6] (116), 1795, 63.
Kinsman, Mary[6] (121), married Bemsley Smith, 1811, 64.
Kinsman, Mary,[6] married John B. Brown[8] (186), 1818, 62, 111.
Kinsman, Mary[7] (138), 1781, 65.
Kinsman, Mary B.[9] (193), married John F. LeBaron, 1870, 69.
Kinsman, Mary C.[7] (151), 1822, 66.
Kinsman, Mary E.[9] (178), 1844, 68.
Kinsman, Mary E.[9] (199), married Edwin W. Hawes, 1908, 69.
Kinsman, Mary F.[9] (183), 1857, 68.

INDEX

Kinsman, Mary Q., wife of Willard F., land, 16, 17.
Kinsman, Mehitable[6] (94), married John Burnham, 1780, 61.
Kinsman, Mercy[5] (65), 1766, 59.
Kinsman, Michael[5] (53); married[1] Sarah Treadwell, 1768; married[2] Mary Knowlton, 1783, 63.
Kinsman, Michael[6] (109), 1794, (112), 1780; (113), 1783, 63.
Kinsman, Moses[5] (58), married[1] Lucy Cogswell, 1780; married[2] Susanna Cogswell, 1809, 63, 64; land, 14.
Kinsman, Moses[6] (127), married Jane Kinsman[6] (130), 1834, 64; land, 14, 15.
Kinsman, Nancy[8] (161), married Stephen Blatchford, 1834, 67.
Kinsman, Nathan[6] (76), married[1] Mercy Wheeler; married[2] Elizabeth Shattuck, 1772, 60.
Kinsman, Nathaniel[4] (29), married[1] Anna Robinson, 1741; married[2] Dorcas Parsons, 1787, 57; land, 23.
Kinsman, Nathaniel[5] (54), married[1] Priscilla Treadwell, 1772; married[2] Elizabeth Choate, 1786, 63.
Kinsman, Nathaniel[5] (68), 1745, 60.
Kinsman, Nathaniel[6] (110), married Deborah Webb, 63.
Kinsman, Nathaniel[6] (128), married Joanna Brown, 1828, 66; farm, 12, 13.
Kinsman, Nathaniel[7] (150), 1819, 66.
Kinsman, Nicholas W.[9] (197), married Margaret Miller, 69.
Kinsman, Oliver D.[8] (172), 1805, 67.
Kinsman, Pelatiah[3] (16), married Sarah Cumbey, 1708, 58.
Kinsman, Pelatiah[4] (30), married Jane Farley, 59; land, 23, 24, 34.
Kinsman, Pelatiah[5] (62), 1760; (64), 1766, 59.
Kinsman, Pelatiah[6] (104), 1785, 63.
Kinsman, Priscilla[6] (109), married Thomas Hodgkins, 1795, 63.
Kinsman, Rebecca[4] (32), 1706, 57.
Kinsman, Rhoda E.[9] (179), 1831, 68.
Kinsman, Rhoda E.[9] (195), 1854, 69.
Kinsman, Rhoda F.[9] (187), 1862. 68; land, 36.
Kinsman, Robert[1] Genealogy of, 55.
Kinsman, Robert[2] (2), wife Mary (Boreman), 55; land, 22, 23; Quartermaster, 35.
Kinsman, Robert, Jr.[3] (15), married[1] Lydia More, 1700; married[2] Rebecca Burley, 1705, 57; land, 34.
Kinsman, Robert[4] (35), 1713, 58.
Kinsman, Robert[5] (69), 1747, 60.
Kinsman, Salome[6] (102), 1775, 62.
Kinsman, Samuel[5] (50), married Martha Smith, 1769, 62; land, 4, 6. 9, 14, 18.
Kinsman, Samuel[6] (100), married Hannah Pearson, 1809, 62.
Kinsman, Sally[7] (141), 1790, 65.
Kinsman, Sarah[2] (4), married Samuel Younglove, 1660, 55.
Kinsman, Sarah[3] (9), married Jacob Perkins, 55.
Kinsman, Sarah[4] (24), married Nathaniel Wells, 1723, 56, 57.
Kinsman, Sarah[5] (49), married William Appleton, 1764, 59.
Kinsman, Sarah[6] (85), 1763, 60.
Kinsman, Sarah[6] (90), married Capt. John Andrews, 1766, 61.
Kinsman, Sarah[6] (107), married David Dennis, Jr., 63.
Kinsman, Sarah[8] (164), married Oliver M. Whipple, 1844, 67.
Kinsman, Sarah M.[9] (190), married Joseph A. Story, 1868, 69.
Kinsman, Simon B.[8] (160), married Elizabeth B. Stone, 1829, 68; farm, 47.
Kinsman, Stephen[4] (17), married[1] Lucy Kimball, 1711; married[2] Lydia Kimball, 1716, 58; farm, 35, 36.
Kinsman, Stephen[5] (38), 1713, 58.
Kinsman, Stephen[5] (40), married Elizabeth Russell, 1739, 60; land, 36.
Kinsman, Stephen[6] (75), married Elizabeth Caryl, 1762, 60.
Kinsman, Susan[8] (163), 1813, 67.
Kinsman, Susan C.[7] (149), married Israel Crafts, 1834, 66.
Kinsman, Susanna[4] (21), married[1] Increase How, 1723; married[2] John Smith, 1762, 56.
Kinsman, Susanna[5] (56), married David Dennis, 1779, 59.
Kinsman, Susanna[5] (72), 1753, 60.
Kinsman, Susanna E.[6] (125), 1793, 64.
Kinsman, Tabitha[2] (7), 55.
Kinsman, Thomas[3] (10), married Elizabeth Burnham, 1687, 56; land, 35.
Kinsman, Thomas[4] (19), 1693, 56; farm, 35.
Kinsman, Thomas[5] (39), married Mary Tilton, 1745, 58.
Kinsman, Willard B.[8] (167), married Harriet Manning, 1844, 69; land, 9, 17, 18, 19.
Kinsman, Willard F.[9] (194), married Mary A. Quincy, 1876, 69; farm, 17.
Kinsman, Willard Q.[10] (201), married Mary E. Nichelsen, 1904, 70.
Kinsman, Willard Q., Jr.[11] (204), 1906, 70.
Kinsman, William[6] (93), married Anna Brown, 1773, 65; farm, 36.
Kinsman, William[7] (144), married Sarah Brown[6] (211*i*), 1802, 66, 107; farm, 36.
Kinsman, William[8] (174), married Nancy D. Green, 69.
Kinsman, William H.[8] (164), married Frances J. Lamson, 1857, 68; farm, 31, 32, 36.
Knight, Francis, married Lydia Kinsman[6] (80), 1768, 60.
Knowlton, Alphonso M., land, 39, 46.
Knowlton, Elizabeth, married Nathan Brown[4] (23), 1737, 97.
Knowlton, Mary, married Michael Kinsman[4] (33), 1736, 74.
Knowlton, Nehemiah, married Susanna Fellows[5] (70), 1771, 76.
Knowlton, Samuel, married Sarah Fellows[4] (33), 1736. 74.
Kunert, Helen, married George F. Brown[9] (504), 1894, 127.

Lafayette, General, in Ipswich, 1824, 64.
Lakeman, Abigail, 1830, 18.
Lakeman, Curtis E., married Katharyn L. Brown[9] (449), 1908, 121.
Lakeman, Elizabeth, married Jonathan Brown[4] (36), 1748, 100.
Lakeman, John P., married Elizabeth Fellows[6] (130), 1830, 80; land, 39.
Lakeman, John R., married Sarah Brown[7] (310), 1820, 112.
Lakeman, Laura A., 1830, 18.
Lakeman, Mary L., married David A. Brown[7] (334), 1845, 120.
Lakeman, Susanna, 1830, 18.

INDEX 145

Lakeman, William, 3d, married Susanna Brown⁶ (201), 1797, 105.
Lakeman, William, 4th, 18.
Lambert, Lucy, married Nathaniel Fellows, Jr.⁶ (101), 82.
Lamson, Frances J., married William H. Kinsman⁸ (164), 1857, 68.
Lamson, Joshua, married Elizabeth F. Brown⁷ (274), 1841, 110; land, 31, 36.
Lamson, Obadiah, land, 31.
Lampson, Sarah, married James Brown⁴ (49), 1751, 101.
Lane, John, married Hannah Fellows⁶ (120), 1798, 79.
Lane, Lakeman's, laid out, 1743, 16.
Lane, Moses, married¹ Mary Fellows⁶ (145); married² Olive Fellows⁶ (142), 1819, 81.
Langdon, Samuel, married Elizabeth Brown⁵ (68), 1746, 98.
Lawrence, Emery, married Lucy A. Brown⁸ (340), 1862, 114.
LeBaron, John F., married Mary B. Kinsman⁹ (193), 1870, 69.
Lee, Ariel P., married Eliza T. Brown⁸ (423), 1848, 119.
Leonard, Mary A., married Otis Brown⁸ (372), 1873, 122.
Libby, Lester E., land, 3, 11.
Lincoln, or Link-horn Hill, 1753, 32.
Lincoln, Levi T., married Mary A. Brown⁷ (326), 1852, 113.
Linnell, Emma L., married Henry H. Brown¹⁰ (527), 1894, 126.
Little, Henry Jr., married Mary Kinsman⁶ (104), 63.
Lonsdale, Henrietta, married Birney Fellows⁸ (235), 1883, 88.
Loomer, Urvilla, married Isaac Fellows⁸ (107), 1852, 83.
Lord, Anna, married John C. Kinsman⁶ (114), 1810, 65.
Lord Charles R., married Sarah Fellows⁷ (208), 1873, 85.
Lord, Josiah, Jr., married Lydia H. Brown⁷ (216), 1845, 107.
Lord, widow Lydia, married Timothy Thornton, 1785, 96.
Lord, Sarah B., married Walter Brown⁸ (436), 1885, 125.
Lord, Dr. Sidney A., farm, 6.
Lord, Susan W., married Joseph P. Brown⁷ (264), 1846, 117.
Low, Alice L., married Clarence E. Brown⁷ (222), 114.
Low, Daniel, land, 1761, 9.
Low, Deborah, married Isaac Randall, 8.
Low, Dorothy, married Thomas Yorke, 9.
Low, Elizabeth, married Timothy Bragg, Jr., 8.
Low's Island, 1757, 45, 49, 50.
Low, John, land, 8, 40, 42.
Low, John C., married Ellen Brown⁷ (281), 1855, 111.
Low, Joseph, 8.
Low, Martha, 9.
Low, Mary, married Nathaniel Foster, Jr., 8.
Low, Nathaniel, married widow Sarah Fellows, 1739, 73; land, 8, 9.
Low, Dr. Nathaniel, sold homestead, 1779, 9.
Low, Nathaniel, of Gloucester, 1773, 78.
Low, Sarah, married Abraham Martin, 8.
Low, Thomas, land, 8, 40.
Low, Thomas, Jr., married Abigail Fellows³ (25), 1721, 73; land, 44.
Low, Thomas, land, 1835, 9, 19.

Low, Thorndike, 1708, land, family, 8.
Low, Winthrop, quitclaim, 1851, 33.
Lufkin, Moses, married Mary Brown⁴ (21), 1733, 95.
Lufkin, Moses, Jr., married Mary Brown⁵ (119), 1780, 101.
Lufkin, ———, married Sarah Brown⁵ (106), 101.
Lufkin, Samuel, Jr., married¹ Elizabeth M. Brown⁷ (330); married², 113, Mary P. Brown⁷ (333), 114.

MacGlashen, Charles E., married Elizabeth G. Kinsman¹⁰ (202), 1909, 70.
Manning, Harriet, married Willard B. Kinsman⁸ (167), 1844, 69.
Manning, Dr. John, land, 1806, 16, 17.
Manning, Dr. Joseph, land, 1739–1743, 16.
Manning, Richard, married Judith Brown⁸ (188), 1819, 105.
Manning, William, land, 1833, 49.
Mansfield, John W., house and lot, 1888, 31.
Marshall, John, house and lot, 1863, 19.
Marshall, Joseph, married Abigail Kinsman⁷ (157), 1860, 66; land, 13, 14.
Martin, Abraham, married Sarah Low, 8.
Mason, Caroline L., married Elbridge Brown⁸ (363), 1865, 122.
Masury, Charles H., married Evelyn A. Fellows⁸ (243), 1877, 87.
Matthias, Joseph, married Jennie S. Brown¹⁰ (526g), 1904, 126.
May, Perrin, married Abigail Fellows⁶ (83), 1789, 77.
Meady, Alexander, married Charlotte Brown⁶ (211), 106.
Meady, Lucy, married George Brown⁶ (208), 1807, 113.
Meady, Rachel, married Stephen Brown⁶ (207), 1805, 106.
Meady, Thomas, house and lot, 1808, 21.
Mears, Susan, married Levi Brown⁷ (307), 1826, 118.
Mellen, Wilder J., married Lucy Brown⁷ (292), 1854, 112.
Merrill, Ezekiel, farm, 1850, 39, 47.
Miller, Margaret, married Nicholas M. Kinsman⁹ (197), 69.
Moody, Joseph, married¹ Dolly P. Fellows⁷ (190), 1838; married² Mehitable P. Fellows⁷ (193), 1843, 84.
Mooney, Philena M., married Henry H. Brown⁸ (440), 1891, 125.
More, Lydia, married Robert Kinsman³ (15), 1700, 57.
Morgan, D. P., married Caroline Fellows⁸ (227), 86.
Morse, Abigail, married Daniel Kinsman⁶ (88), 1768, 61.

Newhall, James R., married Dorcas B. Brown⁷ (251), 1840, 110.
Nichelson, Mary E., married Willard Q. Kinsman¹⁰ (201), 1904, 70.
Norfolk, John R., married Eliza Brown⁷ (336), 1847, 114.
Norman, T. M., house and lot, 1894, 19.
Norwood, Caleb, 1735, family, 75.
Norwood, Jerusha, married Farley Kinsman⁶ (124), 64.

Olive, Marion W., married Karl Brown¹⁰ (531), 1907, 127.
Oliver, Eunice T., married Jonathan Fellows⁶ (95), 1792, 81.

INDEX

Parker, Hannah, married Cornelius Fellows[5] (53), 1794, 77.
Parrott, Tyler, Jr., married Morinda J. Fellows[7] (221), 1859, 86.
Parsons, Caroline A., married Asa Kinsman[7] (154), 1858, 66.
Parsons, Charles C., married Caroline Brown[8] (426), 1854, 119.
Parsons, Dorcas, married Nathaniel Kinsman[4] (29), 1787, 57.
Parsons, Lucy, married David A. Brown[7] (334), 120.
Patch, Benjamin, lot, 1790, 31.
Patch, Benjamin 3d, married Fanny Brown[6] (155), 1816, 103.
Patch, John, Jr., married Mary Brown[6] (167), 1811, 104; farm, 31, 36.
Patch, Samuel, farm, 1767, 31. 36.
Paul, Mary, married Dr. Daniel R. Brown[9] (441b), 1890, 125.
Peabody, Sarah, married Joseph Kinsman[3] (14), 23, 56.
Pearson, Hannah, married Samuel Kinsman[5] (100), 1809, 62.
Pease, Caroline L., married Frank A. Brown[8] (384), 1881, 122.
Peatfield, Susan M., married Charles G. Brown[8] (407), 123.
Pengry, Mehitable, married James Brown[2] (20), 1707, 97.
Perkins, Charles W., married Sarah E. Fellows[8] (238), 1875, 87.
Perkins, Eben., farm, 1878, 31, 36.
Perkins, Elizabeth, married Benjamin Kinsman[4] (31), 1740, 59.
Perkins, Elizabeth (Fellows), widow of Joseph, married Capt. John Kinsman[4] (26), 1753, 58, 73.
Perkins, Elizabeth, married Ebenezer Brown[5] (75), 1768, 103.
Perkins, Elizabeth, married Joseph Brown[5] (84), 1778, 27, 104.
Perkins, Jacob, married Elizabeth Kinsman[4] (18), 1713, 56; lot, 35.
Perkins, Jacob, married Sarah Kinsman[3] (9), 55.
Perkins, James, of Marlborough, 27, 28; married Hannah Kinsman[5] (47), 1762, 59.
Perkins, John, Sen., original lot, 25.
Perkins, John, of Dresden, 28.
Perkins, Joseph, married Elizabeth Fellows[4] (30), 1728, 73.
Perkins, Judith, married Nathaniel Brown[2] (5), 1673, 94.
Perkins, Martha, married Joseph Brown[5] (84), 1806, 104.
Perkins, Mary, married Daniel Kinsman[5] (41), 1740, 61.
Perkins, Capt. Robert, married Elizabeth Brown[4] (41), 1753, 96; farm, 27, 30, 32.
Perkins, Robert, of Woolwich, 28.
Perkins, Sarah, inheritance, 28.
Perley, Annie T., married Isaac Fellows[8] (107), 1823, 82.
Perley, Judith A., married Gardiner A. Brown[7] (268), 1851, 118.
Perrin, Thomas, original lot, 19.
Perry, Albert, married Sophia Brown[8] (374), 1853, 116.
Pert, Hannah S., married Joseph Kinsman[7] (153), 1863, 68.
Philbrook, Eliza A., married E. Newton Brown, 1871, 120.
Philbrook, John W., married Kate S. Brown[8] (383), 1860, 117.

Philips, John, Argilla farm, 1749, 13.
Pierpoint, Hannah, married Gustavus Fellows[5] (52), 1761, 77.
Pierpont, Sarah, married Gustavus Fellows[5] (52), 77.
Pingree, Thomas P., lot, 1869, 31.
Plummer, Jeremiah, married Frances Fellows[6] (89), 77.
Podd, Samuel, wife Grace, land, 1660, 3, 4.
Poland, William, married Betty Brown[6] (211e), 1781, 106.
Poor, Sarah E., married Edward Brown[7] (280), 1858, 118.
Poor, William, married Elizabeth (Brown) Butler[7] (289), 1842, 111.
Post, Mrs. Lucy, married Walter Brown[6] (209), 1838, 114.
Potter, Benjamin, married Anna Kinsman[7] (143), 1794, 65.
Potter, Daniel, Jr., married Eunice Fellows[5] (121), 1796, 79.
Potter, Elizabeth, married Stephen Brown[5] (98), 1770, 106.
Potter, Elizabeth, married John B. Brown[6] (186), 1809, 111.
Potter, James, married Rhoda Brown[7] (242), 1830, 109; land, 3, 12, 18.
Potter, James, married Lucretia B. Brown[6] (376), 1853, 116.
Potter, Lucy, married Jeremiah Brown[5] (62), 1770, 101.
Potter, Mary, married David Brown[5] (92), 1797, 106.
Potter, Moses, married Sarah Fellows[5] (66), 1757, 76; house, 1778, 4.
Potter, Richard, lot, 1838, 15.
Potter, Samuel, Jr., married Lucy Brown[5] (69), 1748, 98.
Potter, Sarah (Fellows), inheritance, 1764, 46.
Potter, Symms, land, 15.
Prime, Abigail (Boardman), inheritance, 1760, 34.
Proctor's Brook, 1740, 43.
Proctor, Hannah, married John Brown[5] (66), 1789, 102.
Proctor, Isaac, lot, 1755, 24.
Proctor, James H., house and land, 1899, 47, 48.
Proctor, Joseph, married[1] Hannah Brown[5] (91), 1773; married[2] Eunice Brown[5] (95), 1808, 99.

Quincy, Mary A., married Willard F. Kinsman[9] (194), 1876, 69.

Randall, Isaac, married Deborah Low, 8.
Raymond, John, married Elizabeth Brown[6] (163), 1791, 103.
Raymond, Sophia, married John Brown[6] (175), 1791, 104.
Redfern, Anna M., married Percival H. Brown[9] (470), 1908, 122.
Reed, Edwin, married Emily P. Fellows[8] (241), 1871, 87.
Remmick, James, married Mary Kinsman[6] (97), 1782, 62; land, 9.
Richardson, Frank C., land, 1901, 39.
Richards, Jabez, married Betsey Burnham, 1809; land, 11.
Ringe, Daniel, married Mary Kinsman[2] (3), 55.
Road, Heart-break, 1809, 6.
Road, Old, in Hobson lot, 1778, 4.
Roberts, Elizabeth, married Elisha Brown Jr.[5] (78), 1759, 103.

INDEX

Roberts, John, farm, 1861, 39.
Roberts, Martha, married Benjamin Brown[5] (87), 1762, 105.
Roberts, Mary, married Isaac Fellows[5] (69), 1764, 79.
Roberts, Thomas, farm, 39, 46.
Robinson, Anna, married Nathaniel Kinsman[4] (29), 1741, 57.
Robinson, Joseph H., married Eliza H. Brown[6] (360), 1857, 115.
Rogers, Daniel, land, 1727, 2.
Rogers, John, son of John, land, 1694, 7.
Rogers, John, wife Martha, son of Samuel, 1694, 7.
Rogers, Martha, married Matthew Perkins, quitclaim, 7.
Rogers, Rev. Nathaniel, land, 6, 14.
Rogers, Samuel, indenture, 1684, 6; land, 14.
Rogers, Sarah, married James Burnham, Jr., quitclaim, 7.
Rolfe, Ebenezer, married Mehitable (Fellows) Moody[7] (193), 1853, 84.
Rollins, Olive E., married Asa Brown[8] (345), 120.
Ross, Daniel, lot, 1824, 15.
Ross, John, original grant, 37.
Rowell, Joseph, land, 1850, 31.
Ruggles, Capt. Nathaniel, married Sarah Fellows[6] (99), 1786, 78.
Russell, Elizabeth, married Stephe Kinsman (40), 1739, 60.
Russell, John L., married Bertha A. Brown[9] (448), 1896, 121.
Russell, Susan M., married Augustine Brown[8] (370), 1871, 122.
Rust, Asa, married Lucy M. Brown[7] (272), 1851, 110.
Rust, John, married Sarah Fellows[2] (6) 71.
Rust, Nathaniel, Jr., married Joanna Kinsman[3] (11), 1684, 55.
Rust, Sarah, widow, married Jonathan Fellows[3] (13), 1716, 74.

Safford, Margaret, married Stephen Brown[5] (111), 1780, 101.
Saltonstall, Forty-acres, 40, 42.
Sanborn, Solomon, married Relief Brown[6] (143), 1820, 102.
Sargent, Epes, land, 1839, 3.
Saul, Joseph, married Elsy Fellows[7] (155), 82.
Saunders, Elizabeth, widow, married Jonathan Fellows, Jr.[4] (29), 1735, 75.
Saunders, Esther A., married George Brown[6] (208), 1813, 113.
Saunders, Moses S., married Esther A. Brown[8] (437), 1866, 120.
Saville, Eliza, married Samuel Brown[6] (145), 1829, 107.
Saw-Mill to Bragg's Hill, way, 1728, 44.
Sawyer, Mary E., married Harry A. Brown[8] (401), 1887, 123.
Sawyer, Samuel, daughters Elizabeth and Susanna, land, 1760, 27, 30, 32.
Scanks, Jacob, farm, 1870, 31, 36.
Scotton, Charles F., married Elsie F. Brown[9] (490), 1904, 124.
Sears, Jonathan T., married Catherine W. Brown[10] (537), 1907, 127.
Seymour, Charles W., married Mary G. Brown[8] (361), 1857, 115.
Shatswell, Martha, married John Fellows[5] (76), 1772, 79.
Shattuck, Elizabeth, married Nathan Kinsman[6] (76), 1772, 60.

Sherwood, Clarence I., married Elva A. Fellows[8] (245), 1905, 87.
Shoemake Island, 1794, 45.
Slaves, 28, 38, 51, 95.
Smith, Alfred, farm, 1865, 14, 15.
Smith, Bemsley, married Mary Kinsman[6] (121), 1811, 64.
Smith, Hannah, married Langley Brown[6] (134), 1811, 107.
Smith, Helen F., married Augustus Brown[8] (355), 1869, 121.
Smith, John, married Susanna (Kinsman) Howe[4] (21), 1762, 56, 57.
Smith, Lucy J.[7] (282), 1826, 111.
Smith, Lydia, married Isaac Brown[6] (183), 1825, 111.
Smith, Martha, married Samuel Kinsman[5] (50), 1769, 62.
Smith, Mary A. G., married Arthur D. Kinsman[9] (189), 1899, 69.
Smith, Susanna, married Nehemiah Brown[6] (176), 1819, 110.
Snelling, Laura B., married Augustus M. Brown[9] (464), 1900, 127.
Somes, Joseph, 1774, 78.
South-Eight, The, 1.
Souther, widow Rebecca, married Benjamin Fellows[4] (40), 1778, 76.
Spencer, Frank H., married Sarah S. Fellows[8] (253), 1900, 87.
Spooner, ——, married Eliza (Brown) Lee[8] (423), 119.
Sprague, Mary L., married John F. Fellows[7] (205), 1843, 85.
Spring, Andrew C., married Julia A. Brown[8] (403), 1868, 117.
Spring, The Great, 1777, 45.
Sproul, Sarah H., married Jesse H. Brown[8] (435), 1884, 125.
Spuyt, Albin M., house and lot, 1903, 3.
Stackpole, Josiah, lot, 1882, 3.
Staniford, Abbie, married Jacob Kinsman[8] (162), 1837, 67.
Staniford, Daniel, lot, 1749, 36.
Staniford, Thoms, married Mary Burnham, 8; lot, 36.
Stanton, Lydia, married Nathaniel Fellows[5] (55), 1774, 78.
Stanwood, Sarah E., married George Fellows[6] (134), 1847, 85.
Staples, Stephen, married Frances Brown[6] (141), 1824, 102.
Start, Ann, married[1] Nathan Fellows[4] (42); married[2] Stephen Brown[4] (32), 1746, 77, 100.
Steeves, Sarah, married Charles D. Brown[9] (505), 124.
Stone, Abby S., wife of Augustine, farm, 1901, 9.
Stone, Elizabeth B., married Simon B. Kinsman[8] (160), 1829, 68.
Story, Alvin, married Charlotte A. Brown[8] (352), 1857, 115.
Story, Joseph A., married Sarah M. Kinsman[9] (190), 1868, 69.
Story, Leonora Abby, married Gardiner A. Brown[7] (268), 1855, 118.
Story, Ruth, married David Brown[5] (110), 1772, 101.
Story, William, land, 22.
Stowe, Joel B., married Lucretia Brown[7] (226), 1838, 108.
Sturtevant, Albert, house and lot, 1878, 19.
Sullivan, John J., married Mary E. Brown[8] (373), 1880, 116.
Swasey, Jennie G., married Edward G. Brown[10] (526a), 1896, 126.

Sweet, John, married Lucy M. Brown[7] (332), 1834, 113; land, 1836, 12.
Symonds, Dep. Gov. Samuel, Argilla farm, 10.

Tanor, Mary, married Nehemiah Brown[4] (31), 1743, 99.
Tappan, Betsey, married Perley Brown[7] (308), 1827, 119.
Tarbox, Abner, dwelling, 1756, 45.
Taylor, Jennie E., married Edward Brown[7] (256), 1859, 117.
Tenney, Jacob B., house and lot, 1869, 18, 19.
Thissell, Nellie M., married Frank W. Brown[9] (445), 1883, 125.
Thorne, Barnard, married Martha Brown[2] (3), 1670, 92.
Thorne, Martha, wife of Barnard, deposition, 1723, 37.
Thornton, James B., lot, 1796, 30.
Thornton, Thomas G., lot, 1796, 30.
Thornton, Timothy, married[1] Eunice Brown[4] (40), 1761; married[2] Lydia Lord, 1785, 96; land, 30.
Throat distemper, 1736, 52.
Thurston, Ella, married A. Story Brown[8] (408), 1879, 123.
Tibbets, Timothy, married Lucy Brown[6] (166), 104; land, 28.
Tilton, Abraham, land, 1740, 36.
Tilton, Benjamin T., married Catherine E. Fellows[8] (236), 1867, 87.
Tilton, Deborah, widow, married Dea. Jonathan Fellows[3] (13), 1733, 74.
Tilton, Elzina A., married George Kinsman[8] (169), 1865, 67.
Tilton, Mary, married Thomas Kinsman[5] (39), 1745, 58.
Todd, William S., farm, 1868, 15.
Trask, Ebenezer, married Lucy Kinsman[6] (89), 1768, 61.
Treadwell, Mercy, married Samuel Fellows[5] (51), 1763, 77.
Treadwell, Priscilla, married Nathaniel Kinsman[6] (54), 1772, 63.
Treadwell, Sarah, married Michael Kinsman[5] (53), 1768, 63.
Trefethen, Benjamin, married Melicent M. Fellows[7] (194), 84.
Troop, Alexander, wife Lucy, land; family, 1787, 4, 15.
Tuck, Robert, married Anna Fellows[6] (140), 1810, 81.
Tucker, Eunice A., married George Brown, Jr.[7] (328), 1836, 120.
Tucker, Richard, married Mary Fellows[4] (36), 1768, 74.
Tuttle, John, original lot, 20.
Tuttle, Olphert, married Sarah Fellows[6] (141), 1820, 81.

Varney, Rachel, married John Fellows[3] (19), 1692, 72.

Wade, Asa, land, 3, 16.
Wade, Isaac, land, 1831, 2.
Wade, John, land, 1763, 2.
Wade, Jonathan, wife Jane, land, 1696, 1, 2, 15, 16, 20.
Wade, Joseph H., land, 1844, 17.
Wade, Mary, 1763; land, 2.
Wade, Col. Nathaniel, 1763; land, 2, 17.
Wade, Nathaniel, son of Col. Nathaniel, land, 2, 17.
Wade, Samuel, land, 1763, 2.
Wade, Capt. Thomas, wife Elizabeth, 1669; land, 1, 2.
Wade, Thomas, son of Capt. Thomas, land, 1737, 2, 44.
Wade, Thomas, son of William, land, 1803, 2, 15.
Wade, Timothy, wife Ruth, land, 1737, family, 2, 3, 44.
Wade, William, wife Eunice, land, 1763, 2.
Wade, William F., married Mary P. Brown[6] (185), 1841, 105; land, 1827, 2, 17.
Wade, William F., Jr., married Susan (Lord) Brown, 1865, 117; land, 2.
Wainwright, Col. Francis, land, 25, 37, 40.
Wainwright, John, land, 1754, 24.
Waite, Samuel, married Ruth Fellows[8] (24), 1717, 73; land, 43.
Waite, Thomas, Jr., married Mary Kinsman[4] (20), 56.
Walker's Swamp Island, 35.
Wall, Henry H., married Frances (Fellows) Cassell[7] (215), 1880, 85.
Wallace, Aretas D., farm, 1901, 9.
Wallis, Hannah, inheritance, 1741, 23.
Wallis, Robert, Jr., married Hannah Kinsman[4] (27), 1735, 56.
Ward's meadow, original lot, 15.
Wardell, Uzall, married Mary Kinsman[2] (3), 55.
Wardwell, I. M., married Eliza (Fellows) Ingraham[8] (226), 1863, 86.
Warner, Hannah, married Ephraim Fellows[3] (12), 1703, 73.
Washburn, Frank R., married Bessie P. Brown[10] (526d), 126.
Way, from saw-mill, 1743, 16, 44; over Saltonstall lot 1658, 41, 42.
Webb, ——, married Harriet Brown[6] (211b), 106.
Webb, Deborah, married Nathaniel Kinsman[6] (110), 63.
Webber, Anna, married Benjamin Pellows, Jr.[5] (78), 1784, 80.
Webster, John, land, sold by son, John, 1652, 22.
Weed, Daniel, lot, 3.
Wells, Abigail, married John Kinsman[5] (45), 1758, 61.
Wells, Eunice, married William Brown[6] (70), 1755, 103.
Wells, James L., married Elizabeth Kinsman[7] (147), 1832, 65.
Wells, John, Jr., married Betsey Kinsman[10] (69), 1796, 62.
Wells, Moses, married Eunice Kinsman[4] (23), 1724, 56, 57; land, 35.
Wells, Nathaniel, married Sarah Kinsman[4] (24), 1723, 23, 56, 57; land, 35, 36.
Wheeler, Henrietta, married Alonzo B. Fellows[7] (216), 1876, 87.
Wheeler, Mercy, married Nathan Kinsman[6] (76), 60.
Whipple, George A., farm, 22, 24.
Whipple, Hervey, married Martha P. Brown[7] (270), 1835, 110; farm, 22, 24.
Whipple, Joseph, original lot, 44.
Whipple, Dea. Matthew, lot, 13.
Whipple, Oliver M., married Sarah Kinsman[8] (164), 1844, 67.
Whitney, Caroline S., married Cornelius Fellows[8] (231), 1874, 88.
Wilderness Hill, Pasture, 31.
Wildes, Edward B., married Harriet M. Kinsman[9] (192), 1870, 69.

Willett, George, land, 1852, 49.
Willett, John, farm, 1793, 11, 21.
Willett, Julia P., inheritance, 15.
Willett, Levi, inheritance, 49.
Willett, Molly, married John Fellows[6] (123), 1804, 79.
Willett, Moses, married Martha Fellows[6] (122), 1804, 79; land, 11.
Willett, Wallace P., land, 3, 15.
Williams, George F., married Susan Fellows[7] (163), 82.
Williams, John S., married Nancy (Fellows) Hunt[6] (104), 78.
Williams, Sarah, married Cornelius Fellows[5] (53), 1763, 77.
Wilson, Margaretta, married Everett K. Brown[8] (351), 1870, 115.
Wing, Emma J., married Jesse F. Brown[8] (435), 1883, 124.
Winthrop, John, Jr., Argilla farm, 10.
Wise, Mary (Wade), 1737, 2.
Witham, Daniel, married Sally Brown[6] (173), 1805, 104.

Wood, John, married Eunice Fellows[5] (72), 1758, 76.
Wood, Mattie A., married Daniel P. Kinsman[8] (170), 1855, 67.
Woodbridge, Mary A., married Charles Brown[8] (346), 120.
Woodbury, Charles W., married Agnes H. Brown[9] (501), 1898, 124.
Woodbury, Hannah, married Benjamin Brown, Jr.[6] (193), 1792, 112.
Woodworth, Florence E., married Elbridge G. Brown[9] (469), 1903, 122.
Worcester, Ira, wife Ruth G., land, 1844, 17.
Wright, Abigail, married Ira Fellows[6] (108), 1827, 83.

Yorke, Thomas, married Dorothy Low, 9.
Younglove, Samuel, married Sarah Kinsman[2] (4), 1660, 55.

www.ingramcontent.com/pod-product-compliance
Lightning Source LLC
Chambersburg PA
CBHW050818160426
43192CB00010B/1808